ReadSmart 2
INTERMEDIATE

Cheryl Pavlik

McGraw-Hill ESL/ELT

ReadSmart 2

Published by McGraw-Hill ESL/ELT, a business unit of The McGraw-Hill Companies, Inc. 1221 Avenue of the Americas, New York, NY 10020.

This book is printed on recycled, acid-free paper containing 10% post-consumer waste.

1 2 3 4 5 6 7 8 9 QPD 9 8 7 6 5 4 3

ISBN: 0-07-283894-9

Editorial director: *Tina B. Carver*
Senior sponsoring editor: *Thomas Healy*
Developmental editors: *Susan Johnson, Annie Sullivan*
Production managers: *Juanita Thompson, MaryRose Bollwage*
Editorial assistant: *Kasey Williamson*
Cover designer: *Martini Graphic Services, Inc.*
Interior designer: *Acento Visual*
Art: *Martini Graphic Services, Inc.*
Photo credits: p 22, © *Duomo/CORBIS;* p 55, © *Royalty-Free/CORBIS;* p 65, *Lashram, Nirba and the "Science Head" icon redrawn with permission from HowStuffworks, Inc.;* p 72, © *Royalty-Free/Antonello Turchetti/Getty Images;* p 77, © *David Turnley/CORBIS* p 135, © *Royalty-Free/Tim Green/Getty Images;* p 137, © *Charles & Josette Lenars/CORBIS;* p 146, © *Royalty-Free/CORBIS;* p 150, © *Stuart Westmorland;* p 189, © *PoodlesRock/CORBIS;* p 224, © *AFP/CORBIS*

McGraw-Hill
ESL/ELT

Table of Contents

Chapter	Reading Topics	Preparing to Read
INTRODUCTION: MECHANICS Page 1		
1 **READING SKILLS AND STRATEGIES** Page 19		• Making predictions about the text • Predicting from genre
2 **URBAN LEGENDS** Page 39	1. Urban Legend 2. Alligators in the Sewers? Not Again! 3. Language Mistakes That Weren't 4. Chain Letters: From Snail Mail to E-Mail	• Making predictions about the text • Predicting from genre
3 **OUT OF THIS WORLD** Page 55	1. Signs of Life in a Rock 2A. Life on Earth...and Beyond 2B. Life in an Extreme Environment 3. Aliens from a Scientist's Imagination 4. Visitors from Outer Space?	• Making predictions about the text • Predicting from genre
4 **CLOTHES MAKE THE MAN (AND THE WOMAN)** Page 72	1. The Importance of Clothes in Society 2. Before You Leave for the Gulf 3A. Why Ties? 3B. How to Tie a Tie 4. Origami Clothing Takes the Shop out of Shopping	• Making predictions about the text • Predicting from genre
5 **READING SKILLS AND STRATEGIES** Page 90		• Predicting from illustrations and photos • Predicting from thesis statements

Reading	Remembering	Vocabulary Strategies
<ul><li>Scanning</li><li>Skimming for gist</li><li>Increasing reading speed</li></ul>		
<ul><li>Reading with a purpose</li><li>Using signal words to predict ideas</li><li>Using background knowledge</li></ul>**Critical reading**<ul><li>Distinguishing fact from opinion</li></ul>	<ul><li>Highlighting and underlining text</li></ul>	<ul><li>Deciding which words are important</li><li>Predicting the next word</li><li>Recognizing internal definitions</li><li>Analyzing a word for meaning</li><li>Guessing the approximate meaning of a word</li></ul>
<ul><li>Using background knowledge</li><li>Reading with a purpose</li><li>Using signal words to predict ideas</li></ul>**Critical reading**<ul><li>Distinguishing fact from opinion</li></ul>	<ul><li>Highlighting and underlining text</li></ul>	<ul><li>Deciding which words are important</li><li>Predicting the next word</li><li>Recognizing internal definitions</li><li>Analyzing a word for meaning</li><li>Guessing the approximate meaning of a word</li></ul>
<ul><li>Using background knowledge</li><li>Reading with a purpose</li><li>Using signal words to predict ideas</li></ul>**Critical reading**<ul><li>Distinguishing fact from opinion</li></ul>	<ul><li>Highlighting and underlining text</li></ul>	<ul><li>Deciding which words are important</li><li>Predicting the next word</li><li>Recognizing internal definitions</li><li>Analyzing a word for meaning</li><li>Guessing the approximate meaning of a word</li></ul>
<ul><li>Using background knowledge</li><li>Reading with a purpose</li><li>Using signal words to predict ideas</li></ul>**Critical reading**<ul><li>Distinguishing fact from opinion</li></ul>	<ul><li>Highlighting and underlining text</li></ul>	<ul><li>Deciding which words are important</li><li>Predicting the next word</li><li>Recognizing internal definitions</li><li>Analyzing a word for meaning</li><li>Guessing the approximate meaning of a word</li></ul>
<ul><li>Using topic sentences to identify main ideas</li><li>Using signal words to predict ideas</li><li>Using referring words and referents to follow ideas</li><li>Using illustrations and photos to aid comprehension</li><li>Using punctuation to aid comprehension</li></ul>**Critical reading** • Evaluating arguments	<ul><li>Paraphrasing</li></ul>	<ul><li>Using a dictionary</li><li>Recognizing names, abbreviations, and acronyms</li><li>Analyzing a word for meaning</li><li>Recognizing common phrases</li><li>Guessing the approximate meaning of a word</li></ul>

Reading	Remembering	Vocabulary Strategies
• Using topic sentences to identify main ideas • Reading with a purpose • Using illustrations and photos to aid comprehension • Using signal words to predict ideas • Using referring words and referents to follow ideas • Using punctuation to aid comprehension **Critical reading** • Evaluating arguments	• Paraphrasing	• Using a dictionary • Recognizing names, abbreviations, and acronyms • Recognizing internal definitions • Analyzing a word for meaning • Recognizing common phrases • Guessing the approximate meaning of a word
• Using topic sentences to identify main ideas • Reading with a purpose • Using illustrations and photos to aid comprehension • Using signal words to predict ideas • Using referring words and referents to follow ideas • Using punctuation to aid comprehension **Critical reading** • Evaluating arguments	• Paraphrasing	• Using a dictionary • Recognizing names, abbreviations, and acronyms • Recognizing internal definitions • Analyzing a word for meaning • Recognizing common phrases • Guessing the approximate meaning of a word
• Using topic sentences to identify main ideas • Reading with a purpose • Using illustrations and photos to aid comprehension • Using signal words to predict ideas • Using referring words and referents to follow ideas • Using punctuation to aid comprehension **Critical reading** • Evaluating arguments	• Paraphrasing	• Using a dictionary • Recognizing names, abbreviations, and acronyms • Recognizing internal definitions • Analyzing a word for meaning • Recognizing common phrases • Guessing the approximate meaning of a word
• Using supporting details to identify main ideas • Using signal words to predict ideas • Reading difficult material **Critical reading** • Making inferences	• Summarizing	• Recognizing jargon • Recognizing common phrases • Analyzing a word for meaning • Guessing the approximate meaning of a word

Acknowledgements

I would like to thank the instructors who reviewed **ReadSmart** during the development of the series for their insightful comments and suggestions.

I would also like to thank Thomas Healy for supporting **ReadSmart** from its inception, Susan Johnson for her invaluable improvements to my ideas, and Annie Sullivan for taking a working manuscript and turning it into a book.

Cheryl Pavlik

To the Teacher

ReadSmart is a three-level reading skills series featuring an innovative approach to reading development. Extensive reading and vocabulary skills instruction chapters, followed by ample opportunities to practice the target skills, help learners to *read smart.*

Features

- **Skills and strategies chapters** present and practice vital **reading strategies**, such as predicting from what you already know, and **reading skills**, such as skimming and scanning.
- **Vocabulary strategies**, such as recognizing internal definitions, recognizing common phrases, and using word forms, help learners to read more fluently.
- **Reading chapters** provide diverse opportunities for learners to practice and apply the target skills and strategies.
- **Self-evaluation activities** make learners aware of the skills and strategies they use when reading.
- **A wide range of reading genres**, including textbook excerpts, magazine features, newspaper articles, encyclopedia entries, and dictionary entries, prepares students for academic reading as well as reading for pleasure.
- **A skills chart** is included in the table of contents of each book.
- **Chapter quizzes** in the Teacher's Manual prepare students for different types of test-taking situations, including standardized multiple choice, matching, true/false, and questions where students must apply the reading strategies and skills to a text.
- **A Teacher's Manual** provides an overview for the teacher, chapter quizzes, and complete answer keys.
- **An optional audio program** with recorded reading passages provides expansion opportunities for teachers.

Components

- **Student Book** has 12 units: three skills and strategies chapters that present and practice both reading and vocabulary skills and strategies, and nine reading chapters that provide diverse opportunities for learners to practice and apply the target skills and strategies.

- **Teacher's Manual** provides the following:
  - Teaching tips and techniques
  - Answer keys for the Student Book
  - Expansion activities
  - Chapter quizzes in a variety of test formats, such as standardized multiple choice, matching, true/false, and questions where students must apply the reading skills and strategies to a text
  - Answer keys for the chapter quizzes.
- **Audio program** contains recordings of the readings in both audio CD and audiocassette formats.

About the Series

ReadSmart is a three-level reading skills series intended for high beginning, intermediate, and high intermediate students who are studying English. The topics, reading genres, and strategies were purposefully chosen to accommodate a wide variety of students. The themes in the reading chapters were chosen to relate to different academic disciplines, although most of the readings themselves are non-academic in nature. Therefore, the series can be used with students who would like to read more effectively for academic, career, or general purposes.

The Philosophy

ReadSmart teaches that there is no single correct way to read. Some strategies work well for some people and not others. Some strategies work well in some situations and not others. The key to success is using the right strategy in each reading situation. Effective readers understand this, and they use a wide variety of reading strategies with great flexibility. Effective readers are not easily discouraged. If one strategy doesn't work, they simply try another. *ReadSmart* therefore introduces students to a great variety of reading and vocabulary strategies. The text then encourages readers to be flexible by providing them with opportunities to practice different strategies in the readings.

The readings represent different topics, genres, and styles. They were carefully chosen to provide reading practice at different levels of difficulty. Some readings may seem relatively easy. These will help students gain confidence and give them a chance to practice the reading skills and strategies in depth. Other readings will be quite challenging, allowing students to see how much they can understand when faced with difficult material. Although the chapters were designed to move generally from easier to more difficult, each reading chapter also offers a mixture of levels of difficulty. For this reason, a reading in Chapter 7 might be easier than a reading in Chapter 4, for example. However, within each chapter, the most challenging reading is last. This structure allows students to gain a fair amount of background knowledge before they tackle more difficult material.

The Reading Process

One of the most important lessons that students studying English have to learn is that reading is not a linear process. Effective readers usually do not begin at the first word in a text and continue without stopping until the end—especially if the reading is challenging. The reading process is much more flexible than that. Effective readers often begin **the reading process** before they actually begin reading and, in some cases, they may start at the end. Then as they are reading, they constantly move forward and backward—predicting, making deductions, checking their guesses, and reacting to the information they are learning.

The reading process does not always go smoothly, and there are often words or sentences that the reader may not completely understand. Effective readers are willing to keep reading, even though they may be confused. They continue to read while looking for clues to help them understand the text.

ReadSmart encourages students to "read through" their confusion and then reread to increase their understanding. Students learn that understanding *approximately* what a word means is often enough. For example, depending on your purpose for reading, it may be enough to know that a carburetor is a part of a car engine without having any idea what it does. Read the following sentence:

> The garage was filled with things that Adam had collected over the years and discarded: an old lawn mower, broken sports equipment, unused tools, cans of dried-up paint, even an old carburetor.

In this sentence, you only need to know that a carburetor is a concrete noun that one might find in a garage.

Reflective Reading and Self Evaluation

Research has shown that **reflective reading** is one of the keys to reading improvement. For this reason, every reading chapter in *ReadSmart* concludes with a section that asks students to review their own reading process, identify the strategies that they used, evaluate their effectiveness, and think about what they might do differently in the future. Students have many opportunities to compare their work with a partner's. The purpose of these activities is to help students share their reading experiences and exchange ideas about the use of the different strategies.

Text Overview

Introduction

Each text begins with an introductory chapter on the mechanics of reading. This chapter provides practice in the physical skills required for scanning, skimming, and reading more quickly. The exercises focus on things such as rapid eye movement, using your hand to move down the page, and so on.

Skills and Strategies Chapters (1, 5, 9)

There are three **Skills and Strategies chapters** in the text (Chapters 1, 5, and 9). These chapters present skills and strategies for improving your reading. Skills and strategies for comprehension are taught in Part 1; skills and strategies for understanding vocabulary are taught in Part 2. The comprehension section is further divided into steps in the reading process: *Prepare, Read,* and *Remember.* Although **ReadSmart** teaches that reading is not necessarily a linear process, these chapters do teach and practice skills and strategies in a logical progression to ensure that students have mastered them in isolation before applying them.

Each strategy is introduced, explained, and then practiced. The exercises in these chapters are controlled so that students benefit from focused practice of individual skills and strategies. Especially useful strategies, such as using signal words to predict ideas, are taught and recycled in every skills/strategies chapter with different material.

Thematic Reading Chapters (2, 3, 4, 6, 7, 8, 10, 11, 12)

There are nine **Reading chapters** in the text (Chapters 2–4, 6–8, and 10–12). Each reading chapter contains four readings on a single topic. The activities accompanying the readings are designed specifically to target the comprehension and vocabulary skills and strategies that students learned in the previous skills/strategies chapter. But rather than provide additional focused practice of individual strategies, the reading chapters ask students to apply the skills and strategies in powerful combinations as they read. As the text progresses, skills and strategies are recycled in the reading chapters naturally.

The reading chapters open with a topical photo and discussion questions. These tools activate students' background knowledge about the topic and prompt them into thinking about the topic in a general way. The four readings in the chapter expand the steps in the reading process: *Prepare, Read, Read Again, Remember,* and *Discuss.*

The comprehension and vocabulary skills and strategies taught in the skills/strategies chapters are embedded in the reading steps. *Post-reading Activities* focus students' attention more closely on strategies appropriate for each reading.

Thinking about Strategies prompts students to reflect on the strategies that they used in each reading.

Appendices

The appendices provide extra reading practice in scanning and learning to read faster. In Appendix 1, students scan realistic items, such as a television schedule, a bus schedule, a class schedule, and a menu, looking for specific information. In Appendix 2, diverse readings are provided, some on topics covered in the text. Each of these readings has a multiple choice comprehension exercise but no other supporting material.

Introduction

The Mechanics of Reading: Scanning, Skimming, and Reading Faster

L earning to read at an appropriate speed is important. Reading speed depends on two things: what you are reading and why you are reading. For example, when you look up a telephone number, you may read thousands of words per minute (wpm) because the only thing that you need to understand is the phone number that you are looking for. Other reading tasks require slow, careful reading. For instance, if you read a business contract, an important report, or a recipe in a cookbook really quickly, you could get a terrible result!

The following reading chart lists different kinds of reading. The fastest kind of reading is at the top of the chart—scanning. The slowest kind of reading is at the bottom of the chart—critical reading.

READING SPEED CHART
Adapted from University of Central Florida Student Development Department (Pegasus)

Type of material	Type of reading	Purpose
Dictionaries, telephone directories	SCANNING	Locating specific information
Newspapers, journals, research	SKIMMING	Reading for main ideas only
Easy textbooks, newspapers, stories, magazines	LIGHT READING	Reading for general understanding of main ideas and details when it is not necessary to remember most of the information
Most textbooks, journals, and technical materials	READING FOR LEARNING	Reading for complete understanding of main ideas; making questions from main ideas; taking notes for material that you must remember
Detailed textbooks that require deep thinking	CRITICAL READING	Evaluating and/or reflecting on content, or following directions as in performing a chemistry experiment

Scanning

One way of reading is called scanning. Scanning is looking at a text quickly to find specific information.

Understanding the Strategy

We scan texts to find a phone number, locate a name, or look up a word. In scanning, your eyes behave like a computer searching a document. That is, you search until your eyes recognize letters, numbers, and words that your mind thinks you should see. Also, you look for meaning, not only for exact words but for synonyms and terms that are related to the question you want answered.

When you scan for information, search for the shape of words or phrases as well as the meaning.

Search Terms

When you want to find specific information, think of the kinds of words you should scan the text for.

Example: If the question is "Where did Mr. Lin go to school?" you would search for the following terms.

- specific school names
- common school terms: university, college, institute, school
- location words: New York, London, Beijing, Paris
- question-related words: study, attended, enrolled, graduated

Commonly Scanned Texts

Most people scan the same types of material. Which of these kinds of texts do you think you might scan?

- a page of movie ads in a newspaper
- a weather map
- instructions on how to repair an engine
- a list of sports scores
- a chapter in a novel
- a bus or train schedule
- a menu
- the label on a can or box of food

See Appendix I for more practice with scanning.

A C T I V I T Y . 1   Look at the word in bold. Move your eyes quickly across the line. Each time you see the word again, draw a line through it.

1. **possible**	passable	possible	passable	plausible	possible	probable	passable
2. **made**	made	make	maid	made	make	mood	made
3. **think**	thank	think	tank	think	thank	thin	tank
4. **night**	night	might	might	night	neat	might	night
5. **touch**	cough	tough	touch	touch	torch	cough	touch
6. **tried**	tired	tried	tired	tries	tires	tried	tired
7. **calm**	calm	clam	clamp	calm	clam	calm	clam
8. **biology**	biologist	biology	biologist	biological	biology	botany	biologist
9. **peach**	peace	peach	preach	peach	peace	piece	preach
10. **reading**	reading	railing	rapping	riding	reading	riding	rapping

A C T I V I T Y . 2   Look at the word in bold. Move your eyes quickly across the line. Each time you see the word again, draw a line through it.

1. **telephone**	telegraph	TelePrompTer	telephone	telegraph	television	telephone
2. **worked**	walked	worked	whiled	world	worked	walked
3. **choose**	choice	chose	choose	choice	chose	choose
4. **tests**	tastes	teeth	tests	tempts	tastes	tests
5. **people**	parable	peephole	pebble	people	parable	peonie
6. **information**	informative	informer	instruction	information	infiltrate	inform
7. **threw**	thrown	true	through	thrash	threw	trowel
8. **electrical**	electoral	elected	electricity	electrical	elected	electoral
9. **required**	required	requisite	renounce	respired	repaired	required
10. **applicant**	appliqué	applecore	applicant	appliance	supplicant	applica

ACTIVITY . **3**   Scan the following lists for the phrase in bold. Each time you see the phrase again, draw a line through it. Work as quickly as you can. Count the number of times you find each phrase.

1. **practice reading faster**

practice riding more	practice reading faster
private reading rooms	playtime stays forever
Patsy reads faster	princess rising fair
physical relief works	practice reading faster
practice reading faster	Patsy reads faster
playtime stays forever	practice riding more
painters working over	pandas roam better
princess rising fair	practice reading faster
practice piano more	painters working over
practice reading faster	princess rising fair
private reading rooms	Patsy reads faster
physical relief works	pandas roam better
painters working over	practice reading faster
practice reading faster	physical relief works

2. **the small red brick house**

the small red-haired mouse	the small red wood house
these small brick houses	the simple red brick house
the small boy's red horse	the small red brick house
the Smalls' red brick house	the smart red-haired horse
the small red brick house	those smart red British hotels
the small red wood house	the small boy's red horse
the simple red bridge house	these small brick houses
the smart red-haired horse	the small red-haired mouse
the small red brick house	the Smalls' red brick house
those smart red British hotels	the small red brick house
the simple red brick house	these small brick houses

 A C T I V I T Y . **4**   Scan these different kinds of texts to find the information.

1. Scan this weather map to find:

    a. the temperature in Cleveland.   ————————————

    b. the weather in Miami.   ————————————

    c. the coldest city on this day.   ————————————

    d. the hottest city on this day.   ————————————

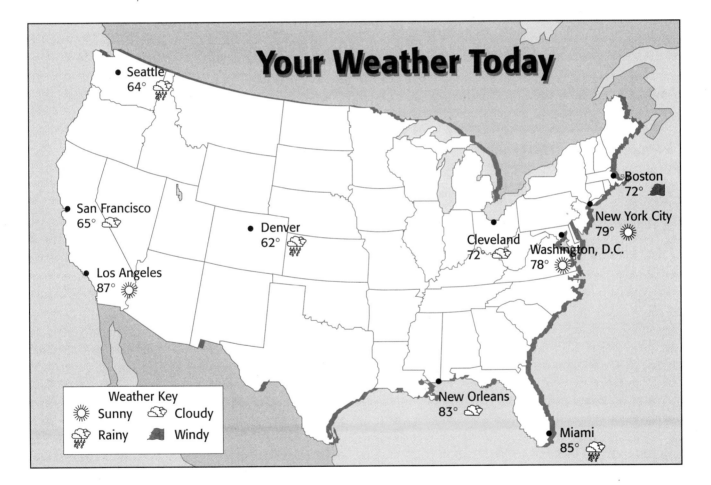

2. Scan this table of contents from a magazine. Move your eyes quickly over the information. Find the article on:

a. moving your business.   _____

b. setting up a new office.   _____

c. hiring skilled people.   _____

Business World

December 2000   Volume 22 Issue 14

TABLE OF CONTENTS

LETTERS 20
Our readers respond.

SCHOOLS WITH A DIFFERENCE 33
Schools that make a profit are becoming increasingly popular in the United States. Read the story of two very different schools that are changing the lives of their students.

INVESTING BASICS 56
Once you start earning money, you have to start learning how to invest it wisely. Our stock expert gives you good advice.

BEST ON THE WEB 78
Looking for new employees? Many companies are going to the Internet to search for résumés. Several new Websites are hoping you will hire them. Here's a list of the best.

HOT CITIES 92
Where is the best place to start your business? In this issue, we rank U.S. cities, big and small.

EMPLOYEES THAT KILL COMPANIES 108
Certain kinds of employees are bad for business, and they aren't always easy to spot. Read about the six kinds of people you don't want to hire.

MOVING MADE EASY 115
Is your business expanding? Do you need to relocate? Don't miss our guide to moving. Plus—instructions on how to set up a new office.

3. Scan this section of the telephone yellow pages. Find:

a. what kind of business Frazier & Son is.   _____

b. the phone number of Green Mountain Interiors.   _____

c. when Furniture Plus is open.   _____

d. who sells Englander mattresses.   _____

4. Scan the following Webpage. Find:

    a. the place where Queen Victoria was born.   _____

    b. how many brothers and sisters Victoria had.   _____

    c. the name of her husband.   _____

    d. how many children she had.   _____

adapted from http:// www.biography.com

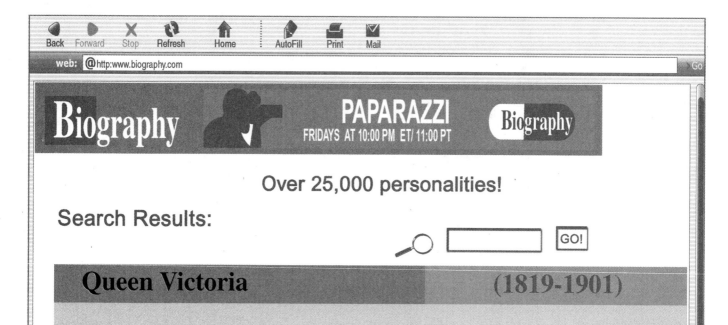

web: @http:www.biography.com

Biography

PAPARAZZI
FRIDAYS AT 10:00 PM ET/ 11:00 PT

Biography

Over 25,000 personalities!

Search Results:

GO!

Queen Victoria   (1819-1901)

Queen of Great Britain (1837–1901) and (from 1876) empress of India, born in London, England. Victoria was the only child of George III's fourth son, Edward, and Victoria Maria Louisa of Saxe-Coburg, sister of Leopold, King of the Belgians. Taught by Lord Melbourne, her first prime minister, she had a clear grasp of constitutional principles and the scope of her own prerogative, which she resolutely exercised in 1839 by setting aside the precedent that decreed dismissal of the current ladies of the bedchamber, thus causing Peel not to take up office as prime minister.

In 1840, Victoria married Prince Albert of Saxe-Coburg and Gotha. The couple had four sons and five daughters. Strongly influenced by her husband, with whom she worked in closest harmony, Victoria went into lengthy seclusion after his death in 1861, neglecting many duties. This decreased her popularity and motivated a republican movement against the Crown. At various points in her long reign, she exercised some influence over foreign affairs, and the marriages of her children had important diplomatic, as well as dynastic, implications in Europe. She died at Cowes, Isle of Wight, England, and was succeeded by her son Edward VII.

Skimming

Skimming is the process of reading to find out the main ideas of a text. There are many reasons to skim a text. For example, one of the best ways to prepare to read a text is to skim it first. At other times, we skim to find out if the text will be useful to us. In which of these situations should you skim a text?

- when you have to memorize a poem
- when you are doing research and need to decide if an article contains important information
- when you are reading instructions on how to use your new computer
- when you are going to have a test in 30 minutes and you still have 20 pages to read

Understanding the Strategy

There are two basic ways of skimming: the whole text method and the beginning and ending method.

When you skim, ignore unfamiliar words. Search only for key ideas.

Whole Text Method

- Read the title.
- Move your eyes quickly over the whole text.
- Read any headings and subheadings.
- Notice any pictures, charts, or graphs.
- Notice any italicized or boldface words or phrases.
- Search for topic sentences.

Beginning and Ending Method

- Read the title.
- Read the introduction or the first paragraph.
- Read the first sentence of every paragraph.
- Read the summary or last paragraph.
- Read headings and subheadings.
- Notice pictures, charts, and/or graphs.
- Notice italicized or boldface words or phrases.

ACTIVITY. **5**   You are trying to decide whether to see the movie *Monster Park II*. Skim the review to find the reviewer's opinion.

> What a difference three years can make! The original *Monster Park* was an almost perfect horror film. Three years later, the makers of that hit have reunited to make a sequel and the results are less than satisfying. Perhaps the worst thing about *Monster Park II* is the change that the insane scientist, Janice Duncan, has gone through since the original. Janice is no longer trying to save the world by creating monsters; now she has a new motive—greed.
>
> Most of *Monster Park II* takes place in Janice's laboratory at a large university. This laboratory has an amazingly small staff, consisting of Janice, two assistants, and one bumbling security guard. Equally odd, there seem to be no students or any other faculty members around even though classes are obviously in session. And judging by the dimness of the lighting, the university hasn't paid their electric bill in some time.
>
> I won't bore you with all of the details of this incredibly silly plot involving a chimpanzee, a robot, and a group of Roman soldiers. I'll just say that the storyline is unbelievable, even for a genre like horror where realism is not the most important factor.

ACTIVITY. **6**   Skim the article. Answer the questions that follow.

A. Skim the following newspaper article to find the main ideas. Use the *whole text method* or the *beginning and ending method*.

International

A Nation Demands 'Give the Parrot Back!'

JULY 26, 2002 11:02 AM ET

SYDNEY (Reuters) — Australian police have issued an APB (All Parrots Bulletin) for Hector the galah, a talkative pink and gray bird they fear was stolen from a Sydney pet shop.

Hector had sat cheerfully at the front door of Doug Eyre's suburban pet shop for 31 years, delighting passers-by with cheerful chatter that included "Give me a kiss," "Hector's got a cough," and "See you later, mate." But the galah, a bird similar to a cockatoo, went missing last Saturday.

Police issued a statement earlier this week that said Hector was last seen being carried off in his cage by a gray-haired woman in her fifties and placed into a car. "Police are investigating reports that the galah may have been freed by a welfare group concerned at Hector's caging," the statement said. "Hector is still missing," a police spokesman said on Thursday.

Eyre fears his feathered friend has become an ex-parrot. "Our family is not taking this too well, but a lot of people have been coming in, asking where he's gone and crying when they find out he was stolen," Eyre said.

Hector's cause has been championed by *The Daily Telegraph*. The Sydney tabloid ran a front-page photo of the bird on Wednesday next to the headline "Give the Parrot Back."

"What kind of people steal a talking galah that has been part of a community for 31 years?" the newspaper demanded. On Thursday, *The Daily Telegraph* ran another front-page story containing pleas for the bird's return from high-profile community members including Prime Minister John Howard.

"I urge the culprit to return Hector for the continuing enjoyment of local passers-by," Howard told the newspaper. The New South Wales state premier, Bob Carr, added: "My simple plea is this: Bring Hector back safe and well."

Galahs are found across the Australian mainland and can live for up to 80 years. In rural Australia flocks of hundreds of galahs are regarded as pests who eat stock feed.

B. Answer these questions. Do not look back at the article.

1. What is a galah?
2. Where did the parrot used to live?
3. What happened to the parrot?
4. Why was this parrot so important?
5. Who is upset about the disappearance of the parrot?

A C T I V I T Y **. 7**   Skim the Webpage. Answer the questions that follow.

A. Skim the following Webpage for key ideas. Use one of the skimming methods.

NEWS ONLINE

Archive | Classified | Shopping | promotions | Games | My news | news

Email this article   Printer friendly version

Crawling Snakehead Fish Face Poison in Maryland

July 26, 2002 02:54 PM ET

By Tom Doggett

WASHINGTON (Reuters) — A panel of scientists on Friday recommended that Maryland game officials use poison to kill snakehead fish found in a local pond to prevent the fish from moving into the state's waterways. An unusual fish, the snakehead, which grows up to three feet, eats other fish and its own offspring, and can crawl across land, was discovered this summer by a fisherman in a pond in Crofton, Maryland.

After nearly 100 baby snakeheads were later found in the pond, state officials created the panel to figure out the best way to destroy the fish. The panel recommended the use of the pesticide rotenone. The poison would be mixed into the pond and kill the snakeheads quickly, said John Surrick, spokesman for Maryland's Department of Natural Resources. "The experiments that we did in the lab earlier this week indicated that the fish would die within an hour," he said. The department will decide by the end of next week whether to proceed with the poisoning proposal, Surrick said.

Several other solutions were looked into. Draining the pond would run the risk that "baby snakeheads could escape in the water pumped into a nearby river," officials were quoted as saying. Other options such as largescale netting or electro-shocking the water were also unworkable.

Snakeheads have been found in at least six other states: Hawaii, Florida, California, Maine, Massachusetts, and Rhode Island, according to the Interior Department.

The freshwater snakehead has a huge appetite, often eating all other fish in a lake and even eating its young. When there is nothing more to eat, the fish can "walk" across land, staying out of water for up to three days, to find new sources of food. Snakeheads have even attacked people in China who got too close to snakeheads' egg-nesting areas, Norton said. The fish is also native to Africa.

Two snakeheads were dumped in the Maryland pond by a local resident who bought them from a live fish market to make soup for a sick relative. Snakeheads are sold in fish markets and some restaurants in Boston and New York, where they are legal. The fish have also been sold through aquarium fish retailers over the Internet.

B. Answer these questions. Do not look back at the article.

1. What is the problem?
2. Who is trying to solve the problem?
3. What do they plan to do about the snakehead fish?
4. Why is the snakehead fish unusual?
5. How did the snakehead get into the pond?

A C T I V I T Y . **8**   Read the textbook passage. Answer the questions that follow.

A. Read the following passage at your own speed. Try to understand as much as you can.

Hunter-gatherers in Southern Africa

For thousands of years before the arrival of European colonists, small groups of people were spread over most of southern Africa. These were the hunter-gatherers, nomads who do not farm. These hunter-gatherers moved constantly, living by hunting animals and gathering food that they found. They lived successfully in even the driest and wettest areas of the subcontinent. In recent times these early inhabitants of the subcontinent have been called the Khoisan people.

There were many different groups within the Khoisan people, however, each with its own name and language or dialect. Despite differences in language and way of life, Khoisan people shared common patterns of kinship, territorial organization, rituals, and religious beliefs.

Between the 18th and early 20th centuries, the Khoisan population underwent major changes. They lost control over their land and its natural resources because of European colonization. This made an independent existence impossible. Many Khoisan people were killed in warfare with European colonists and with other African people. A considerable number also died from new diseases, such as smallpox. The survivors became domestic servants, farm laborers, and industrial workers. In the western and northwestern parts of southern Africa, some Khoisan people settled around mission stations. There they were able to maintain a semi-independent farming life until as late as the 1950s. By then, however, in the central areas of southern Africa there were only a few Kalahari San groups still dependent on hunting and gathering for a livelihood.

Over the years, most Khoisan people have become Europeanized. As a result, the descendents of the Khoisan people can be found at nearly all levels of society throughout southern Africa. Since the extensive political and social changes in South African and Namibian society began in the 1990s, some people of Khoisan origin have been attempting to revive their cultural heritage.

B. Answer these questions. Do not look back at the passage.

1. Who are the Khoisan people?

    a. European colonists
    b. a tribe in southern Africa
    c. landowners in Africa

2. How did they used to live?

    a. as nomads
    b. on farms
    c. in caves

3. When did their lives change?

    a. when the Europeans came
    b. when Africa became industrialized
    c. when South Africa became independent

4. Today most Khoisan people are _____.

    a. hunter-gatherers
    b. living on farms
    c. no longer a tribal group

Reading Faster

Increasing reading speed has benefits. It will improve your skill at scanning, skimming, and reading large amounts of material for main ideas. At times some of us read too slowly, even for difficult material. Reading for speed can improve every reader's skill. There is one point to always keep in mind, however, when reading for speed: Reading quickly doesn't mean reading well.

Understanding the Strategy

To increase your reading speed, start by finding out how fast you read now.

Increase your reading speed and improve your scanning and skimming skills. And remember: comprehension decreases as speed increases.

Time yourself as you read the following two texts. Divide the number of words in the text by the number of minutes it takes you to read the text. Then average the numbers. This is your reading speed.

Of course, reading is not a race. The purpose of reading is to get information. It's useless to read quickly if you don't understand what you are reading. To test your level of comprehension with your reading rate, answer the five questions that follow. If you miss more than two of them, you are reading too quickly.

Example		Number of correct answers
Text 1	369 words ÷ 3 minutes = 123	5
Text 2	452 words ÷ 3.5 minutes = 129	4
Average		126 words per minute

Calculate your normal reading rate in the activity below. Then see Appendix II for articles you can use for speed-reading practice.

A C T I V I T Y . **9**   Read each text at your regular rate, and time your reading. Answer the comprehension questions that follow, and do not look back at the text. Then calculate your normal reading speed.

1. Text 1 - 369 words

International

Armstrong Hopes for More Tour Victories

July 28, 2002 02:31 PM ET

PARIS—Lance Armstrong won his fourth Tour de France on Sunday, but the American has made it clear that he has no thoughts of retiring. The 30-year-old said during the Tour that he plans to continue racing for at least two more years, although he was quick to say that that does not necessarily mean two more victories. "I'll never say I'm going to do this or want that. My personal goals are my business, and it would be suicide to announce that I'm definitely going to win the Tour," Armstrong said after riding into Paris on Sunday.

"I think it's best not to make bold predictions. When I come to the start of the Tour de France, I say, 'I think I'm ready, I think the team's ready, and I hope we win.' I don't go further. But I think I'll be around for another couple of years. This is not my last Tour. I love what I do. I still feel strong, I still feel like I'm not getting weaker, but it's hard to win the Tour de France year after year because so many things can happen," added the U.S. Postal rider. "Fortunately I have a great team around me. An individual can make a silly mistake, but when he's got a great team around him, it's hard to make a mistake."

"I like what I do. For me, it's a hobby and a job. I'm passionate about cycling. I get a lot of enjoyment out of trying to win the Tour de France. It's not only the three weeks in July, it's the whole process, all year round."

Asked if he thought he had dominated this year's Tour, Armstrong admitted he had rarely been troubled. "It's fair to say there weren't many attacks; we've all seen that, but the Tour is still challenging," he said. "The route, the length of the stages, the mountains we've climbed—it's all been hard, perhaps mentally hard more than anything, but still hard. I don't want to criticize the competition. They were strong, but I felt great. I think we prepared well and the team was great and we were lucky enough to do what we set out to do."

Comprehension Questions

1. When was this article written?
   a. after Armstrong's fourth Tour de France victory
   b. at the beginning of Armstrong's fourth Tour de France
   c. during Armstrong's fourth Tour de France

2. What does Armstrong predict?

    a. He is going to win two more tours.

    b. He plans to retire after this race.

    c. He is going to race for two more years.

3. Armstrong feels that _____.

    a. his team is getting stronger

    b. he isn't getting weaker

    c. the race is getting harder

4. Armstrong believes that _____.

    a. his team never makes mistakes

    b. individuals rarely make big mistakes

    c. his team helps him a lot

5. Armstrong says that the Tour _____.

    a. is more difficult mentally than physically

    b. isn't physically difficult

    c. is the hardest race in the world

2. Text 2 - 452 words

THE CITY

VOL. CLII No 45,378   THURSDAY, FEBRUARY 6, 2003   ONE DOLLAR

Asteroid May Hit Earth, but Don't Worry

LAST UPDATED: JULY 24, 2002 11:00 AM ET

LONDON—British space expert Dr. Benny Peiser of John Moore's University in northern England said Wednesday that a huge asteroid is on a collision course with Earth and could hit our planet in 17 years. The asteroid—the most dangerous object ever detected in space—is 2 km (1.2 miles) wide. If it hits Earth it could be the end of life as we know it.

However, Dr. Peiser is quick to add that people should not panic. "Objects of this size only hit Earth every one or two million years," he explains. Peiser and other space experts say they are pretty confident this nightmare scenario will not come about. "If it did hit Earth it would cause a continental-size explosion . . . but it is a fairly remote possibility."

The asteroid—named 2002 NT7—was discovered earlier this month by the United States Linear Sky Survey Program. Since then, Peiser said scientists on the U.S. National Aeronautics and Space Administration's (NASA) near-Earth objects team and at Pisa University in Italy have been doing calculations to figure out the probability of a collision.

Their calculations show it could hit Earth on February 1, 2019. Although the probability of such a collision is below one in a million, it has gotten a positive risk rating because the first date is so early—only 17 years from now—and the object could cause such destruction. This asteroid is the first object that has ever gotten a positive rating.

Peiser said 2002 NT7 would continue to be monitored by space experts across the world, and that these observations would probably lower the probability even further. "In all likelihood, in a couple of months additional observations will eliminate this object from the list of potential impacts," Peiser said. "I am very confident that additional observations over time will . . . show that it is actually not on a collision course with Earth."

But he warned that the world should start preparing for an asteroid hit in the future. "Sooner or later—and no one can really tell us which it will be—we will find an object that is on a collision course," he said. Space scientist Sir Arthur C. Clarke agrees. He recently told a group of reporters that ". . . an asteroid impact is inevitable sooner or later. Admittedly, this is most unlikely to wipe out the human race, but it could send us back to the Stone Age."

At the moment, scientists estimate that it could take at least 30 years to find a way to deal with such a threat. That is why many of them are saying that we should begin now.

Comprehension Questions

1. When is this event going to happen?
   a. in 2019
   b. in 2017
   c. in 2007

2. What will happen if the asteroid hits Earth?
   a. Everyone on Earth will die.
   b. Our lives will change completely.
   c. All of Earth will explode.

3. What are scientists doing now?
   a. They are trying to stop the asteroid.
   b. They are not paying attention to the asteroid.
   c. They are making more accurate calculations.

4. Why is this asteroid considered so dangerous?
   a. Because it is large, and the time is short.
   b. Because an asteroid has never hit Earth before.
   c. Because it is traveling very fast.

5. What are the chances that the asteroid will actually hit Earth?
   a. about one in a thousand
   b. less than one in a hundred
   c. less than one in a million

Keys to Faster Reading

Keep the following points in mind when you are trying to read more quickly.

- **Don't read word by word. Read words in groups. This will not only improve your reading speed, it will help you understand the text.**

Don't read like this:

Scientists   have   discovered   many   interesting   plants   in   the   rain   forest.

Read like this:

Scientists   have discovered   many interesting plants   in the rain forest.

- **Use your peripheral vision to read groups of words.**

City planners help design cities. They decide the height of buildings, the width of

streets, and the number of street signs. They even decide on the design and location of

"street furniture" such as bus stops, lamp posts, and wastebaskets. Deciding how a city is

set up involves creativity, and a career in city planning demands a knowledge of basic

engineering principles, the ability to compromise, political diplomacy, and financial

expertise.

Reading Skills and Strategies

1

Overview of the Strategies

PART 1 . COMPREHENSION STRATEGIES

Prepare

Making Predictions about the Text

Good readers know that it is important to learn about a text before reading it. Doing this helps you evaluate the text and your reading needs. You can predict the answers to the following questions about any kind of reading material.

- What is it about?
- What kind of information does it give about the topic?
- How is the information organized?
- Is the reading for students or specialists, children, or adults?
- Is the reading for fun or to give facts?

Understanding the Strategy

Certain features of reading material reveal key information in the text. It is possible to guess the topic, main ideas, the author's purpose in writing about the topic, and the audience the reading is intended for. You may also be able to guess the special kind of information given and the reading's level of difficulty. Read the list of features. Work in small groups. How do these features of a text help you predict answers to the previous questions?

Before you read, look at the text and make predictions.

- title
- subtitles
- pictures
- charts and graphs
- size of the letters
- length of the article
- author's name / title

A C T I V I T Y . 1   Review the features of the story in Activity 3 on page 22. Which of these predictions can you make?

_____ what the reading is about

_____ how difficult the reading is

_____ why the author wrote it

_____ who the author wrote it for

_____ where the information you are looking for is located

Predicting from Genre

Newspapers, textbooks, magazines, and encyclopedias give information in unique ways. Each treats the same topic differently.

Understanding the Strategy

Writers write to inform, persuade, instruct, and entertain. They may describe, argue, or explain their ideas. Or they may classify items or try to solve a problem. Reading material is shaped according to genre and the author's purpose. Match the following titles with the genres of reading material.

Before you read, consider the writer's purpose and the kind of text it is.

1. science textbook
2. weekly news magazine
3. magazine for scientists
4. tabloid newspaper
5. newspaper editorial

a. Cloning Must Be Stopped
b. Chapter Four: Human Reproduction
c. First Cloned Cow Gives Milk
d. The Use of Deoxygenated RNA in Cloning
e. Scientist Produces First Catdog

A C T I V I T Y . **2**

A. In the chart, check the description that applies to each genre.

	Accuracy	Explanations, Definitions	Unreliability	Personal Opinion	Difficulty of Vocabulary	Current Topics Only
1. science textbook extract						
2. tabloid newspaper story						
3. weekly news magazine article						
4. newspaper editorial						
5. scientific journal						

B. Which of the genres would you choose to read:

a. for fun?   _____

b. to write a school report?   _____

c. for general information?   _____

Read

Reading with a Purpose

Reading is an interactive process. This means the reader communicates with a text. If you ask a text questions, it will provide answers. Read with a purpose: read to learn ideas, to get specific data, or to get answers.

Understanding the Strategy

Texts may give specific details connected to a topic. The details may include statistics, dates and times, type, and location of people, places, or things. Ask specific questions about details that might be given in a reading, in addition to general questions about main ideas, the audience, or the writer's purpose. Work with a partner. For each title that follows, think of a general question and a specific question the article might answer.

> Read with questions in mind. As you find the answers, think of more questions.

1. A Bear's Best Friend
2. What Really Works for Small Businesses
3. Ten Perfect Family Vacations

A C T I V I T Y . **3**

A. Look at the title of the following reading. Think of two or more general questions it may answer. Then read to find the answers.

Tiger Woods: A Golf Legend at 27

1   Eldrick (Tiger) Woods, now 27 years of age, has had an incredible career. Most professional golfers would be happy to retire with his statistics. The difference is, Tiger is not even 30. Since he became a professional in 1996, he has won 50 tournaments, including the 1997, 2001, and 2002 Masters Tournaments, the 1999
5   and 2000 PGA Championships, the 2000 and 2002 U.S. Open Championships, and the 2000 British Open Championship. In 2001, Tiger became the first golfer ever to hold all four professional major championships at the same time. He has won more championships than any active golfer, even though most are much older than he is.

This amazing young man is the son of Earl Woods and his wife, Kultida, a native
10 of Thailand. He was nicknamed Tiger after a Vietnamese friend of his father, Vuong Dang Phong, to whom his father had also given that nickname. Born on December 30, 1975, Tiger Woods grew up in Cypress, California. His interest in golf was obvious from the time he was only six months old, as he watched his father hit golf balls into a net and copied his movements. At the age of two he was on television, and at three he had a score of 48 for nine holes.

B. Write three to five specific questions that the reading answers. Read the paragraphs again and find the answers.

C. The two paragraphs are the beginning of a magazine article on Tiger Woods. Think of more questions the article may answer. Share your questions with the class.

Using Signal Words to Predict Ideas

Signal words connect ideas. They tell what kind of idea is coming, and how it relates to the idea that came before it.

Understanding the Strategy

Signal words are divided by purpose. For example, they can add ideas, compare or contrast ideas, show cause, or give examples. Study the following signal words and the sample sentences. Then answer the questions by filling in the blanks with the correct signal words.

Use signal words to help you predict the ideas that are coming.

Categories and sample signal words

Addition:	*and, in addition*
Cause or reason:	*because, since*
Contrast:	*but, however*
Effect or result:	*therefore, consequently*
Example:	*for example, for instance*

Sample sentences

The team played well; **in addition,** they played politely.

The team played well. **However,** they will have to play better.

The team played well, **but** they didn't win.

The team played well. **For instance,** the outfield made no mistakes.

The team played well **since** the game was important.

The team played well. **Consequently,** they won the championship.

Which signal word introduces:

a. a reason?   _____

b. an addition?   _____

c. a contrasting idea?   _____

d. an example?   _____

e. a result?   _____

A C T I V I T Y . 4   For each item, read the sentence(s), and complete the meaning. Circle the letter of the correct answer, and underline the idea that the signal word connects it to.

Example: The American poet Emily Dickinson was born in 1830, when women were expected to get married. However, _____ .

    a. she had no children

    (**b.**) she stayed single her whole life

    c. she was a great poet

1. Many books contain photos that photographers take. An editor helps decide which photos will be used. In addition, _____ .

    a. the photographer develops the photos

    b. the editor and photographer never work together

    c. the editor decides where to put each photo on the page

2. No problem facing American public schools has been more difficult to deal with than integration. Consequently, _____ .

    a. Americans have still not found a good solution

    b. all schools are now integrated

    c. it is a socioeconomic issue

3. The legend of King Arthur began with an ordinary boy, and _____

    a. it was not true

    b. a sword

    c. he was king

4. Some people made millions of dollars on new Internet companies in the 1990s. However, _____ .

    a. technology was very important

    b. many of their companies no longer exist

    c. they are rich

5. There are several different kinds of environmentally friendly vehicles available today. For example, _____ .

    a. people don't like to spend money on gas

    b. electric cars are gaining in popularity

    c. they are often inconvenient

A C T I V I T Y . **5**   Work with a partner. Read each item. Note the signal word, and complete the sentence.

Example: Harry wanted the job. However, *he didn't get it*.

1. Science has helped find cures for diseases. In addition, _____

_____.

2. Kansas isn't a wonderful place for a vacation. However, _____

_____.

3. Astronauts have to be in excellent physical condition since _____

_____.

4. Alexander Graham Bell was a famous inventor. For instance, _____

_____.

5. Christopher Columbus sailed west, but _____

_____.

Using Background Knowledge

Background knowledge is what you already know about a topic. This knowledge helps you understand a text without understanding every word. Using background knowledge as you read builds reading speed, confidence, and understanding.

Understanding the Strategy

When you meet familiar terms in a reading, ask this question: What do I know about this? Think of your experience and knowledge. Do you know inventors? Do you invent things? Read the following paragraph and answer these questions.

As you read, think of what you already know about the topic.

- What did George Stephenson invent?
- What background knowledge did you use to guess his invention?

George Stephenson was the son of a poor coal miner. He began working in a mine at the age of 15. Stephenson conceived the idea of a machine that could pull trucks of mined coal instead of men pulling them. In 1814, he tried out his invention. It was not long before he thought of using the invention for passenger travel.

ACTIVITY. **6**

A. Read the paragraph about Peter Black, a scientist who flew into a hurricane. Do not try to guess the meaning of unfamiliar words. As you read, find answers to these questions.

- Was it difficult to fly the plane? Why?
- What example shows how strong the wind is?

As the airplane flew into Hugo's eye, the wind increased from 67 to 184 mph in less

than two minutes. A _____ of strong _____

and _____ shook the plane _____. As the

plane flew into the edge of the _____, it _____

air moving upward at 45 mph and then four seconds later, air moving downward at 18

mph. While all of this was going on, the _____ turned off one of the

airplane's four _____ that suddenly began turning too quickly. Black

was _____ in next to a _____ life raft that

broke loose from the _____ holding it to the floor. It flew up and

_____ a one-inch steel pipe in the ceiling.

B. Compare your answers with your classmates'. Do you have knowledge or experience of airplanes and hurricanes? If so, explain how it helped you understand the reading.

Critical Reading: Distinguishing Fact from Opinion

Reading critically means evaluating the information you are reading. It is especially important to separate facts from opinions. Facts refer to what can be measured or proven. Opinions are judgements, usually about the value, appearance, usefulness, or appeal of a person, place, or thing. Facts and opinions are often mixed in reading articles.

Understanding the Strategy

Facts are often stated in the simple present or past tense. Opinions may be stated like a fact, or may be signaled by words such as *think, believe,* and *seem.* Study the examples, then work with a partner. Find at least one fact and one opinion for each of the following statements.

As you read, constantly evaluate the information you are reading. Separate fact from opinion.

Examples: Fact: It is 38°C today. The teacher gave the test on Monday.
Opinion: John is handsome. The tea tastes terrible, I think.

1. James Freeman's first novel, *The Truth about Life,* shows amazing skill for a new author.

2. There are fantastic new medicines today; however, high prices make them too expensive for the people who need them most.

3. Antonín Dvorak's ninth symphony, *From the New World,* his most popular work, is among the most beautiful pieces of music ever created.

A C T I V I T Y. 7   Read each paragraph. For each underlined phrase, write fact or opinion in the blank.

1. India is one of the most interesting countries in the world. In my opinion, its geography

   a   b

   is one reason why. The country has jungles filled with monkeys and other animals.

   c

   It also has hot, dry deserts, fertile river valleys, and tall, snow-covered mountains

   d

   that are the most beautiful you will find.

   e

   a. _____   d. _____

   b. _____   e. _____

   c. _____

2. In many ways, India is like two countries. The cities are highly industrialized. They are

   f

   crowded, although only 30 percent of the population live in them. By contrast, the villages

   are farming communities where people still use primitive agricultural methods. About

   g

   70 percent of the population live outside the cities, and 40 percent of them live in

   h   i

   poverty. Although India is beautiful and fascinating, it can be a sad place to visit.

   j

   f. _____   i. _____

   g. _____   j. _____

   h. _____

Remember

Highlighting and Underlining Text

When you are reading for fun, it is all right to forget what you read. When you are reading to learn, however, you must remember important information. Marking important words and ideas in a text helps you remember them.

Understanding the Strategy

If you highlight or underline too much, you won't be able to find important points. Examine the two paragraphs. Which paragraph's highlighting will better help you study for an anthropology test?

> Underline or highlight important points as you read.

A. What is culture? For some people, culture refers to the great books, music, and works of art that a group of people have created over time. This is sometimes also called high culture. In anthropology, however, culture is the way of life of a group of people. It is the total of their learned behavior, beliefs, and material things. Furthermore, culture must be transmitted from one generation to the next by learning and experience.

B. What is culture? For some people, culture refers to the great books, music, and works of art that a group of people have created over time. This is sometimes also called high culture. In anthropology, however, culture is the way of life of a group of people. It is the total of their learned behavior, beliefs, and material things. Furthermore, culture must be transmitted from one generation to the next by learning and experience.

ACTIVITY. **8**

Imagine you are writing a report on Sigmund Freud's achievements. Highlight the important points of the reading.

1   Sigmund Freud, the founder of psychoanalysis, was born on May 6, 1856, in Freiberg, now in the Czech Republic. At the age of four, his family moved to Vienna, where he lived and worked for most of his life. Freud attended medical school at the University of Vienna. In 1881, he received his medical degree and eventually started a private practice in the treatment of psychological disorders.

5   Freud's greatest achievements are based on his new ideas. Freud developed the idea of the unconscious. He believed many psychological disorders were caused by childhood experiences buried in the unconscious. He claimed that patients could be cured if they faced the experiences. In 1894, he published this controversial theory. Freud also believed that dreams represent unconscious desires. In 1900, he published *The Interpretation of Dreams,* based on this now-famous theory. Many people believe that this is Freud's greatest work.

10   Another of Freud's great achievements was his model of the human mind. He developed this model in 1923. He said the mind consists of three elements—the *ego,* the *id,* and the *superego.* During his life, Freud published over 20 books of theory and studies based on this model. In these, he named now-familiar concepts such as libido, subconscious, and inferiority complex.

  In 1886, Freud married Martha Bernays. They had six children. In 1937, he went to live in England. He
15 lived there until his death in 1939.

P A R T 2 **: VOCABULARY STRATEGIES**

Deciding Which Words Are Important

To highlight the key ideas in a text, you must be able to recognize them. When you are reading in a foreign language, texts are filled with words you don't know. Grasping main ideas often only requires about 50 percent comprehension of a reading. It is not necessary to understand every word, but you must understand the important ones.

Understanding the Strategy

Remember that all words are not equal. To decide if a word is important, consider the following list.

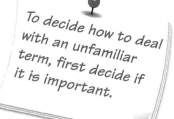

To decide how to deal with an unfamiliar term, first decide if it is important.

Important words

- Words in the title. Titles often sum up main ideas.
- Repeated words. Good writers repeat key words.
- Words that appear in various forms. If the writer uses *accelerator, accelerate,* and *acceleration,* the concept is probably important.

A C T I V I T Y . 9

Only one underlined word is a key term in the story. As you read, answer these questions.

- Which underlined word is the most important?
- What is the approximate meaning of this word?

1 Andy Evans was up before dawn. He <u>tiptoed</u> around the kitchen, getting his breakfast and making a lunch. This was Saturday, and he had to <u>harvest</u> the corn. It was going to be a <u>rough</u> all-day job. He needed an early start.
   Breakfast was over. He closed the <u>damper</u> on the stove. He stacked the dishes in the sink, got his matches
5 from the <u>cupboard</u>, and put on his mosquito <u>repellent</u>. He got his <u>knife</u> and <u>ax</u> from the barn. He was ready to go. Last year, he was able to pick most of the corn. He made almost 2,000 dollars. He hoped to make more money this season.

Predicting the Next Word

In Part 1, you learned to make predictions before you read. It is also important to predict as you read. Predicting ideas helps you grasp the general meaning of a text. Predicting words helps you grasp the meaning of each sentence and connect ideas.

Understanding the Strategy

Descriptions are stated near the person, thing, or place they describe, and usually before it. Look at this phrase, and predict the word that is coming:

As you are reading, think of the words that might be coming.

the little red _____

Will the next word be *tomorrow, quickly, gave?* Could it be *idea* or *hat?* The next word will be a noun—a noun that we can describe as *little* and *red*.

A C T I V I T Y . 10   Work with a partner to finish these sentences. There may be many ways to finish them, or only one or two. Discuss with classmates which words are important and why.

1. Dave was upset when he saw the terrible _____.

2. Everyone likes a lot of _____.

3. Gary wants to marry a wonderful _____.

4. We had a meal that was _____.

5. On holidays, the children are _____.

Recognizing Internal Definitions

Recognizing definitions is a valuable skill. It helps you build vocabulary and read quickly and effectively at the same time. Look for internal definitions. A term is often defined within the text itself.

Understanding the Strategy

Internal definitions usually occur near the new term. Learn to find the clues. Clues that a definition is coming are often given by these means:

When you find an unfamiliar word, look for an internal definition.

Repeating and defining the term in a succeeding sentence

repeating and defining   Avalanches are common in the Himalayas. An avalanche is a large mass of snow that suddenly slides down a mountain.

Explaining what the term is not

not   Avalanches are not the speed that snow tumbles down a mountain.

Single words or phrases

or   People once thought that water would dilute or weaken chemicals and other pollutants.

that is   Champagne—that is, the sparkling white wine from the Champagne region of France—can be very expensive.

Punctuation

a long dash (—) Two astronomers work at the planetarium—a dome-shaped building that uses a machine to project pictures of stars on the ceiling.

a comma   In the 19th century, women wore bustles, or frames that made their dresses stick out in the back.

A C T I V I T Y . **11**   Underline the internal definitions, and circle the words they define.

1. A lightbulb gives off light from a glowing metal. The thin, coiled wire inside the bulb, or the filament, is made from a metal that can be heated to high temperatures.

2. To compare unlike things, poets use simile, a figure of speech using *like* or *as,* and metaphor, a figure of speech that doesn't use a signal word. "He ate like a wolf" is a simile, but "He wolfed down his food" is a metaphor.

3. In thinking about political culture, it is important that we understand not only what it is, but what it is not. Political culture does not refer to the actions of the government. Political culture is how people feel about the actions of their government.

4. Migration, that is, movement of people from one place to another, has always involved a heavy cost. This is particularly true for migration from the country to the city, which usually brings more crime and pauperism or poverty.

5. He entertained the group by playing the ocarina—a simple wind instrument shaped like an egg.

Analyzing a Word for Meaning

To understand or guess the meaning of a word, good readers analyze it carefully. They relate unfamiliar words to words they already know, and they examine the words' parts to see how meaning changes.

Understanding the Strategy

Words of similar meaning may have similar spelling. That is, they may have the same root meaning, or stem, but occur in different forms. Endings and beginnings change the basic meaning of a word, and they may also change the part of speech.

When you find an unfamiliar word, relate it to familiar words. Analyze the parts to determine changes in basic meaning.

Suffixes

Suffixes are endings added to a whole word or to a stem. They change the part of speech. For example, you can change a verb to a noun and a noun to an adjective by adding a suffix.

Example:	**Verb**	**Noun**	**Adjective**
	connect	connect**ion**	connect**able**
		connect**or**	

Prefixes

Prefixes are attached to the beginning of a word or a stem. They do not change the part of speech. They change the meaning.

Example:	**re**connect	to connect again	(**re** means "again or back")
	disconnect	to cut a connection	(**dis** means "not")
	misconnect	to connect incorrectly	(**mis** means "wrong")

Stems

Stems represent the basic or root meaning of a word. A stem can be at the beginning, the middle, or the end of a word.

Example:	**graph**	means "write"
	graphology	the study of handwriting
	tele**graph**ing	sending a message over a telegraph system
	picto**graph**	a message written in the form of a picture

A C T I V I T Y . 12   Work in groups or pairs. Complete the chart. Complete the columns with related words.

	Verb	Noun	Adjective
1.	beautify		
2.		collection	
3.			powerful
4.			organized
5.	inform		

A C T I V I T Y . 13   For each item, study the word parts and the meanings of the words. Then guess the meaning of the italicized root, prefix, and/or suffix, and write your answer in the blanks.

1. **bi cycle**   a vehicle with two wheels

   cy clone   winds that go in a circle
   bi ped   an animal that walks on two feet
   pedo meter   an instrument that measures how far you walk
   baro meter   an instrument that measures air pressure

   a. *bi-*   probably means _____.

   b. *ped*   probably means _____.

   c. *cy-*   probably means _____.

2. **bio logy**   a study of living things

   bio graphy   the story of someone's life
   audi ology   the study of hearing
   audi torium   a large room where an audience attends meetings,
                  plays, etc.
   nata torium   a large room with an indoor swimming pool

   a. *bio-*   probably means _____.

   b. *aud*   probably means _____.

   c. *-orium* probably means _____.

3. **astro logy**   the study of predicting the future by looking at the stars and planets

   astro nomer   a person who studies the stars and planets
   golf er   a person who plays golf
   carpent er   a person who builds things from wood
   found er   a person who begins or establishes something

   a. *-(o)logy* probably means _____.

   b. *astro*   probably means _____.

   c. *er*   probably means _____.

4. **micro scope**   an instrument for seeing very small things

micro film   a process for copying a document by reducing its size
tele scope   an instrument for seeing things that are far away
tele phone   an instrument that allows people in different places to talk to each other
phone etics   the study of speech sounds

a. *micro-* probably means _____.

b. *tele-* probably means _____.

c. *phon* probably means _____.

5. **geo graphy**   the study of the land on the earth

geo thermal   heat that comes from the earth
geo ology   the study of the earth's crust
therm ometer   an instrument that measures temperature
bar ometer   an instrument that measures air pressure

a. *geo* probably means _____.

b. *therm* probably means _____.

c. *-meter* probably means _____.

ACTIVITY. **14**   Read the following sentences, and analyze the italicized words. Guess the meaning, and write your answers in the blanks.

1. We spent most of the semester studying 20th-century *geopolitics*.

Geopolitics probably means _____.

2. We have a *bimonthly* meeting in New York.

Bimonthly probably means _____.

3. Learning to fly a *hydroplane* is very exciting.

Hydroplane probably means _____.

4. Dr. Edwina James teaches *phonology*.

Phonology probably means _____.

5. You're driving too fast. Look at the *speedometer*.

Speedometer probably means _____.

Guessing the Approximate Meaning of a Word

It is often possible to guess the approximate meaning of a word without analyzing it. Guessing lets you continue reading. Reading continuously helps you keep the main idea in mind.

Understanding the Strategy

Look for context clues to the approximate meaning of unfamiliar words. You may find these clues by using logic, by drawing from your general background knowledge, or by using synonyms and antonyms. Study the following examples.

When you read a new word, look for clues to guess its approximate meaning.

Logic

Example: Bob didn't go out in the rain because he didn't have his *wellies,* his *bumbershoot,* or his *mackintosh.*

You may not have any idea what the words *wellies, bumbershoot,* or *mackintosh* mean. However, you can guess that they are things that people use or wear when it's raining. In many cases, this approximate meaning will be enough to let you continue reading. In fact, the italicized words are British English terms for boots, an umbrella, and a raincoat.

General Background Knowledge

Example: Like Aesop, the French writer La Fontaine wrote many amusing *fables.*

The clue to the meaning of *fables* is based on your general background knowledge. If you know who Aesop (or La Fontaine) is, then you probably know what type of stories they wrote, and therefore, the meaning of *fables.*

Synonyms and Antonyms

Example: She found the story *humorous,* and I also thought it was <u>funny</u>.

The important clue is the word "funny". The writer's opinion is **like** the other person's opinion, but she uses the word "funny". Therefore, if you know the meaning of "funny", you can guess the meaning of its synonym. *Humorous* is the same as "funny".

Example: My own problems are <u>small</u> compared with her *enormous* difficulties.

The important clue is the word "small." The writer contrasts his problems with those of another person. His are "small", **not** like the other person's. Therefore, if you know the meaning of "small", you can guess the meaning of its antonym. *Enormous* is "big" or "great", the opposite of "small".

ACTIVITY . 15   For each item, search for context clues to the meanings of the underlined words. Then fill in the blanks with your answers.

1. Elizabeth Enright's mother was an artist and her father was a <u>cartoonist</u>. After she finished studying at the School of Applied Art in Paris, she began <u>illustrating</u> children's books. Her first book, which she wrote and <u>illustrated</u>, was honored for its <u>literary content</u> as well as its art.

    a. *Cartoonist* probably means _____.

    b. *Illustrated* probably means _____.

    c. *Literary content* probably refers to _____.

2. Frank was a great bus driver. He didn't get <u>annoyed</u> at passengers. He was always friendly, even though he had a <u>lousy route</u>. Going to Chicago, he had to stop at tiny towns along the way: Clinton, Fullerton, Farmer City, Gibson.

    a. *Annoyed* probably means _____.

    b. *Lousy* probably refers to _____.

    c. *Route* probably means _____.

3. Cotton growing brought <u>prosperity</u> to the South. Every year, more land was planted with cotton. However, the riches were temporary because growing cotton ruined the farmland. It <u>depleted</u> the soil of all its nutrients, making it unfit for <u>cultivation</u>.

    a. *Prosperity* probably means _____.

    b. *Depleted* probably means _____.

    c. *Cultivation* probably refers to _____.

4. Managers of teams that <u>conquer</u> problems are good interviewers. They know that finding <u>competent</u> people is only one goal of interviewing. In addition to ability, they look for willingness in an interviewee. If they find willingness, they analyze the <u>candidate's</u> judgement and emotional maturity.

    a. *Conquer* probably means to _____.

    b. *Competent* likely means _____.

    c. *Candidate* probably refers to _____.

5. Camels used to be wild animals but they are now <u>domesticated</u>. Camels are <u>herbivores</u>, or plant eaters. They are usually <u>placid</u> but have a <u>bad temper</u> if disturbed or upset.

    a. *Domesticated* probably means _____.

    b. *Herbivores* possibly means _____.

    c. *Placid* probably means _____.

A C T I V I T Y . **16**   In Activity 6, you read about the scientist Peter Black. Now read the story again with the missing words filled in. Then complete the chart.

As the airplane flew into Hugo's eye, the wind increased from 67 to 184 mph in less than two minutes. A **series** of strong **updrafts** and **downdrafts** shook the plane violently. As the plane flew into the edge of the **eyewall,** it **encountered** air moving upward at 45 mph and then four seconds later, air moving downward at 18 mph. While all of this was going on, the **flight engineer** turned off one of the airplane's four **turboprops** that suddenly began turning too quickly. Black was **strapped** in next to a **bundled** life raft that broke loose from the **straps** holding it to the floor. It flew up and **dented** a one-inch steel pipe in the ceiling.

A. Put a check mark in the correct column.

Unfamiliar Words	A I know this word.	B I guessed the meaning of this word.	C I can't guess the meaning, but it probably isn't important.	D I can't guess the meaning and it may be important.
1. series				
2. updrafts				
3. downdrafts				
4. eyewall				
5. encountered				
6. flight engineer				

Unfamiliar Words	A I know this word.	B I guessed the meaning of this word.	C I can't guess the meaning, but it probably isn't important.	D I can't guess the meaning and it may be important.
7. turboprops				
8. strapped				
9. bundled				
10. straps				
11. dented				

B. Compare your chart with a partner's, and answer the questions.

1. How many words were you able to guess?
2. What do you think the words that are new to you mean?
3. What clues did you use to guess the approximate meanings of the words?
4. Did you check any words in column C? Look up these words in a dictionary. Were they important after all? Why or why not?
5. Did you check any words in column D? Look them up in a dictionary. Decide if they are important, and why or why not.

C. Join another pair. Compare and discuss your answers to the questions as a group.

Reading:
Urban Legends

Getting Started

Discuss these questions in pairs or small groups. Share your ideas with the class.

1. Read the chapter title and look at the photo. Then look at the titles of the readings in this chapter. What do you think this chapter is about?

2. What is a myth? A legend?

3. Do you believe in any myths? Why or why not?

Strategies Reminder

Comprehension Strategies

Prepare
- Making Predictions about the Text
- Predicting from Genre

Read
- Using Background Knowledge
- Reading with a Purpose (with Questions in Mind)
- Using Signal Words to Predict Ideas

Critical Reading
- Distinguishing Fact from Opinion

Remember
- Highlighting and Underlining Text

Vocabulary Strategies
- Deciding Which Words Are Important
- Predicting the Next Word
- Recognizing Internal Definitions
- Analyzing a Word for Meaning
- Guessing the Approximate Meaning of a Word

1 · READING

Prepare

Work with a partner. Describe the features of the text. Complete the following predictions, and explain your choices to the class.

1. This reading is from _____.
   a. a newspaper
   b. an encyclopedia
   c. a tabloid

2. Most of the information in this reading will be _____.
   a. facts
   b. opinions
   c. about current topics only

Read

Think of what you already know about urban myths. Read the text to get a general idea of the meaning. Don't try to figure out unfamiliar terms. While you are reading, find the answer to this question.

What is an urban legend?

Urban Legend   345

Urban Legend:

a usually apocryphal story about events of the recent past, often including humor and horror, that spreads quickly and is popularly believed to be true.

Some begin from a real event but change significantly passing through society; others begin with misinformation. Another common feature of urban legends is their mysterious origin. Many urban legends relate to certain geographic areas, but sociologists cannot say specifically where the phenomenon begins. Third, they have common purposes. Urban legends are always told in order to surprise, shock, frighten, disgust, or elicit laughter. The legends spread rapidly through interpersonal communication. They are passed by word of mouth and over the Internet. Another key feature is the indirect connection between storyteller and story; the teller commonly claims the experience happened to a friend of a friend. Stating that the story is true, the teller at the same time changes small features of it to suit his or her purposes. Researchers observe that the personal communication and believability are the reasons that the legends spread. Last, a selection process is probably involved. Psychologists have found that people are more likely to believe and pass on stories that are consistent with their fears and experience. For instance, if a person is afraid of dogs and hears a story about dangerous dogs, he is more likely to pass the story on. As a general rule, if an urban legend expresses a fear that is common in society, it will spread quickly. *(See psychology of groups, mythology.)*

Read Again

Read the text again and do the following:

1. Think of two or three more questions and read to find the answers.
2. Predict ideas. Use signal words from Chapter 1 and other clues to help you.
3. Note unfamiliar words. Decide if they are important. If so, try to figure out their meanings, and notice which vocabulary strategies you are using.

Post-Reading Activities

A. Comprehension Check

Answer these questions about the reading.

1. Are most urban legends true or false?
2. What is the origin of urban legends?
3. What are the common purposes of urban legends?
4. How do urban legends spread?
5. What are some features of an urban legend?
6. Do people who pass on urban legends believe them?

B. Vocabulary Check

Each of the following words is in Reading 1. Write the prefix, suffix, or root of each word.

1. researchers   _____

2. geographic   _____

3. relate   _____

4. misinformation   _____

5. indirect   _____

6. interpersonal   _____

7. connection   _____

8. mythology   _____

Remember

Pretend that you are studying for a psychology test on urban legends. Highlight or underline the important parts of the reading.

Discuss

1. How is an urban legend different from a myth or fairy tale?
2. Do you know any urban legends? Do you believe them? Share an urban legend, and explain the reasons you do or do not believe it.

Thinking About Strategies

What did you do with unfamiliar words in Reading 1? Complete the chart and answer the questions. Then compare your answers with a partner's.

A. Check each column that applies. The first one is done for you. See step B for column B1.

Unfamiliar Words	A I knew this word.	B I was able to guess the approximate meaning.	B1 I used this vocabulary strategy.	C I couldn't guess the meaning, and it was an important word.	D I couldn't guess the meaning, but it wasn't an important word.
1. sociologists		✓	2		
2. phenomenon					

Unfamiliar Words	A I knew this word.	B I was able to guess the approximate meaning.	B1 I used this vocabulary strategy.	C I couldn't guess the meaning, and it was an important word.	D I couldn't guess the meaning, but it wasn't an important word.
3. mysterious					
4. apocryphal					
5. interpersonal					
6. indirect					
7. origin					
8. psychologists					
9. consistent					
10. society					

B. How did you figure out the meaning of the words checked in column B? Read the following list. In column B1, write the number of the strategy you used. If you are not sure, or if you used a strategy not listed, write "5."

    1. background knowledge

    2. context clues

    3. word analysis

    4. internal definition

    5. other

C. Did you find out the meaning of the words checked in column C? If so, how?

2 · READING

Prepare

Work with a partner. Look at the title of Reading 2. Make predictions about the following questions, and explain your choices to the class.

1. Where would you find this reading?

    a. in a textbook   **b.** in a scientific journal   **c.** in a newspaper

2. Does the author believe this urban legend? Why or why not?

Read

Read the text to get a general idea of the meaning. Don't try to figure out unfamiliar words and phrases. While you are reading, find the answers to these questions.

When did this legend start?

How did the legend continue?

Alligators in the Sewers? Not Again!

When tourist Mary Brown was charged with carrying a concealed weapon on the streets of New York, she explained that she had brought the gun from her home in Texas because she needed a weapon to kill the alligators. And so the legend lives on. One of millions, Mary Brown has become a victim of one of the oldest and most famous urban legends in the United States—the belief that there are alligators in the sewers under New York City.

This ridiculous legend has stayed alive for nearly 75 years. Why? The story itself might explain. According to the legend, when New Yorkers went to Florida on vacation, they often bought baby alligators as pets for their children. When the alligators got too big, people flushed them down the toilet. A few of the alligators survived and began to reproduce in the sewers. It's absurd, but yet the story spreads. "It must be true," Mary Brown frowned. "After all, New Yorkers often go to Florida on vacation." But the fact that so many New Yorkers visit Florida every year isn't the only reason for the legend's long life.

The media itself has contributed to the continued popularity. The legend has been encouraged by a number of news reports over the years. The one documented case appeared in the *New York Times* on February 10, 1935, with a headline that read: "Alligator Found in Uptown Sewer." The story reported two teenaged boys finding an eight-foot-long alligator in a manhole in Upper Manhattan. The only explanation given was that the alligator, half-dead from the cold, had fallen off a ship in the East River. The story received its biggest boost from a book published in 1959 called *The World Beneath the City.* The book was intended as a work of nonfiction. Unfortunately, author Robert Daley relied on a sewer official named Teddy May for information about life under the city. May's imaginative stories of seeing alligators in the sewers were amusing but false. The sewer official even claimed that he was responsible for killing hundreds of alligators. Instead of dispelling the legend, the book kept it alive. Even the logic of science has failed to stop the tale. "It is a well-known fact that alligators cannot survive in cold, dark sewers," says Dr. J. M. Harvey, reptile expert at the Bronx Zoo.

Read Again

Read the text again and do the following:

1. Think of two or three more questions, then read to find the answers.

2. Predict ideas. Use signal words from Chapter 1 and other clues to help you.

3. Note unfamiliar words. Decide if they are important. If so, try to figure out their meanings, and notice which vocabulary strategies you are using.

Post-Reading Activities

A. Comprehension Check

Answer these questions about the reading. Read each question carefully.

1. Does the writer think people should believe this legend? Why or why not?
2. Why does the writer think that people believe this legend?
3. What truth is there in this story?
4. How did *The World Beneath the City* keep this story alive?
5. Who was Teddy May?
6. What did Mr. May claim?

B. Vocabulary Check

Answer parts (a) and (b) for each question. In part (a), circle the letter of the correct answer.

1. **(a)** The meaning of *absurd* in paragraph 2 is ———————————.

 a. believable   **b.** important   **c.** silly

 (b) Find and mark another word in the reading that is a synonym for *absurd*.

2. **(a)** Two words that are important to the main ideas of the reading are

 ——————————— and ———————————.

| alligator | documented | sewer |
| claim | flush | toilet |

 (b) What do these two words mean? In which paragraphs do you find them?

C. Critical Reading Check

Find three places in the reading where the author's opinion of the legend is revealed.

Remember

If you spread the legend of alligators in the sewers of New York, what will you say? Highlight or underline the legend.

Discuss

1. Have you heard this urban legend? Who told it to you, and why?
2. What is the most ridiculous urban legend you have heard? Did you believe it?

Thinking About Strategies

What did you do with the unfamiliar words in Reading 2? Complete the chart, and answer the questions. Then compare your answers with a partner's.

A. Check each column that applies. See step B for column B1.

Unfamiliar Words	A I knew this word.	B I was able to guess the approximate meaning.	B1 I used this vocabulary strategy.	C I couldn't guess the meaning, and it was an important word.	D I couldn't guess the meaning, but it wasn't an important word.
1. concealed					
2. weapon					
3. victim					
4. ridiculous					
5. survived					
6. reproduce					
7. sewers					
8. media					
9. popularity					
10. documented					
11. boost					
12. relied					
13. dispelling					

B. For each word checked in column B, read the following list. In column B1, write the number of the strategy you used. If you are not sure, or if you used a strategy not listed, write "5."

1. background knowledge
2. context clues
3. word analysis
4. internal definition
5. other

C. Did you find out the meaning of the words checked in column C? If so, how?

3 ⟩ READING

Prepare

Work with a partner. Review the title and the format of the reading. Make predictions about the following questions, and explain your choices to the class.

1. Two parts of the text are indented. What kind of information is this? How is it different from the rest of the text?

2. What is the author's purpose?

Read

Think of what you already know about language mistakes. Read the text to get a general understanding of the meaning. Don't try to figure out unfamiliar words and phrases. While you are reading, find the answers to these questions.

What were the "mistakes"?

Who made the "mistakes"?

Language Mistakes That Weren't

1 Don't believe everything you read—especially if the writer is making fun of famous people or corporations. Here are two urban legends that have to do with language use. The first is a story that appeared in newspapers in 1963 after John F. Kennedy's visit to Berlin.

In 1963, Berlin was a divided city that had many problems. Kennedy wanted to make a friendly
5 speech. The speech was made in English, but the president, who did not speak German, said one sentence in German: "I am a doughnut," said President John F. Kennedy yesterday during his speech to Berliners. Kennedy's embarrassing "Ich bin ein Berliner," should have been, "Ich bin Berliner." A Berliner, Mr. President, is a kind of doughnut made in Berlin.

The story is amusing, but the critics were wrong. Germans say that "Ich bin ein Berliner" is correct. Experts
10 agree that Kennedy's German grammar was perfect. In fact, a professional translator told him exactly what to say.

People in business commonly hear stories of international business blunders. The stories appear in business textbooks. Experts at business seminars recount them. One particular blunder concerns the way product names can create cross-cultural problems. Of course, the classic example of a bad automobile name goes to General
15 Motors Corporation. Here is a popular legend about it, as it is usually told. This version was recounted by two experts on international business in their book *Kiss, Bow or Shake Hands.*

General Motors Corporation wanted the Chevy Nova marketed in Latin America without a name change. Technically, the word *nova* means the same in English and Spanish: an exploding star. But when spoken aloud, it also sounds like the Spanish phrase *no va,* which means "it does
20 not go." Sales were poor in Latin America until GM changed the model's name to Caribe.

A bad name can affect a product's sales, but the Nova story is not a good example of that fact. Why? First, Nova is not pronounced as "no va." Nova has an accent on "no," and "no va" has an accent on "va." Spanish speakers would not confuse the two. Second, GM did not change the name of the Nova. The Caribe wasn't a GM car; it was a Toyota. Finally, one of the strongest pieces of evidence that this story is absurd comes

25   from Pemex, the Mexican oil company. Pemex sells a successful gasoline product in Mexico called
Nova. Everyday, Mexicans buy thousands of gallons of Nova. Is it possible they believe they are
fueling their cars with "no va" gas?

Read Again

Read the text again and do the following:

1. Think of two or three more questions, and read to find the answers.
2. Predict ideas. Use signal words from Chapter 1 and other clues to help you.
3. Note unfamiliar words. Decide if they are important. If so, try to figure out their meanings, and notice which vocabulary strategies you are using.

Post-Reading Activities

A. Comprehension Check

Answer these questions about the reading.

1. What did President Kennedy say in German in Berlin?
2. According to Kennedy's critics, what should he have said?
3. What company is the subject of the second story?
4. What did the company name one of their cars?
5. According to the authors of *Kiss, Bow or Shake Hands,* what was GM's blunder?
6. Why does the author of this reading say don't believe everything you read? What examples does the author give?

B. Vocabulary Check

Scan the reading for the following items. Write your answers on the lines.

1. Find a synonym that means "mistake." _____

2. Find a phrase that means "laughable." _____

3. Find a synonym for *tell.* _____

C. Critical Reading Check

In Reading 3, legends are presented, then disproved. Find the evidence against each legend. Which is strongest? Why?

Remember

Imagine that you are preparing a one-minute talk on language blunders. Highlight or underline key points in the article.

Discuss

1. Have you ever heard a foreigner make a funny mistake in your language? What was it?
2. What are some foreign products' names that sound funny or odd in your language?

Thinking About Strategies

What did you do with the unfamiliar words? Complete the chart and answer the questions. Then compare your answers with a partner's.

A. Write the unfamiliar words from the reading in the left column. Then check each column that applies. See step B for column A1.

Unfamiliar Words	A I was able to guess the approximate meaning.	A1 I used this vocabulary strategy.	B I couldn't guess the meaning, and it was an important word.	C I couldn't guess the meaning, but it wasn't an important word.

B. For each word checked in column A, read the following list. In column A1, write the number of the strategy you used. If you are not sure, or if you used a strategy not listed, write "5."

1. background knowledge
2. context clues
3. word analysis

4. internal definition
5. other

C. Do you now know the meaning of the words checked in column B? If so, how?

4 READING

Prepare

Work with a partner. Review the title, subtitles, and other features of the reading. Make predictions about the following questions, and explain your answers to the class.

1. Do you understand the title? Where else can you look for clues?
2. Parts of the article are set in computer screens. What kind of information is in these sections? How is it different from the rest of the text?

Read

Think of what you already know about chain letters. Read the text to get a general idea of the meaning. Don't try to figure out unfamiliar terms. While you are reading, find the answers to these questions.

What are chain letters?

What is snail mail?

Chain Letters: From Snail Mail to E-mail

1   Chain letters as we know them have been around for at least a hundred years. Examples are even found in ancient literature. In the 19th century we first find the letters being sent by mail. Simply defined, chain letters are letters that ask you to copy them and send them on: "Please copy this message and send it to ten other people."

Chain Snail Mail

One of the first modern examples of the chain letter is the Good Luck of Flanders letter. It is a classic example
5   of the original snail mail chain letter. The Good Luck of Flanders letter promised that everyone who copied and sent it to four other people within twenty-four hours would have good luck. In addition, it warned that those who "broke the chain" would have bad luck. In chain letters, there is always a promise of a reward for continuing the chain. The sender will receive blessings, good luck, money, or a clear conscience. However, if you break the chain, beware! It is not unusual for chain letters to have statements such as the following: "One person did not
10 circulate this letter and died a week later."

Chain E-Mail

The Internet has been the greatest help to chain letter writers since the invention of the photocopy machine. It's faster than regular snail mail and a lot cheaper. E-mail messages, which can be sent to multiple people with the click of a mouse button, are perfect for chain letters. It's not surprising that the Internet is full of messages saying, "Send this to everyone you know."

15   However, the Internet has also changed chain letters. Before the Internet, most chain letters promised good fortune or asked for help for a needy person. Now they also spread fear. Many letters warn about everything from criminal activities to health threats. They include little or no evidence. Their purpose is to cause fear rather than to inform. People may send them with good intentions, but they cause unnecessary worry. Here is an example of a fear-mongering e-mail.

20   Warning: If you receive an e-mail message titled "Urgent News," do not open it! This powerful e-mail message will destroy your hard drive and actually "bake" your computer system and, perhaps, even cause a fire in the room. The Federal Computer Virus Response Authority (FCVRA) has documented thirteen instances of serious injury as the result of this virus.

The Internet hasn't changed chain letters entirely, though. People still send e-mail chain letters that ask you to
25 help others—usually sick children. Take a look at this one:

This little girl has six months left to live, and as her dying wish she wants to send a chain letter telling everyone to live his or her life to the fullest, since she never will. She'll never graduate from high school, or get married and have a family of her own. But you can give her and her family a little hope,

30 because with every name that this is sent to, the American Cancer Society will donate three cents to her treatment and recovery plan. One guy sent this to 500 people!!!! So, I know that we can send it to at least five or six. Come on, you guys . . . It's not even your money, just your time.

The good fortune chain letter continues to be sent. Below is one of the most famous examples—completely untrue, of course:

bbrozino@amol.com

Subject:	Please send this to everyone you know!
From:	GatesBeta@microsoft.com
Attach:	Tracklog@microsoft.com/Track883432/ ~TraceActive/On.html

List address
- Wendy
- Cindy
- An ony

Send Stop
Save as
Attach

Hello Everyone,
35 And thank you for signing up for my Beta Email Tracking Application, or BETA for short. My name is Bill Gates. Here at Microsoft we have just produced an email tracing program that tracks everyone who gets this message. It does this through a unique IP (Internet Protocol) address logbook database.

We are experimenting with this and need your help. Send this to everyone you know and if it
40 reaches 1,000 people, everyone on the list will receive $1,000 and a copy of Windows98 at my expense. Enjoy.

Note: You will be notified by email with further instructions once this email has reached 1,000 people. Windows98 will not be sent until it has been released to the general public.

Your friend,
45 Bill Gates & The Microsoft Development Team

Chain letters have a long, and sometimes a dangerous, history. If you receive a chain letter by snail mail or by e-mail, remember this:

If it seems too good to be true, it probably is.
If there is no way to check the information, it is likely to be false.

Read Again

Read the text again and do the following:

1. Think of two or three more questions, and read to find the answers.

2. Predict ideas. Use signal words from Chapter 1 and other clues to help you.

3. Note unfamiliar words. Decide if they are important. If so, try to figure out their meanings, and notice which vocabulary strategies you are using.

Post-Reading Activities

A. Comprehension Check

Answer these questions about the reading.

1. What is a chain letter?
2. How long have people been sending chain letters?
3. What are two characteristics of chain letters?
4. How has the Internet helped people who send chain letters?
5. How has the Internet changed chain letters?
6. What are three types of chain letters?
7. What does the first email chain letter warn?
8. What does the second letter ask you to do and why?
9. Who is the sender of the first letter?
10. What promise does the third letter make?

B. Vocabulary Check

Match the words with their definitions.

Words	Definitions
1. beware	a. many
2. multiple	b. letters sent by regular mail
3. warning	c. to tell
4. purpose	d. watch out
5. inform	e. luck
6. fortune	f. making people afraid without reason
7. fear mongering	g. reason
8. snail mail	h. advice that something bad may happen

Remember

Would you send a chain letter? Why or why not? Find evidence in the reading to support your reason. Highlight or underline it. Be sure to separate facts from opinions.

Discuss

1. Have you ever received a chain letter? If so, what did you do with it?
2. Do you think chain letters are harmful? Why or why not?

Thinking About Strategies

What did you do with the unfamiliar words? Complete the chart, and answer the questions. Then compare your answers with a partner's.

A. Write the unfamiliar words from the reading in the left column. Check each column that applies. See step B for column A1.

Unfamiliar Words	A I was able to guess the approximate meaning.	A1 I used this vocabulary strategy.	B I couldn't guess the meaning, and it was an important word.	C I couldn't guess the meaning, but it wasn't an important word.

B. For each word checked in column A, read the following list. In column A1, write the number of the strategy you used. If you are not sure, or if you used a strategy not listed, write "5."

1. background knowledge

2. context clues

3. word analysis

4. internal definition

5. other

C. Do you now know the meaning of the words checked in column B? If so, how?

Reviewing Your Reading

A. Look at the following list of readings in this chapter. Check the column that shows how easy or difficult the material was for you.

Name of Reading	Type of Reading	Easy	Average	Difficult
1. Urban Legend	encyclopedia entry			
2. Alligators in the Sewers? Not Again!	newspaper article			
3. Language Mistakes that Weren't	magazine article			
4. Chain Letters: From Snail Mail to E-mail	magazine article			

B. Read the following list of strategies that you have practiced in this chapter. Review the readings. Which strategies did you use, and how often did you use them? Check your answers in the chart.

Strategy	Always	Often	Sometimes	Never
Prepare				
Making predictions about the text				
Predicting from genre				
Read/Read Again				
Using background knowledge				
Reading with a purpose				
Using signal words to predict ideas				
Critical Reading				
Distinguishing fact from opinion				
Remember				
Highlighting and underlining				
Vocabulary Strategies				
Deciding which words are important				
Predicting the next word				
Recognizing internal definitions				
Analyzing a word for meaning				
Guessing the approximate meaning of a word				

C. Compare your chart with a partner's.

D. Did you use any other strategies while reading? If so, share them with the class. Explain where you learned them.

Reading:
Out of this World

3

Getting Started

Discuss these questions in pairs or small groups. Share your ideas with the class.

1. Read the chapter title and look at the photo of the spaceship. Then look at the titles of the readings in this chapter. What do you think this chapter is about?
2. Is there life on other planets? Why or why not?
3. Have you ever seen a UFO (Unidentified Flying Object)?
4. What do you think living things on other planets might look like?

Strategies Reminder

Comprehension Skills

Prepare
- Making Predictions about the Text
- Predicting from Genre

Read
- Using Background Knowledge
- Reading with a Purpose (with Questions in Mind)
- Using Signal Words to Predict Ideas

Critical Reading
- Distinguishing Fact from Opinion

Remember
- Highlighting and Underlining Text

Vocabulary Strategies
- Deciding Which Words Are Important
- Predicting the Next Word
- Recognizing Internal Definitions
- Analyzing a Word for Meaning
- Guessing the Approximate Meaning of a Word

1 ? READING

Prepare

Work with a partner. Review the title of the reading. Complete the following predictions, and explain your choices to the class.

1. This article talks about _____.
   a. rocks
   b. life on Mars
   c. space travel

2. This article came from a _____.
   a. tabloid newspaper
   b. magazine for the general public
   c. scientific magazine

Read

Think of what you already know about Mars. Read the text to get a general idea of the meaning. Don't try to figure out unfamiliar terms at this time. While you are reading, find the answers to these questions.

What rock are they talking about?

Why is the rock important?

The Science Times

WEDNESDAY, JANUARY 18, 2003

Signs of Life in a Rock

A new study says there may have been life on Mars.

WAS THERE EVER LIFE on Mars? Scientists have debated this question for years. Last week researchers announced there is new evidence that life may have existed on the Red Planet.

5 Scientists at the Johnson Space Center in Houston, Texas, examined a 46 billion-year-old meteorite from Mars. The meteorite had landed in Antarctica. Using a powerful microscope, they found tiny crystals. Crystals are made in two ways: by a 10 chemical process, or by living things. The shape of the crystals in the meteorite suggests that a living creature made them.

Some scientists believe that they were formed by a one-celled animal. "I am convinced that this is evidence of ancient life on Mars," says Kathie 15 Thomas-Keptra, microbiologist and head of the study. "If it existed there before, we could even expect it to exist today," she adds. Not all scientists agree with her conclusion; however, others are eager to do more research on the Mars rock. 20

Read Again

Read the text again and do the following:

1. Think of two or three more questions, and read to find the answers.
2. Predict ideas. Use signal words from Chapter 1 and other clues to help you.
3. Note unfamiliar words. Decide if they are important. If so, try to figure out their meanings, and notice which vocabulary strategies you are using.

Post-Reading Activities

A. Comprehension Check

Answer these questions about the reading.

1. Where is the rock from?
2. How old is the rock?
3. What did the scientists find in the rock?
4. Do scientists agree about the importance of the rock?
5. There is another name for Mars in the reading. What is it?
6. Does Kathie Thomas-Keptra think that an animal made the crystals? Why or why not?

B. Vocabulary Check

Match the words with their definitions.

Words	Definitions
1. shape	a. 1,000,000,00
2. sign	b. looked at carefully
3. ancient	c. formally argued
4. examined	d. form
5. billion	e. very old
6. debated	f. evidence
7. eager	g. enthusiastic

C. Critical Reading Check

Read the article again, and read it critically. Find three facts and one opinion. Share your choices with the class.

Remember

Was there life on Mars? Imagine that you are debating the question. Underline or highlight key points for and against. Compare your points with a partner's.

Discuss

1. Is discovering life on Mars important? Why or why not?
2. Should your country explore space?

Thinking About Strategies

What did you do with the unfamiliar words in Reading 1? Complete the following chart, and answer the questions. Then compare your answers with your partner's.

A. Check each column that applies. The first one is done for you. See step B for column B1.

Unfamiliar Words	A I knew this word.	B I was able to guess the approximate meaning.	B1 Vocabulary strategy I used.	C I couldn't guess the meaning, and it was an important word.	D I couldn't guess the meaning, but it wasn't an important word.
1. debated	✓	✓	3		
2. evidence					
3. tiny					
4. meteorite					
5. crystals					
6. ancient					
7. eager					

B. For each word checked in column B, read the following list. In column B1, write the number of the strategy you used. If you are not sure, or if you used a strategy not listed, write "5."

   1. background knowledge

   2. context clues

   3. word analysis

   4. internal definition

   5. other

C. Did you find out the meaning of the words checked in column C? If so, how?

2 · READING

Prepare

Reading 2 is a long article. It is divided into two parts. Look at the features of Part A and Part B. Work with a partner. Make predictions about the following questions and explain your answers to the class.

   1. What genre is Reading 2?

   2. Who is the audience? How do you know?

   3. What can you predict from the reading's title?

   4. What can you predict from the section or part titles?

Read Part A

Think of what you already know about how we define "life." Read the text of Part A. Read only to get the general meaning. There are several scientific terms. Do not stop to figure out unfamiliar words. Keep reading! While you are reading, find the answer to this question.

How is the study of life on earth connected to the study of life on other planets?

Unit 8

Life on Earth . . . and Beyond?

Introduction

1   When you think of an alien, that is, a creature from another planet, you probably think of E.T. or Darth Vader, aliens with a human type of body. However, the human body plan — bilateral symmetry with one head, two legs, and two arms — is unlikely in an alien. To understand how a real alien might look, we turn to astrobiology.

5   Astrobiology is the scientific study of life in the universe. It combines biology, chemistry, physics, geology, and astronomy. Astrobiologists study the origins of life on Earth, the organization of life, and what makes a planet suitable for living things. Often, astrobiologists must use their knowledge of life on Earth to guide their study of life on other planets. Let's examine some of our knowledge about life on Earth.

1 What Is Life?

10   It is difficult to completely define life. Most biologists agree, however, that all living things share certain characteristics:

Organized	Living things are made of atoms and molecules organized into cells. The cells are organized into tissues, organs, and systems.
Homeostatic	Living things function in homeostasis, a state of constancy. For example, some systems in the body keep its temperature from changing too much—you shiver if you're cold, you sweat if you're hot.
Reproduce	Living things make copies of themselves. They make exact copies by asexual reproduction, or similar copies by sexual reproduction.
Grow	Living things grow and develop from smaller and/or simpler forms. For instance, a human begins life as a fertilized egg, develops into an embryo, a fetus, and then a baby. The baby then grows into a toddler, an adolescent, and then an adult.
Take in energy	Living organisms use energy to remain in a relatively constant state. Humans and other animals get energy from the food they eat.
Respond to stimuli	Living things respond to their environment. If something causes you pain, you move away from it. Likewise, if you put a plant near light, it grows toward the light.
Adapt to their environment	Living things are suited to their environment. For instance, the fins of a dolphin are flat for swimming. The wings of a bat are like the dolphin's fins, but in addition, have a thin cover that enables the bat to fly.

15

20

25

30

Read Again

Read Part A again and do the following:

1. Think of two or three more questions and read to find the answers.

2. Predict ideas. Use signal words from Chapter 1 and other clues to help you.

3. Note unfamiliar words. Decide if they are important. If so, try to figure out their meanings, and notice which vocabulary strategies you are using.

Read Part B

Think of what you already know about extreme environments. Now read to get the general idea of Part B. Do not stop to figure out unfamiliar terms. While you are reading, find the answers to these questions.

What does *extreme* mean?

Is this environment different from Earth's? How?

2 Life in an Extreme Environment

1   Until about 30 years ago, scientists believed that all life on Earth depended upon energy from the sun. They also believed life could not survive in extremely hot or cold temperatures.

     These ideas changed when oceanographers explored
5   hydrothermal vents. Hydrothermal vents are openings in the ocean floor where extremely hot, mineral-rich water erupts from the earth. On the ocean floor, the temperature is at or near freezing, it is absolutely dark, and pressure is high. Yet around these vents scientists found clams, crabs, and giant tubeworms that were six feet (two meters)
10   long. The water coming out of these vents is 230° to 662° Fahrenheit (110° to 350° Celsius).

     How can living things survive under these extreme conditions? Scientists discovered the answer in the water. They found a kind of bacteria that takes energy from the water to make organic compounds. These bacteria live in the tubeworms. The clams eat the bacteria, and the crabs eat the tubeworms.

15   Life has been found in other extreme environments as well. Lichens called cryptoendoliths were discovered in rock samples from the Antarctic desert. In the Antarctic, temperatures often drop to 100 degrees below zero Fahrenheit, and there is little or no liquid water. In contrast, thermophilic or heat-loving bacteria have been found in hot springs where temperatures are higher than the boiling point of water.

20   The discovery of hydrothermal-vent communities has changed science. We now know life can exist in extreme environments, even without light. Encouraged by the discovery, scientists are thinking more seriously about alien life. Researching other planets, astrobiologists are investigating Europa, a moon of Jupiter, which may have a water ocean beneath its icy surface.

Read Again

Read Part B again and do the following:

1. Think of two or three more questions and read to find the answers.
2. Predict ideas as you read. Use signal words and other clues to help you.
3. Note unfamiliar words. Decide if they are important. If so, try to figure out their meanings, and notice which vocabulary strategies you are using.

Post-Reading Activities

The following activities cover both parts of the reading.

A. Comprehension Check

Answer these questions about the reading. Then share your answers with the class.

1. What is an astrobiologist?
2. A living thing must be able to _____.

    a. move   **b.** think   **c.** take in energy

3. What is an extreme environment?
4. What are some examples of extreme environments?
5. Why are astrobiologists interested in the discovery of life in extreme environments?

B. Vocabulary Check

The following chart lists terms from Part B of the reading. Match the words with their definitions.

Words	Definitions
1. extreme	**a.** completely
2. survive	**b.** openings or holes
3. oceanographer	**c.** comes out of forcefully
4. hydrothermal	**d.** a scientist who studies the ocean
5. vents	**e.** very intense
6. erupts	**f.** relating to hot water
7. absolutely	**g.** continue to live

C. Critical Reading Check

Think about the reading and its genre. Answer these questions.

1. Does "Life on Earth . . . and Beyond?" contain mostly facts or opinions? Why?
2. Can you check the facts? How?

Remember

What is life? Underline or highlight the key ideas of the definition in Part A of Reading 2. Compare your work with a classmate's.

Discuss

1. Do we need to know if life exists on other planets? Explain your opinion.
2. Compare machines with living things. How are they alike? How are they different?

Thinking About Strategies

A. Read the following terms from Part B. Guess their approximate meanings. Is an approximate meaning useful for these terms? Why or why not?

| bacteria | crabs | lichens |
| clams | cryptoendoliths | tubeworms |

B. Find these signal words in Part A. What ideas do they introduce? Complete the last column.

Word	Line	Idea introduced
1. however	2	
2. for instance	28	
3. in addition	30	

C. Many words in Reading 2 use stems and affixes that you learned in Chapter 1. Write their meanings in the blanks. Look back at pages 31–32 to help you remember.

1. *bi-* _____

2. *astro* _____

3. *-ology* _____

4. *re-* _____

5. *hydro* _____

3 · READING

Prepare

Look at the title and the pictures for Reading 3. Work with a partner. Make predictions about the following questions, and share your ideas with the class.

1. Where would you find this article?

2. Who will probably read the article?

3. What knowledge or experience does the author(s) have with the topic?

Read

Have you ever thought about what aliens might look like? Read the text to get a general idea of the meaning. Don't try to figure out unfamiliar terms at this time. While you are reading, find the answers to these questions.

What is *HowStuffWorks*? What did they do?

Are the ideas about alien worlds believable?

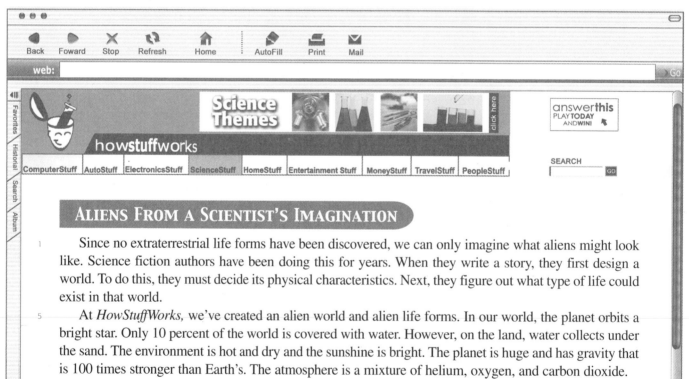

ALIENS FROM A SCIENTIST'S IMAGINATION

1   Since no extraterrestrial life forms have been discovered, we can only imagine what aliens might look like. Science fiction authors have been doing this for years. When they write a story, they first design a world. To do this, they must decide its physical characteristics. Next, they figure out what type of life could exist in that world.

5   At *HowStuffWorks,* we've created an alien world and alien life forms. In our world, the planet orbits a bright star. Only 10 percent of the world is covered with water. However, on the land, water collects under the sand. The environment is hot and dry and the sunshine is bright. The planet is huge and has gravity that is 100 times stronger than Earth's. The atmosphere is a mixture of helium, oxygen, and carbon dioxide.

       The two life forms that we created for this world are animals that live around the few small bodies of
10   water. Both aliens are short, about 1 foot (30 centimeters) tall. And they both have strong limbs to support their weight against the strong gravity. Both also have thick skins to conserve water. To gather information, one depends on its eyes, while the other uses taste and smell.

THE LASHLARM: AN ALIEN ANIMAL

The Lashlarm is our first alien. It looks like a walking toilet bowl. The mouth portion is supported by three thin legs
15 connected to a flat top. Underneath it has scales like a snake. The scales help it slide across the surface of the sand. It has several sensory arms that allow it to hunt by taste and smell. It locates prey by tasting the sand and water for other animals. When it finds prey, the Lashlarm crouches down and glides
20 up to it. It then opens its large mouth and jumps down on the animal.

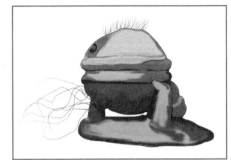

THE NIRBA: AN ALIEN PREDATOR

The Nirba is a little larger than the Lashlarm. It lives in shallow water. The Nirba hunts animals that come to the water, especially the Lashlarm. It has a
25 large head with nostrils located on top of its nose so it can breathe while mostly under water. The Nirba has thick skin and big, muscular front legs with large claws for killing its prey. A long tail helps it swim in the water. The end of its tail is shaped like an
30 arrowhead. This is useful in hunting and defending its territory.

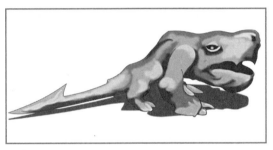

Read Again

Read the text again and do the following:

1. Think of two or three more questions and read to find the answers.
2. Predict ideas. Use signal words and other clues to help you.
3. Note unfamiliar words. Decide if they are important. If so, try to figure out their meanings, and notice which vocabulary strategies you are using.

Post-Reading Activities

A. Comprehension Check

Answer these questions about the reading. Then share your answers with the class.

1. How is this world different from ours?
2. Would humans weigh more or less on this planet? Why?
3. How are the alien life forms alike? How are they different?
4. Describe the Lashlarm or the Nirba to a partner. Look only at the pictures. Do not look at the text.

B. Vocabulary Check

Find words in the reading that match the following definitions. Write them on the lines.

1. not from the earth _____

2. to travel around _____

3. a combination _____

4. leg or arm _____

5. save _____

6. a hunter _____

7. an animal that is food
   for another animal _____

8. to find _____

9. nails _____

C. Critical Reading Check

How believable are the ideas in Reading 3? Should they be believable? Should they be factual? Explain your opinion to the class.

Remember

Imagine that you are giving a talk on science fiction. Highlight or underline information in Reading 3 to share with your science club.

Discuss

1. Could human beings survive on the world described in the article? Why or why not?
2. Could other Earth animals survive on this planet? Support your opinion with facts from the reading.

Thinking About Strategies

Work with a partner. Complete the following items.

A. Find the descriptions of the two aliens in the reading. Label their parts in the illustrations. Compare your work with your partner's. Did the pictures help you understand the text?

B. What did you do with unfamiliar words? Write the five most difficult new words from Reading 3 in the left column. Check each column that applies.

Unfamiliar Words	A I was able to guess the approximate meaning.	A1 I used this vocabulary strategy.	B I couldn't guess the meaning, and it was an important word.	C I couldn't guess the meaning, but it wasn't an important word.

C. For each word checked in column A, read the following list. In column A1, write the number of the strategy you used. If you are not sure, or if you used a strategy not listed, write "5."

1. background knowledge
2. context clues
3. word analysis
4. internal definition
5. other

D. Compare your chart with your partner's.

4 . READING

Prepare

A. Work with a partner. Review the features of the reading. Make predictions about the following questions, and explain your answers to the class.

1. What genre is this reading?
2. Who is the audience?
3. What is the article about? If you don't understand *UFO,* what should you do?
4. What are the subtitles? What are these sections going to be about?

B. With your partner, write one or two additional general questions the reading might answer. Then share your questions with the class. Add or change questions if you wish.

Read

Think of what you know, or have read, about UFOs. Read the text to get a general idea of the meaning. Don't try to figure out unfamiliar terms. While you are reading, find the answers to the questions that you wrote in number 4 of the *Prepare* section.

Visitors from Outer Space?

One Night in Nova Scotia

1   One of Canada's most famous UFO incidents happened in Nova Scotia on October 4, 1967. On that night, hundreds of people saw an unidentified object fly 300 kilometers southwest along the coast until it eventually crashed into Shag Harbour. "I saw this strange orange light tracing the shoreline," recalls Chris Styles, who was 12 at the time. "My first reaction was fear. I had never seen anything like that before."

5   Styles never forgot this event and in 1999, he and writer Don Ledger wrote a book about it. During their research they interviewed police and military officers who worked on the official search. The authors discovered that police records called the crash a UFO incident. "I know many people involved want an investigation," says Styles. "UFOs are a worldwide phenomenon and these few cases that are well-corroborated should be looked into."

Other Alien Visits

10   Some people say they have actually met aliens. Some of them claim that they have been temporarily abducted or kidnapped by aliens. Larry, a successful 50-year-old Ontario businessman, is normal in every way except one: Aliens began visiting him when he was 16. Larry says he never realized that he was an abductee until 20 years later when he saw a program about people who were abducted by aliens. Now he knows that he has experienced a number of alien abductions.

15   A typical abduction was described in the 1987 book *Communion* by American writer Whitley Strieber. Apparently, aliens abduct people every few months—usually at night. During the abduction, the abductee cannot move. He or she may see bright lights. After people are abducted, they almost always have sensation of lost time. Many of these people say that their abductors have performed medical experiments on them.

     Are abductions real? Some people believe that extraterrestrials are trying to help us. Others think
20   that aliens want information only to destroy us. Still others believe that UFOs and aliens do not exist at all except in the imaginations of people who want them to be real.

Read Again

Read the text again and do the following:

1. Think of two or three more questions and read to find the answers.
2. Predict ideas. Find signal words and other clues to help you understand ideas.
3. Note unfamiliar words. Decide if they are important. If so, try to figure out their meanings, and notice which vocabulary strategies you are using.

Post-Reading Activities

A. Comprehension Check

Answer these questions about the article. Share your answers with the class.

1. What did people in Nova Scotia see in the sky on October 4, 1967?
2. What happened to this unidentified flying object?
3. Did the Canadian government investigate?
4. Did they tell everyone the results of their investigation?
5. What happens when aliens abduct people?

B. Vocabulary Check

Find words in the article that match the following definitions. Write them on the lines.

1. unidentified flying object   _____

2. where the ocean meets
   the land   _____

3. ordinary   _____

4. understood   _____

5. found   _____

C. Critical Reading Check

This reading contains a lot of facts and some opinions. Check the correct column for each of the following statements.

Statement	True	Possibly True	Fact or Opinion
1. Something flew over Nova Scotia on October 4, 1967.			
2. This thing was a UFO.			
3. The thing crashed into Shag Harbour.			
4. Styles and Ledger wrote a book.			
5. Many people want an investigation of UFOs.			
6. Some people believe that they have met aliens.			
7. Aliens abduct humans.			
8. Aliens are trying to help us.			

Remember

If you are searching for information about alien abductions, how could Reading 4 help? Underline or highlight key facts and opinions.

Discuss

Debate these questions with a partner or in small groups. Discuss your views with the class. Be sure to support your opinion.

1. Do UFOs visit Earth?
2. What should we do if aliens do visit our planet?

Thinking About Strategies

Work in pairs or small groups, and complete the following questions.

A. How accurately did you predict? Answer these questions.

1. Did you find answers to most of your questions?
2. How important were questions that the article did not answer? Should this information be included?

B. Did you use word analysis to guess the meanings of related words? The following words occur in paragraph 4 of the reading. Match the words with their definitions.

Words	Definitions
1. abductee	a. someone who takes another against his or her will
2. abduction	b. the taking of someone against the person's will
3. abducted	c. a person taken against his or her will
4. abductor	d. took or taken against a person's will

Reviewing Your Reading

A. Look at the following list of readings in this chapter. Check the column that shows how easy or difficult the material was for you.

Name of Reading	Type of Reading	Easy	Average	Difficult
1. Signs of Life in a Rock	newspaper article			
2A. Life on Earth . . . and Beyond?	textbook			
2B. Life in an Extreme Environment	textbook			

Name of Reading	Type of Reading	Easy	Average	Difficult
3. Aliens from a Scientist's Imagination	Website			
4. Visitors from Outer Space?	newspaper article			

B. Read the following list of strategies that you have practiced in this chapter. Review the readings. Which strategies did you use, and how often did you use them? Check your answers in the chart.

Strategy	Always	Often	Sometimes	Never
Prepare				
Making predictions about the text				
Predicting from genre				
Read/Read Again				
Using background knowledge				
Reading with a purpose				
Using signal words to predict ideas				
Critical Reading				
Distinguishing fact from opinion				
Remember				
Highlighting and underlining				
Vocabulary Strategies				
Deciding which words are important				
Predicting the next word				
Recognizing internal definitions				
Analyzing a word for meaning				
Guessing the approximate meaning of a word				

C. Compare your chart with a partner's.

D. Did you use any other strategies while reading? If so, share them with the class. Explain where you learned them.

Reading:
Clothes Make the
Man (and the Woman)

4

Getting Started

Study the men in the photo. Look at what they are wearing. Discuss these questions in pairs or small groups. Share your ideas with the class.

1. What kinds of clothes do you recognize?

2. Why do you think the men in the photo are wearing the type of clothes that they are wearing?

Strategies Reminder

Comprehension Strategies

Prepare
- Making Predictions about the Text
- Predicting from Genre

Read
- Using Background Knowledge
- Reading with a Purpose (with Questions in Mind)
- Using Signal Words to Predict Ideas
  Critical Reading
  - Distinguishing Fact from Opinion

Remember
- Highlighting and Underlining Text

Vocabulary Strategies
- Deciding Which Words Are Important
- Predicting the Next Word
- Recognizing Internal Definitions
- Analyzing a Word for Meaning
- Guessing the Approximate Meaning of a Word

1 ⟩ READING

Prepare

Work with a partner. Describe the features of the text. Complete the following predictions, and explain your choices to the class.

1. This reading is from a ——————————.
   a. newspaper
   b. textbook
   c. fashion magazine

2. The writer is a(n) ——————————.
   a. fashion designer
   b. businesswoman
   c. anthropologist

Read

Think of ways clothing is important in society. Read the text to get a general idea of the meaning. Don't try to figure out unfamiliar terms. While you are reading, find the answer to this question.

   What is the importance of clothes in society?

The Importance of Clothes in Society

Why Do We Wear Clothes?

1   At first, this may seem like a silly question. We wear clothes because society expects us to. While this is true, clothes must still serve some kind of purpose. In fact, anthropologists have identified five primary reasons that people in every culture wear clothes and adornments— even in societies where people wear little, if any, clothing, they still decorate their bodies with paint, feathers, and 5   other objects.

Five Uses of Clothing

Protection: One of the most basic reasons we wear clothes is for protection. Soldiers used to wear metal armor to protect themselves in battle. Divers put on wet suits that enable them to enter freezing water. Firefighters wear flame-retardant clothing to avoid getting burned. Chemists wear protective goggles, and even cooks use oven mitts so they won't burn their hands.

10   **Sexual attraction:** Sexual attraction is another reason people wear clothing. Both men and women use clothes to appear desirable to other people. For a woman, sexual attraction often means wearing clothing that reveals certain parts of her body while concealing others. Each society determines which parts it is acceptable to reveal. For example, in many parts of the Middle East, hair is considered sensual, so women cover their heads. Some tribes in Africa felt 15   no need for women to cover their breasts until the arrival of Europeans. Men also use clothing to attract the opposite sex. In the 15th century some men wore a piece of clothing called a codpiece to enhance the appearance of sexual prowess. Today, bodybuilders wear tight clothing that reveals their muscles for much the same reason.

Status: Clothing can also be used to show status in the community. It can show wealth, often an 20   important indicator of status. This is why some people like to wear clothing with designer labels. Designer clothing is usually expensive, and therefore shows the high economic status of the owner. In the West, men in management positions traditionally wore white shirts, whereas men who worked with their hands wore blue shirts. The terms white-collar and blue-collar jobs refer to high-status office work versus low-status manual labor.

25   **Identification:** Uniforms of all kinds are examples of clothing used for identification. Military uniforms are some of the best examples. They identify the wearers as soldiers in a specific military group. In addition, there is a clear code that tells colleagues their status in the military. Other examples of clothing as identification include uniforms for nurses and doctors, students, police officers, and waiters. In some countries, tellers in banks, department store clerks, and 30   government workers have distinctive uniforms. Even clothing that is not a uniform can still serve to identify the wearer as a member of a certain group. For instance, people often adopt clothing styles that distinguish them from other groups in their society.

Ceremonial Purposes: Special clothing that people wear for ceremonies takes many forms. Priests and monks often wear special clothes when they are performing religious ceremonies. In 35   China, most people wear special white clothing for funerals. The robes that many students wear on graduation day are another example of ceremonial clothing. In addition many cultures have specific clothing for weddings. In the West, brides usually wear long white dresses. In Palestine, brides wear black dresses covered with multicolored embroidery.

Read Again

Read the text again and do the following:

1. Think of two or three more questions and read to find the answers.
2. Predict ideas. Use signal words from Chapter 1 and other clues to help you.
3. Note unfamiliar words. Decide if they are important. If so, try to figure out the meanings, and notice which vocabulary strategies you are using.

Post-Reading Activities

A. Comprehension Check

Answer these questions about the reading.

1. Do people in all societies use clothing for the same reasons?
2. What are the five reasons that people in every culture wear clothes?
3. Think of two pieces of clothing that protect us.
4. What kind of clothes do women wear to attract men?
5. What kind of clothes do men wear to attract women?

B. Vocabulary Check

Complete the chart by following the example in number 1.

Word in the Reading	Part of Speech	Related Word	Part of Speech
1. anthropologist	noun	anthropology	noun
2. adornment			
3. protection			
4.		sex	
5. attraction			
6.		desire	
7. acceptable			
8. identification			
9.		ceremony	
10. graduation			

Remember

As you read, did you underline important words or phrases? If not, do so now. Highlight the information that you think will be useful in a general discussion of the uses of clothing.

Discuss

1. Name types of clothing in your society that fit in each of the five categories.
2. Do you agree that many people care less about physical appearance than status in the community?

Thinking About Strategies

Were you able to use your background knowledge? There are several words in the reading that are probably unfamiliar. The reading may not give you a lot of clues. However, the topic is one that is easily understood from everyday life. Were you able to guess the meanings of the following words using your general knowledge and experience?

Word	Line	Meaning
1. desirable	11	
2. reveals	12	
3. status	19	
4. uniforms	25	

2 . READING

Prepare

Work with a partner. Look at the features of the text. Make predictions about the following questions, and explain your answers to the class.

1. What is the writer's purpose?
2. Who is the expected audience?
3. Look at the words in italics. What kinds of words are these?
4. Does the writer expect that readers will understand Arabic?

Read

Think of what you already know about the Gulf nations, such as Saudi Arabia, Kuwait, and the United Arab Emirates. Read the text to get a general idea of the meaning. Don't try to figure out unknown words and phrases. While you are reading, find the answer to this question.

What are typical Gulf Arab forms of dress?

Before You Leave for the Gulf

How Not to Be an "Ugly" American in the Gulf States

1   There is a saying in English: "When in Rome do as the Romans do." When it comes to dress in the Gulf Arab states, visitors need not do exactly as the Arabs do. However, they should modify their clothing so they do not offend their hosts or make them feel uncomfortable. Here is some information on what Gulf Arabs expect of you and what you should expect of them. If you
5 follow this advice, you are likely to have a more satisfying time abroad.

Foreign Dress

The religion and customs of Gulf Arab countries such as Saudi Arabia, Kuwait, and the United Arab Emirates dictate conservative dress for both men and
10 women. Foreigners are given some flexibility in their dress, but they still must be careful not to offend people. As a general rule, foreign men should wear long trousers and shirts that cover their chests.
15 Foreign women should wear loose-fitting skirts and dresses that fall below the knee. Sleeves should be at least elbow length and the neckline modest. The best fashion guideline is "conceal rather than reveal."
20 Foreign women sometimes also wear *abayahs* to show respect for the local customs, but this is usually not required. Teenagers should be particularly careful to dress modestly in public places. Jeans
25 should not be tight, and low necks and tank tops are not recommended. Shorts and bathing suits should never be worn in public.

Arab Dress

Men in the Gulf still wear their traditional clothing. The long-sleeved one-piece dress that
30 covers the whole body is called a *dishdashah* or *thoub*. In the summer, men usually wear white
dishdashahs. Cotton is the most common fabric. However, *dishdashahs* made of other more
expensive fabrics show the status of the wearer.

Dishdashahs are extremely practical for living in the desert because they allow air to circulate
near the skin. This helps cool the body during the hot summer days. Their white color also
35 reflects the sunlight. Because they are ankle-length, they protect the body from blowing sand.
During ceremonies and official visits, government officials and important businessmen may also
wear a transparent black robe with gold edges over the *dishdashah*.

In addition to the *dishdashah,* Gulf Arab men wear a head cover. A tight-fitting white cap
holds the hair in place. This is covered with a large, square cloth. A white headscarf, called a
40 *gutrah*, is worn in the summer, and a red-and-white-checked headscarf, called a *shumag,* is worn
in winter. This protects the head from the sun and can be used to cover the mouth and the nose.
Finally, a black band, called an *ogal,* holds the cap and cloth in place. Male children begin
wearing the head covering when they reach puberty. Normally Arabs do not cover their heads
inside their homes; however, head coverings are often worn as a sign of respect while receiving
45 guests.

When Gulf Arab women appear in public, they normally wear large black cloaks called
abayahs. In addition, they wear scarves over their hair and full-face veils. However, women's
fashions do not stop with the *abayah.* Beneath the black cloak, most modern Arab women wear
fashionable clothing and take great pride in their appearance. They often prefer clothing in bright
50 colors made of beautiful, fancy fabrics. In addition, jewelry has long been a favorite accessory of
Arab women. Historically, women of desert tribes have worn their family's material wealth in the
form of their bracelets, earrings, rings, and necklaces. Although most people now keep their
money in banks, women are still fond of wearing expensive jewelry.

Read Again

Read the text again and do the following:

1. Think of two or three more questions, and read to find the answers.

2. Predict ideas. Use signal words from Chapter 1 and other clues to help you.

3. Note unfamiliar words. Decide if they are important. If so, try to figure out their meanings, and notice which vocabulary strategies you are using.

Post-Reading Activities

A. Comprehension Check

1. Look at the following picture. Which people are wearing appropriate clothes for the Gulf?
2. Label the different parts of the Gulf Arab man's clothing in the picture.
3. What is an *abayah*?
4. When do Arab women in the Gulf wear abayahs?
5. Do foreign women in the Gulf have to wear abayahs?

1. _____

2. _____

3. _____

B. Vocabulary Check

Match the words with their approximate meanings.

Words	Definitions
1. dictate	a. cloth
2. flexibility	b. to cover up
3. modest	c. pure
4. conceal	d. to show
5. fabric	e. ability to change easily
6. circulate	f. to move around
7. reveal	g. demand

Remember

You are preparing to go to Saudi Arabia. What should you pack? What should you leave home? In the reading, underline things to remember about appropriate clothing.

Discuss

1. How important is it that visitors to a country follow the customs of that country?
2. Have you ever been surprised at the clothing tourists wear? What surprised you?

Thinking About Strategies

Did you use your knowledge of the world and/or Gulf Arab countries to help you understand the following words?

conservative   modest   puberty   veil

3 READING

Prepare

Reading 3 is a long article. It is divided into two parts. Work with a partner. Make predictions about the following questions, and explain your answers to the class.

Look at the features of Part A, including the title and the subtitles.

1. Where would you find the following article? What genre is it?
2. Who is the expected audience?

Examine the features of Part B.

1. What is the author's purpose?

2. Who is the expected audience?

Read Part A

Think of what you already know about ties. Read to get a general idea of the meaning. Don't try to figure out unknown words and phrases. While you are reading, find the answers to these questions.

Where did the custom of wearing neckties come from?

Why are ties still so popular?

Why Ties?
by Alan Flusser

History

1   According to historians, neckties date back to 1660. In that year, a group of soldiers from Croatia visited Paris. These soldiers were war heroes whom King Louis XIV admired very much. Impressed with the colored scarves that they wore around their necks, the king decided to honor the Croats by creating a military regiment called the Royal Cravattes. The word *cravat* comes from the word *Croat*. All the soldiers in this regiment wore

5   colorful scarves or cravats around their necks.

This new style of neckwear traveled to England. Soon all upperclass men were wearing cravats. Some cravats were quite extreme. At times, they were so high that a man could not move his head without turning his whole body. There were even reports of cravats that were so thick, a sword could not go through them. The cravats were made of many different kinds of materials from plaid to lace, which made them suitable for

10   any occasion. People also tied them in a variety of ways. At one point there were almost 100 different kinds of knots in use.

Continuing Popularity

How can we explain the popularity of neckties? For years, fashion historians and sociologists have predicted that men would stop wearing ties because they seemed to have little or no function. It may be that men continue to wear them because ties are now a tradition. As long as world and business leaders continue

15   to wear ties, the young executives will follow them and ties will remain popular. However, the apparel does have a different kind of appeal. Neckties cover the buttons of the shirt and emphasize the length of a man's body. They also add color and adornment to men's clothing, which is often plain and serious.

Today, there are tens of thousands of designs of ties available. There are ties for special occasions—hearts for Valentine's Day, fireworks for the Fourth of July, and pumpkins for Halloween. There are ties that tell you

20   about a man's interests—pictures of tennis rackets, motorcycles, airplanes, fishing rods, or musical instruments, to name a few. There are even ties for different occupations such as accountants, firefighters, and police officers. And funny ties are becoming ever more popular. You can get ties covered with colorful frogs, pictures of Elvis Presley, and bottles of beer. If you enjoy rock music, you can even find a tie in the shape of a guitar!

Funny or formal, wide or narrow, it's clear that ties are going to be around for a long time.

Read Again

Read the text again and do the following:

1. Think of two or three more questions and find the answers.
2. Predict ideas. Use signal words from Chapter 1 and other clues to help you.
3. Note unfamiliar words. Decide if they are important. If so, try to figure out their meanings, and notice which vocabulary strategies you are using.

Read Part B

Read to get a general idea of the meaning. Don't try to figure out unknown words and phrases. While you are reading, look at the pictures to help you understand the instructions.

How to Tie a Tie

The Four-in-Hand Knot

Of all the different types of knots, this is the most basic. Note that these instructions are given for a right-handed person. If you are left-handed, reverse the words right and left.

1. Get ready. Button your collar at the neck. Then fold it up so that you can slip the tie easily around your neck. This helps you tie it in the right spot the first time.

2. Put the tie around your neck and adjust the length. It is important that the wide or broad end of the tie be a little longer than the narrow end, so you need to measure. One measuring trick is to let the broad end hang down twice as long as the narrow end.

3. Hold the narrow end about three inches (8 cm) down from your neck with your left hand. This is the spot where you will make the knot. Take the broad end with your right hand and pass it across and over the spot, and hold it there with your left hand.

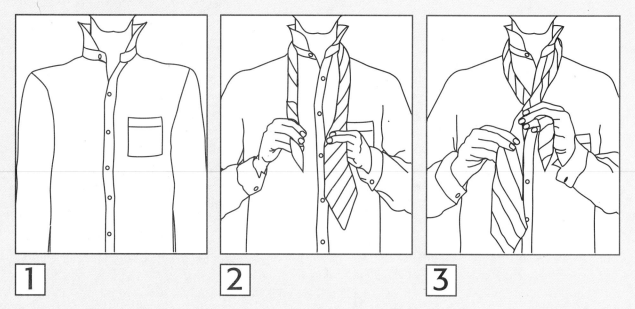

4. Bring the broad end around behind the spot, then around and over again. Then pull the broad end behind the spot and up through the "V" at the top.

5. Let the broad end flop over and hang down. Now put it between the top wrap of the tie and the place you have been holding. Use both hands to straighten the knot and pull it tight.

6. Pull the knot gently but firmly. Look at the tie in the mirror. Is it straight? Does the broad end cover the narrow end? Loosen the tie if you need to, and readjust the length of the narrow end as needed. The four-in-hand knot will be slightly larger on one side than the other. The knot should be smooth, not wrinkled or folded.

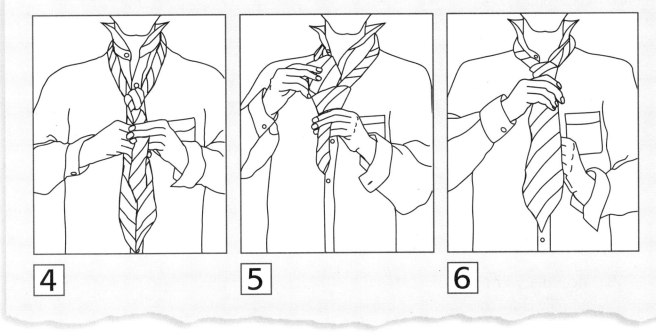

Read Again

Read the text again and do the following:

1. Now that you have a general idea of the meaning, read the text again and closely match the pictures to the instructions.

2. Do the motions as you are reading to help you understand the instructions.

3. Note unfamiliar words. Decide if they are important. If so, try to figure out their meanings, and notice which vocabulary strategies you are using.

Post-Reading Activities

A. Comprehension Check

Complete the questions for both parts of the reading.

Part A

1. What famous person made cravats popular?

2. Where did non-military people begin wearing cravats?

3. What kind of men wore cravats?

4. What are two possible reasons why ties are still popular?

5. What are some different kinds of ties that men can buy?

Parts A and B

Read the statements from each part of the reading. What do the underlined words or phrases refer to? Write your answers on the lines.

Part A

1. At times, <u>they</u> were so high that a man could not move <u>his</u> head without turning his whole body.

_____

2. There are ties <u>that</u> tell you about a man's interests.

_____

Part B

3. Of all the different types of knots, <u>this</u> is the most basic.

_____

4. Then fold <u>it</u> up.

_____

B. Vocabulary Check

Match the word with its definition for both parts of the reading.

Words	Definitions
1. was impressed with	a. make something longer or shorter
2. regiment	b. a kind of fabric
3. cravat	c. group of soldiers
4. plaid	d. correct place
5. function	e. wide
6. right spot	f. admired
7. adjust the length	g. use
8. broad	h. tie

Remember

Have you ever shown anyone how to tie a tie? Underline or highlight the important words and phrases in Part B that you should use. Choose a partner and take turns explaining. Try not to look at the text again, and try to use the terms you highlighted.

Discuss

1. Do men in your country wear ties?
2. Do you think that men should wear ties with suits? Why or why not?

Thinking About Strategies

Work alone or with a partner. Answer these questions. Share your answers for questions 2 and 3 with the class.

1. How did you deal with unimportant words?
2. In paragraphs where there are several words you don't know, could you understand the main idea without knowing these words? If so, how?
3. Which strategy worked best for understanding the instructions? Was it easier to look at the pictures, or to do the motions with your hands? Did you do both?

4 · READING

Prepare

Work with a partner. Look at the features of the text. Make predictions about the following questions, and explain your choices to the class.

1. What genre is this reading? How do you know?
2. Who is the expected audience?

Read

Think of what you already know about origami. Read the text to get a general idea of the meaning. Don't try to figure out unknown words and phrases at this time. While you are reading, find the answer to this question.

What is origami clothing?

THE CITY

VOL.CLII No 45,378   THURSDAY, FEBRUARY 6, 2003   ONE DOLLAR

Origami Clothing Takes the Shop out of Shopping

UPDATED: FRI, NOV. 16 7:45 AM EST
By Sinead O'Hanlon

LONDON (Reuters) — A London designer has come to the aid of people who hate to shop: self-assembly clothing that you buy from a vending machine.

Swedish-born Helena Rosen's clothing collection is more like origami, the Japanese art of paper folding, than typical fashion design. Her T-shirts, dresses, bags, and skirts have no seams, zippers,

snaps, or buttons. The wearer will buy them from a
10 vending machine and put them together by folding and tucking.

"I was amazed to realize how much can be achieved by simple folding, cutting, and gathering techniques," Rosen told Reuters.

15 The first "AnyWear" collection includes bags, T-shirts, skirts, and dresses. But the concept of vending machine trousers was still a little difficult, she said.

Rosen thinks that the clothing will be bought by
20 people who need a quick change of clothes, hate to shop, or just want an instant makeover.

The pieces, made of synthetic fabrics, are semi-disposable and designed to last for a short time.

"For people on the move, I think the future is for virtually instant clothing that adapts to your lifestyle 25 and how you use technology," she said.

Rosen, 25, is based at the Design Laboratory at the St. Martin's College of Art and Design in London.

Rosen said that while sales planning was still in the early stages, she hopes one day to see vending 30 machines installed in many public places such as airports, train stations, and hotels.

She hopes the trend will take off internationally, and sees Japan, where the vending machine lifestyle is already very popular, as a particularly interesting 35 market.

Rosen estimated a T-shirt will cost about $14.80, with other items being slightly more expensive.

Read Again

Read the text again and do the following:

1. Think of two or three more questions and read to find the answers.

2. Predict ideas. Underline signal words as you are reading, then predict the type of idea that is coming.

3. Circle unfamiliar words. Decide if they are important. If so, try to figure out their meanings, and notice which vocabulary strategies you are using.

Post-Reading Activities

A. Comprehension Check

Answer these questions about the reading.

1. Who is Helena Rosen?

2. Why does the author say that these clothes are like origami?

3. Where will people buy these clothes?

4. What kind of clothes is Rosen going to sell?

5. What kind of clothing isn't the designer going to sell at first?

6. Why does Rosen think her idea will be successful?

7. Where will you be able to find the clothing vending machines?

8. What will the price of a T-shirt be?

9. Explain the title.

B. Vocabulary Check

Complete the paragraph with the following words.

collection   instant   take off
disposable   self-assembly   vending machines

A Japanese designer has designed a line of _____. clothing.
                                                    1

You just fold and tuck, and you have _____ clothing. The clothes
                                                    2

are actually _____. They aren't meant to last for a long time.
                    3

In addition to their unusual design, the clothing will also be sold in a unique way. You will

be able to buy them from _____. The designer hopes that the
                                        4

_____ will really _____.
            5   6

Remember

This evening you are giving a one-minute oral report on one aspect of the future of clothing.
You have only a few minutes to prepare. Highlight or underline key terms in the reading.

Discuss

1. Would people in your country buy clothes from a vending machine?
2. What would be some advantages and disadvantages of disposable clothing?

Thinking About Strategies

What kind of words are these? What do they have in common? Is it necessary to
understand exactly what each one means? Why or why not?

buttons   seams   tucking
folding   snaps   zippers

Reviewing Your Reading

A. Look at the following list of readings in this chapter. Check the column that shows how easy or difficult the material was for you.

Name of Reading	Type of Reading	Easy	Average	Difficult
1. The Importance of Clothes in Society	textbook			
2. Before You Leave for the Gulf	pamphlet			
3A. Why Ties?	magazine article			
3B. How to Tie a Tie	instructions			
4. Origami Clothing Takes the Shop out of Shopping	newspaper article			

B. Read the following list of strategies that you have practiced in this chapter. Review the readings. Which strategies did you use, and how often did you use them? Check your answers in the chart.

Strategy	Always	Often	Sometimes	Never
Prepare				
Making predictions about the text				
Predicting from genre				
Read				
Using background knowledge				
Reading with a purpose				
Using signal words to predict ideas				
Critical Reading				
Distinguishing fact from opinion				

Strategy	Always	Often	Sometimes	Never
Remember				
Highlighting and underlining				
Vocabulary Strategies				
Deciding which words are important				
Predicting the next word				
Recognizing internal definitions				
Analyzing a word for meaning				
Guessing the approximate meaning of a word				

C. Compare your chart with a partner's.

D. Some of the best strategies are the ones that we think up ourselves. Did you use any other strategies while you were reading? If so, share them with the class.

Reading Skills and Strategies

5

Overview of the Strategies

PART 1
Comprehension Strategies

Prepare
- Predicting from Illustrations and Photos
- Predicting from Thesis Statements

Read
- Using Topic Sentences to Identify Main Ideas
- More Practice Using Signal Words to Predict Ideas
- Using Referring Words and Referents, or Antecedents, to Follow Ideas
- Using Illustrations and Photos to Aid Comprehension
- Using Punctuation to Aid Comprehension

Critical Reading
- Evaluating Arguments

Remember
- Paraphrasing

PART 2
Vocabulary Strategies
- Using a Dictionary
- Recognizing Names, Abbreviations, and Acronyms
- More Practice Analyzing A Word for Meaning
- Recognizing Common Phrases
- More Practice Guessing the Approximate Meaning of a Word

P A R T **1** **COMPREHENSION STRATEGIES**

Prepare

Predicting from Illustrations and Photos

Illustrations and captions (the words under the illustrations) will help you figure out new words and concepts in a reading. In addition, for long texts, illustrations may help you easily locate a section without reading the entire text, saving you valuable time.

Before you read, look at pictures, maps, and charts. Read the captions, and note the points or ideas that are illustrated.

Understanding the Strategy

Visual aids to a text illustrate its key points or important data. This is true for every genre. Look at the following list of reading texts. Write the type of information that might be illustrated for each. The first one is done for you.

Text	Illustration
1. business article on Japan's economy	*factors influencing the economy*
2. story of the journey of a boy and his dog	_____
3. article on the climate of Venezuela	_____
4. English dictionary	_____
5. newspaper article on a typhoon in Korea	_____
6. report on the Khoisan tribe of Africa	_____
7. Website about houses for sale in Europe	_____

A C T I V I T Y . 1

Each illustration is from a different article. Guess what the article is about by looking at the illustration. Write your guess on the line under each.

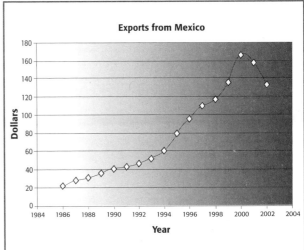

1. _____

2. _____

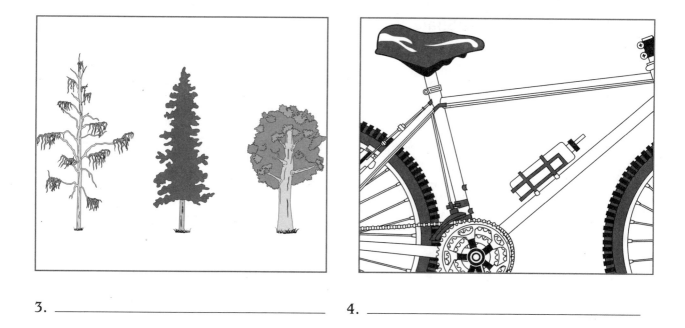

3. _____   4. _____

Predicting from Thesis Statements

A thesis statement tells you two things: the topic of the reading, and the main point that the writer wants to make about that topic.

Understanding the Strategy

A thesis statement is the key statement for an essay, article, book chapter, or entire book. Study the list of thesis statement characteristics and the two examples.

> Use thesis statements to predict the information in a reading.

Thesis statements:

- state the topic and indicate what aspect of it will be discussed.
- usually occur near the end of the introduction.
- often contain words of opinion or persuasion such as *should, terrible, best, have to.*
- are not "bare facts." Compare *Microsoft is a multibillion-dollar corporation.* (fact) with *One of the richest corporations in this decade, Microsoft has not always competed fairly.*

Examples

If you think you can learn how to learn a language, you are right.

American tastes in food are changing and not for the better.

A C T I V I T Y . 2   For each item, read the statement and the list of predictions. Decide how likely it is that the thesis will discuss each idea. After each prediction write *certain, possible,* or *probably not.*

1. The native peoples of the American continents had complex languages and highly developed cultures.

   Predictions

   This reading will describe:

   a. the lives of Native Americans today.   _____

   b. Native American languages.   _____

   c. native cultures in other places.   ____*probably not*____

   d. Native American society in the past.   _____

2. Five methods of studying for the graduate English exam get the best results.

   Predictions

   This reading will:

   a. describe the English exam.   _____

   b. tell you which study methods are best.   _____

   c. explain why people use different methods.   _____

   d. discuss math tests.   _____

3. New York's booming industry is due to open tax laws Ohio has refused to pass.

   Predictions

   This reading will:

   a. compare the industries of New York and California.   _____

   b. talk about industry in Ohio.   _____

   c. describe the geography of Ohio.   _____

   d. discuss industry in the United States.   _____

4. A recent development in Western art, landscape painting grew out of the development of formal gardens in the seventeenth century.

Predictions

This reading will:

a. discuss Asian painting. _____

b. talk about the beginning of landscape painting. _____

c. give the names of some landscape painters. _____

d. tell you where to see landscape painting. _____

5. While computers were arguably the most important invention of the 20th century, the lowly lightbulb had an even greater effect on 19th century life.

Predictions:

This reading will:

a. talk about the invention of lightbulbs. _____

b. explain how lightbulbs work. _____

c. compare types of lightbulbs. _____

d. list the parts of a lightbulb. _____

Read

Using Topic Sentences to Identify Main Ideas

In order to read well, you must be able to identify the writer's main ideas in a reading. Every paragraph has a main idea. This idea is stated in the topic sentence.

Understanding the Strategy

Learn to identify and locate a topic sentence. Read the definition and study the following example essay outline. Then try to find the topic sentence in the paragraph after the example.

Find the writer's most important ideas by identifying topic sentences.

A topic sentence:

- states the topic of the paragraph and the aspect of it that the paragraph will discuss or develop.
- is usually the first or second sentence in a paragraph but can occur in the middle or even at the end.
- is the most general statement in a paragraph, like an umbrella that covers all of the other statements.

- is similar to a thesis statement; however, a thesis statement relates to the entire text, and a topic sentence only relates to one idea.

Example

Computers in Our Lives

Thesis statement: Far from being miracles, computers have actually made our lives much more difficult.

Paragraph 1: Computers make us feel guilty when we aren't productive.

Paragraph 2: Computers have isolated us from friends and family.

Paragraph 3: The world was a much friendlier place before the dawn of the personal computer.

Find the topic sentence of the following paragraph.

Have you ever wondered why you study but never pass a test? Why you come to class every day but never get an A? Three qualities of character contribute the most to a student's success. The first is concentration. You must have the ability to focus. If you are continually distracted, you can't learn. The second is humility. Humility means you are willing to learn. An open attitude allows you to accept new information. Third, and perhaps the most important of all, is determination. If you are easily frustrated, you will never be able to master difficult material.

A C T I V I T Y . 3   Read the paragraphs and underline the topic sentence of each.

1. Before the early 1800s, few people swam; however, by 1900 the first bathing suits were on the market. Every year styles changed more drastically. Now, two hundred years later, few people would recognize the first swimsuits. Women's bathing suits were dresses with high necks and elbow-length sleeves. Women also had to wear stockings and canvas shoes. Men's bathing suits were not quite as uncomfortable, but like the women's suits, they were almost as impractical for swimming.

2. How did the American flag come to have 50 stars but only 13 stripes? After the Declaration of Independence, the American people wanted to have their own flag. The design of the flag was approved on June 14, 1777. This day is now celebrated as Flag Day. The first flag had 13 stripes and 13 stars—one star and one stripe for each state. When Vermont and Kentucky joined the Union, in 1791 and 1792, two stars and two stripes were added. Soon, however, many new states wanted to join the Union, and Congress realized that if a new stripe was added for each state, the flag would grow too large. In 1818, Congress decided that the flag would always have 13 stripes but that a star would still be added for each new state.

3. Sound can travel through any form of matter, but it travels through different matter at different speeds. The speed of sound in air is about 340 meters per second. Sound travels about four times as fast in water as in air. And sound travels fastest through solids, such as steel. The speed of sound in steel is about 15 times as fast as in air. The

5 fact that sound travels relatively slowly in air allows us to "hear" the direction that a sound is coming from. Sound waves reach the ear that is closest to the source of the sound before they reach the other ear. A swimmer underwater can hear sounds but cannot tell which direction the sound is coming from because the sound waves reach both the ears at almost the same time.

1 **4.** Ernest Hemingway is one of the greatest American writers of the 20th century. He was born in Oak Park, Illinois, in 1889. His first novel, *The Sun Also Rises,* was published in 1926 and was a great success. Many people consider Hemingway a very masculine writer. He enjoyed hunting and fishing, and most of his works were about brave men in
5 dangerous situations. He was fond of living dangerously himself. He became a war correspondent during the Spanish Civil War. Two of his most famous novels, *A Farewell to Arms* and *For Whom the Bell Tolls,* took place during that war. Hemingway's life ended tragically. Sick and depressed, he committed suicide in 1961.

1 **5.** When you look at the pages of any modern fashion magazine, you are reminded that "thin is in." More than any other magazine, fashion magazines repeat the messages of popular culture in words that are loud and clear. However, for women today, it is not enough to be thin. The successful modern woman is sexy, a mother, and a prosperous
5 businesswoman. These expectations make many women feel inadequate. In some cases it can lead to two serious illnesses: anorexia and bulimia.

1 **6.** Golden retrievers and young children are a great match. Not only do children love to play with them, they learn from them. Retrievers are easygoing, active, and alert. They are wonderful playmates for children because they love to interact with kids. Retrievers have been bred to "retrieve," that is, bring things back. This makes them good "ball
5 players." Children can learn a sense of control from a golden retriever by giving the dog commands. And like any pet can do, retrievers teach children in another way. Golden retrievers have long hair and they need to be groomed regularly. If children are given this job, their pet can also teach them responsibility. If you have young children and are planning to get a dog, seriously consider the golden retriever.

More Practice Using Signal Words to Predict Ideas

As you learned in Chapter 1, signal words connect ideas. Chapters 5 and 9 introduce more signal words for you to learn and practice. Study the signal words below and the sample sentences. Then answer the questions by filling in the blanks with the correct signal word(s). Note the punctuation: Some of these can begin an independent clause; some cannot.

Categories and sample signal words

Comparison:	*in comparison*
Contrast:	*although, even though, in contrast*
Counterargument:	*nevertheless*
Effect or result:	*as a result*
Emphasis of truth:	*in fact*

Sample Sentences

Tom passed the math test **although** he didn't study

Tom passed the math test **even though** he thought he would fail.

Tom passed the math test; **nevertheless**, he failed the course.

Tom passed the math test. **In comparison**, Greg failed it.

Tom passed the math test. **In contrast**, he failed the history test.

Tom passed the math test. **As a result**, he passed the course.

Tom passed the math test. **In fact**, he got an A!

Which signal word(s) introduce(s):

a. a comparison? _____

b. a contrasting idea? _____ _____ _____

c. a counterargument? _____

d. a result? _____

e. an emphasis on truth? _____

A C T I V I T Y . 4

For each item below, read the sentences(s) and complete the meaning. Circle the letter of the correct answer. Then underline the idea that the signal word connects it to.

1. Many people know that working too hard can lead to health problems. Nevertheless, _____.

   a. hard workers are healthy
   b. health problems are the result
   c. they continue to put in 60- and 70-hour workweeks

2. Citizen Kane is a black-and-white film made in 1941. It is considered one of the best examples of American filmmaking. In fact, _____.
   a. it is still at the top of many lists for the greatest films of all time
   b. no one watches it today
   c. there have been many other films that are better

3. Asia is home to more than half of the world's population, and it is a political and economic power in today's world. As a result, _____.
   a. many people in the West are studying Asian languages
   b. Asian cities are very crowded
   c. Asians enjoy traveling to Europe and the United States

4. About two-thirds of all Americans regularly carry a balance on their credit cards even though _____.
   a. they enjoy shopping
   b. interest rates are high
   c. no one uses credit cards

5. Ann Waigland and her husband spent only $450 for a hotel during their one-week stay in France. In contrast, _____.
   a. the Johnsons spent $2,000
   b. they wanted to go to Germany
   c. the hotel wasn't very good

6. Recent studies show that there are significant physical, mental, psychological, and economic benefits to keeping plants in your home and your office. As a result, _____.
   a. people have stopped growing house plants
   b. sick people should never be near plants
   c. more and more people are buying plants

7. After years of drilling, the 31-mile tunnel under the English Channel finally opened. Now, the 300-mile trip from Paris to London takes about three hours by train. In contrast, _____.
   a. a direct flight takes about one hour
   b. the tunnel opened in 1994
   c. planes are more expensive

Using Referring Words and Referents to Follow Ideas

When you are reading, you must be able to follow the writer's ideas. This can be difficult since writers vary their key terms. As a reader, it is important to recognize which noun a pronoun, noun substitute, or phrase refers to. If you do not, you can misunderstand a sentence, a paragraph, or even an entire article.

Understanding the Strategy

Pronouns and noun substitutes are two types of *referring terms.* These terms refer to a *referent,* which can be a person, place, or thing.

> Be sure to connect pronouns and other referring words to their correct referents as you read.

Types of Referring Words and Phrases

1. **Pronouns.** Personal pronouns refer forward or back. What do each of the following personal pronouns refer to?

   Tom is my best friend. **He** lives next door.

   I gave him the instructions, but he didn't understand **them.**

   Although **her** suitcase was very heavy, Sara refused to let anyone carry it.

It is sometimes the subject of a sentence without being a referring word. Look at these two examples. Which pronoun is a referring word?

it had a dead battery.

My car didn't start this morning because

it was too cold outside.

2. **Noun substitutes.** Noun substitutes rename the person, place, or thing. Note the noun substitutes that refer to *David Riley* in the first sentence of the example.

From the time he was young, David Riley was one of the foremost runners in our state. **The farmboy** began running competitively at the age of 13. By the age of 15 he entered his first adult race, and no one was able to defeat **the determined youngster.** In 1978, **the 22-year-old** became the first graduate of our school to enter the Olympics.

Referents

A referent is the noun to which a pronoun or noun substitute refers. They are also called antecedents. In the following example, what is the referent of *this*? (What does *this* refer to?)

It was impossible for Helen to get up on time. **This** usually made her late for class.

A C T I V I T Y . 5   Draw an arrow from the underlined referring word to its referent. Draw an "X" over it if there is no referent.

1. The tiger lives only in Asia. <u>It</u> is found in mountains and forests.

2. The plumbing system in a house consists of pipes carrying water. <u>Some of them</u> supply clean water for drinking, washing, or heating.

3. Plants usually grow from the end of the stem, but grasses grow from the bottom. <u>This</u> means grasses can be cut and still continue to grow.

4. When Europeans first arrived in Australia, about 300,000 Aborigines lived on the continent, but <u>they</u> were hunted and killed.

5. Advertisements give us information and amusement. We are so used to them that <u>it</u> is hard to imagine life without them.

6. The first airplane was called Flyer I. <u>Its</u> wings were made of wood and cotton.

7. Millions of passengers are carried every year by airliners. <u>These airborne buses</u> have helped to shrink our world.

8. Astronauts go through very special training before they go into space. <u>This</u> gives them as much experience as possible.

9. <u>Some</u> are very quick and <u>others</u> aren't, but all of my students are special.

10. Stringed instruments make sounds when their strings are hit, rubbed, or pulled. Three <u>types</u> are violins and cellos, harps, and guitars.

Using Illustrations and Photos to Aid Comprehension

Textbooks, magazine articles, instruction manuals, and other genres use illustrations for a similar purpose: to show key points, facts, statistics, events, and ideas discussed in the printed text.

Understanding the Strategy

As mentioned in Chapter 1, before reading, always look at a text's illustrations. Look at them as you read as well. When you read a reference to a photograph, chart, or map, reread the reference and look at the illustration. Mentally connect the two. The illustration is a visual aid, a way to sum up, emphasize, and help you "see" and remember the point.

Use the text to help you understand the illustration and the illustration to help you understand the text.

 **6**   Work with a partner, and complete Parts A and B. For Part A, decide what is being illustrated. For Part B, discuss what is not illustrated.

A. For each item, read the text and look at the accompanying illustration(s). Then answer the question that follows.

1. If a person is unable to move or use an injured arm, follow these steps.

   Step 1: Support the injured area above and below the site of the injury.

   Step 2: Place a triangular bandage under the injured arm and over the uninjured shoulder to form a sling.

   Step 3: Tie the ends of the sling on the side of the neck.

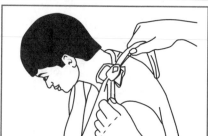

Circle the parts of the pictures that help you understand the following words.

     bandage   site   sling   support

2. An organism depends on its cells to get energy from food. Cell respiration takes place inside cells. During cell respiration, a cell uses energy and oxygen to break down nutrients. Energy escapes as the nutrients split apart. The illustration shows how the cell gains energy during respiration. A cell uses energy to pull certain nutrients through its membrane. A cell also uses energy to break down nutrients in order to gain more energy.

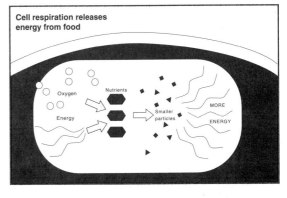

What point is being illustrated? _____

3. Imagine attending a concert with thousands of people. When the concert is over, everyone moves toward the doors. You can hardly move because so many people are around you. Molecules are packed into a solid material in a similar way. Molecules in a solid, such as ice, cannot move very much. When heat energy is added to ice, the ice slowly changes to a liquid. This change occurs because the heat allows some molecules to escape the holding effect of the nearby molecules. These molecules are still close together, but they can move around one another. As more heat is added to water, the molecules move faster and faster and the temperature of the water rises. Molecules begin to break away from the surface of the liquid and mix with the gas. They form bubbles of gas under the surface. The water is boiling or rapidly changing to a gas.

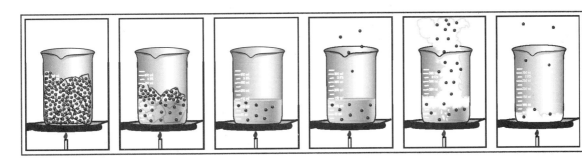

What point is being illustrated? _____

4. Caffeine increases your heart rate and your blood pressure. Doctors today often suggest that people, especially those with heart problems, avoid caffeine as much as possible. Unfortunately, several popular drinks contain caffeine, although some are worse than others. Strong coffee contains the most—nearly 200 milligrams in each cup. Drinking weak coffee is better. It contains less than half the amount of caffeine. In fact, weak coffee and strong tea contain an equal amount of caffeine per cup—80 milligrams. Weak tea and cola drinks

come next. If you need an energy boost but are afraid of caffeine, the best thing to drink is cocoa, which has only 10 to 17 milligrams of caffeine per cup.

What point is being illustrated? _____

B. What information do the previous paragraphs not illustrate? Should the information be illustrated? Why or why not?

Using Punctuation to Aid Comprehension

In addition to the comma and the period, there are a number of other types of punctuation. Punctuation reveals a lot about a reading. It "interprets" the writer's statements, predicts what is coming next, connects ideas, and explains who said what.

Understanding the Strategy

Punctuation is used as a signal. It can signal the end of a thought, the beginning of a list, the addition of an idea, or even an emotion or attitude. Study the following types of punctuation and their uses.

Pay attention to punctuation. It gives valuable information about the text.

Colon, Dash, Italics, and Quotation Marks

Colon

A colon is a punctuation mark indicating that more information is coming. The information can further explain, support, or give examples of the statement before the colon. The colon differs from the semicolon. An independent clause does not have to follow.

Example
My town has a lot to recommend it: good schools, friendly people, and beautiful neighborhoods.

Dash

A dash is often used to signal an afterthought or to stress a point.

Example
The scientist became angry—if a frown can communicate anger—and walked out of the room.

Italics

When a word is printed in italics, the author is trying to call attention to it. For example, when a non-English word is used in an English text, it is often italicized.

Example
Pan fa is to make do with what you have.

Quotation Marks

Quotation marks are used to indicate two things: one, that a person is speaking, and two, what his or her exact words are. However, this punctuation can also be used like italics. Quotation marks may be put around a single word or phrase. In this case, they indicate that the word(s) are being used in an unusual way.

Example
We left when the man pulled out a gun to give us a "friendly" warning.

A C T I V I T Y . 7   Work with a partner or in small groups. Read the paragraph and answer the questions.

There are good reasons why a parent will choose to send a child to private school—not that it's anyone else's business. Private schools offer a number of advantages that public schools do not: small classes, wonderful facilities, and well-behaved students. Of course, private education can cost as much as college, but public education isn't free. Students "pay" in different ways. High school teachers complain that more than half of their time is spent on disciplining students. That means that 49 percent or less of their time is spent on teaching. Clearly, for some students the "cost" of public education will be *trop cher*.

1. Decide why each type of punctuation is used, and support your opinion.
2. Can you determine the writer's attitudes toward public and private schools? Toward discussing the topic? Does the punctuation help indicate these things?

Critical Reading: Evaluating Arguments

We live in the Information Age. More and more information comes to us every day—over the Internet, in books, and in hundreds of magazines and newspapers. Often we do not know who the author is but see only what he or she has written. In addition to identifying facts and opinions, it is important to evaluate a writer's opinion. A critical reader needs to be able to recognize illogical arguments and weak support.

Understanding the Strategy

Responsible authors try to give readers the best information they can. While you are reading, ask yourself the following questions.

Don't believe everything you read. Evaluate the writer's arguments.

1. Does the writer give evidence to support an opinion, and are his or her conclusions valid and reasonable? Some types of evidence might be statistics from reliable sources, real-life examples, or relevant quotations.

   Example
   People in favor of banning cigarette smoking in restaurants are against smoking anywhere anytime. Soon they will try to outlaw cigarettes altogether.

   Question: What is the evidence for the claim stated in the second sentence?

2. Is the evidence relevant* and the conclusion logical?

   Example
   Mike stopped smoking last year and he died six months later. It must be unhealthy to quit smoking.

   Questions: Do the first two events (the "evidence") relate?
   Does the conclusion logically follow? That is, is it a logical result of the events?

Relevant means that the information is closely connected and appropriate.

3. Do the writer's statements sound unreasonably broad? A writer may claim to speak for everyone. Does the writer limit the situations or number of people affected by these claims? Does the writer use many general terms such as "everyone" or "no one"? Or does he or she use limiting terms such as "some" and "a few"?

Example

Cigarette smokers are selfish. They don't care about the health of others. All they want is their own pleasure.

Questions: Is the claim broad or limited?
         Are these statements true of all cigarette smokers?

4. Does the writer seem biased against or for the subject? How does he or she describe the subject? Are any or many value judgement terms used?

Example

Len Davis is leading the fight to ban smoking in restaurants. Everyone knows that he is a liberal fanatic.

Questions: Is the writer attacking Len Davis's ideas or Len Davis himself?
         Does the language seem objective or biased against Len Davis?

5. Does the writer state opinion as if it were fact, or does he or she clearly distinguish the two?

Example

Smoking is the most unhealthy habit in the world today.

Questions: Is this a fact or simply the writer's opinion?
         Do you believe that this is true?

A C T I V I T Y . **8**   Read the point that the writer is trying to make. Then read the question(s) about each supporting statement and circle the answer(s).

Argument: Smoking should not be allowed in restaurants and public buildings.

1. Studies conducted by the University of Maryland's Medical Research Department show that even non-smokers can be hurt by breathing air that contains tobacco smoke.

Is the evidence relevant and logical?	yes	no
Would the evidence be dependable?	yes	no

2. Smokers are dirty and insensitive.

Is the claim too broad?	yes	no

3. If non-smokers have the right to choose not to smoke, then smokers should have the right to choose to smoke.

Is the statement logical?	yes	no

4. My uncle has been smoking for 40 years and he's very healthy.

Is the statement relevant and logical?   yes   no

5. People become ill when they smell cigarette smoke.

Is the statement too broad?   yes   no

6. My cousin works in a restaurant and he has lung cancer even though he has never smoked. He must have gotten lung cancer from smokers at work.

Is the statement logical?   yes   no

A C T I V I T Y . **9**   Read the following paragraph. Evaluate the arguments.

Act Now to Save Our School!

1   The idea that students should participate in the running of our college is stupid. The people who are in favor of this proposal do not have any interest in getting a good education. They only want to make trouble. Students do not have enough experience in the world in order to make good decisions. It is a well-known fact that teenagers are irresponsible, so how can we allow them to make all of these important decisions? The college

5   administration knows how to run a school, and it is made up of educational experts. If immature students are allowed to participate in making decisions, they will soon be running the school. They will ruin it by abolishing grades and firing professors who teach difficult classes. Our college is well known for its high standards. Allowing students to run it will destroy its good name and destroy the future of every student who attends it. Our college is great because the decision makers are mature and well informed. College students are neither;

10   therefore they should not be allowed to participate in the decision-making process.

Remember

Paraphrasing

Restating an idea in your own words makes the idea clearer to you and helps you retain it. Not only that, paraphrasing encourages you to write more simply and to write fewer words.

Understanding the Strategy

Study the characteristics of paraphrases (restatements). Then read the original sentences and their paraphrases. Write simple paraphrases of the last two.

Paraphrase to check comprehension and increase retention.

A good paraphrase:

- may be about the same length of the original passage or shorter.
- uses synonyms for terms except for proper nouns.
- may use some quotes from the passage, but not many.
- says the same thing but in a different way.
- is written while not looking at the original passage.

1. Benjamin Franklin was one of the most famous Americans of the 18th century.

   Benjamin Franklin was a famous American who lived in the 18th century.
   Benjamin Franklin was a famous 18th-century American.

2. He was born of poor parents, and he was mostly self-educated.

   His family was poor. He didn't go to school.
   His family was poor, and he educated himself.

3. As a young man, he began publishing his own newspaper, the Pennsylvania Gazette.

   When he was young, he started a newspaper.
   When young, he started a newspaper.

4. In time, he rose to prominence in Pennsylvania politics.

   In time, he became an important politician in the state of Pennsylvania.
   He became important in Pennsylvania politics.

5. Franklin was also very interested in physics and carried out many experiments, especially in the area of electricity.

   _____

6. By 1775, he was so well known that the men who were creating the new American republic asked him his opinion on the Declaration of Independence and the American Constitution.

   _____

A C T I V I T Y. 10   Write simple paraphrases of each paragraph. Then compare your paraphrases with a classmate's. How are they the same? How are they different?

1. Soon after AIDS appeared on the world scene, doctors began to find more types of bacteria that do not respond to ordinary antibiotic medicine. Four decades of use and overuse of antibiotics had allowed the development of bacteria that these medicines cannot kill. Although there were not many of them at first, there are now hundreds of types of antibiotic-resistant bacteria. In a sense, these bacteria have learned to cope with the attempts of humans to destroy them.

_____

_____

_____

_____

_____

_____

_____

2. Today the world is divided into technological haves and have nots. Some people call this the "digital divide." The digital divide exists between countries. In some places a high percentage of businesses, schools, and homes have access to digital technology such as the Internet. The digital divide also exists within countries. Rich people can afford this technology, while many of their poorer neighbors cannot.

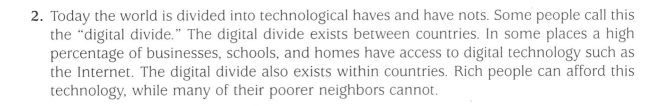

_____

_____

_____

_____

_____

_____

PART 2 **VOCABULARY STRATEGIES**

Using a Dictionary

Did you know that all dictionaries are not alike? "Abridged" dictionaries contain a limited number of entries; for example, sometimes only 2,000 out of hundreds of thousands of words. Translation dictionaries often contain insufficient, even inexact, definitions. Student dictionaries contain fewer words and simpler definitions than regular dictionaries.

Understanding the Strategy

Choose a dictionary that will be accurate and useful. Look at the advantages that an English-English dictionary can offer a student of English.

Use an English-English dictionary for accurate definitions.

All good English-English dictionaries give this information

- the meaning or meanings of the word
- the part of speech
- the pronunciation of the word
- grammatical information such as count/non-count nouns
- an example phrase or sentence

A C T I V I T Y. 11   Read the following entry from an ESL English-English dictionary and answer the following questions.

per fect /p rfikt/ adj. 1. the best possible: *Three hundred is a perfect score in bowling.* 2. complete and faultless with nothing wrong or missing: *The computer is in perfect condition.* 3. appropriate and satisfactory in every respect: *This house is perfect!* 4. Total, complete: *It was foolish to lend money to a perfect stranger.* —v. /perfikt/ to make perfect, excellent: *It took him ten years to perfect his invention.*

    1. What parts of speech are given in the definition?
    2. How many definitions are there for *perfect* as an adjective?
    3. What is the sample sentence for definition 2?
    4. What is the difference in pronunciation between *perfect* as an adjective and a verb?

milk /milk/ n. [U] a white liquid produced by female mammals: *Most children drink cow's milk.*—v. 1. To take milk from (cows, goats, etc.): *Farmers milk their cows every day.* 2. To take s.t. valuable from s.t. usu. in a bad way: *The owners milked their company of its profits.* 3. **to cry over spilled milk:** to be angry over s.t. one cannot change: *The sofa is ruined, but there's no use crying over spilled milk. We'll buy a new one.*

> **1.** What does [U] mean?
> **2.** Can you guess the meaning of the abbreviations "s.t." and "usu."?
> **3.** Can you find the idiom in the definitions?

Recognizing Names, Abbreviations, and Acronyms

Proper names, abbreviations, and acronyms can easily confuse a reader. These are used especially in business and technology, but will be found in every genre. It is not always important to know their meanings, but it is necessary to understand that they are not ordinary words.

Learn to recognize names, abbreviations, and acronyms.

Understanding the Strategy

Names

Names are usually easy to recognize. They begin with capital letters.

Texas Instruments   Memorial Stadium   Fastwork Car Repair

Abbreviations

Abbreviations are shortened forms of words. Abbreviations are usually formed with the first or first few letters of the word or words. Abbreviations of proper names are capitalized.

United States of America	USA
General Motors Corporation	GMC or GM
United Nations	UN
Saint Mary's Ferry	St. Mary's Fry.
Highway 57	Hwy. 57
New York City	NYC
Post Office Box 153	P.O.B. 153

Abbreviations of common nouns and phrases are not capitalized.

kilobyte	k
personal computer	pc
as soon as possible	asap
disc jockey	dj

Acronyms

Acronyms are abbreviations that are pronounced like words rather than letters. Acronyms of proper nouns are capitalized.

National Aeronautics and Space Administration   NASA
United Nations International Children's Emergency Fund   UNICEF

Acronyms of common nouns are not capitalized.

random access memory   ram

A C T I V I T Y . 12   Rewrite each sentence. For 1–3, use abbreviations or acronyms for the underlined words. For 4–5, spell out the underlined abbreviations and acronyms. If you aren't sure, make a guess.

1. The director of the <u>United States Agricultural Commission for the Southern Region</u>, <u>Doctor</u> Stanley Williams, is the guest lecturer.

   _____

2. <u>Mister</u> Ortega's <u>personal computer</u> broke, and he wants it fixed <u>as soon as possible</u>.

   _____

3. After 7:00 <u>in the evening</u>, the <u>disc jockey</u> plays rock and roll on the <u>Saint</u> Louis station.

   _____

4. Send the letter to <u>Prof.</u> Ha Jong at <u>Univ.</u> of Missouri, <u>P.O.B.</u> 14, Thomasville <u>Hwy.</u>, <u>St.</u> Louis, <u>MO</u>.

   _____

5. Did you interview for a job with <u>UNICEF</u>?

   _____

More Practice Analyzing a Word for Meaning

You learned in Chapter 1 to analyze words to help you figure out their meanings, and to compare them with other words that appear similar. Many English words are related by their roots, prefixes, and suffixes. Chapters 5 and 9 present more practice for analyzing words.

A C T I V I T Y . 13   Study the following words. Then guess the meanings of the italicized roots, prefixes, and stems.

1. chronometer   an instrument that keeps time
   chronology   a time line; in order of time
   chronic   continuing for a long time

   a. *chrono*   probably refers to _____.

   b. *–ic*   is probably the ending for _____ (part of speech)

2. unfair   not fair
   nonsmoker   a person who doesn't smoke
   illegal   not legal
   insane   not sane
   disloyal   not loyal

   a. *un-*   probably means _____.

   b. *non-*   probably means _____.

   c. *il-*   probably means _____.

   d. *in-*   probably means _____.

   e. *dis-*   probably means _____.

3. superwoman   a very powerful woman
   supermarket   a large market
   superior   excellent; first-rate
   superscript   a letter or number written above others (8th)
   script   the written text of a play or a movie

   a. *super-* probably means _____.

   b. *script*   probably means _____.

4. hypercritical very critical
   hyperactive   very active
   criticize   to judge; to judge severely
   popularize   to make popular

   a. *hyper-* probably means _____.

   b. *crit*   probably means _____.

   c. *–ize*   is probably the ending for a _____ (part of speech)

5. misinform — to give incorrect information
misbehave — to behave badly
mistake — an error
misplacement — loss
maltreatment — abuse; bad treatment
malfunction — not working correctly

   a. *mis-* and *mal-* probably mean _____.

   b. *–ment* is probably the ending for a _____ (part of speech)

6. precede — to come before
predict — to say what is going to happen in the future
predictable — able to be predicted
predictably — as expected
diction — a way of speaking
dictionary — a book that defines words

   a. *pre-* probably means _____.

   b. *dict* probably refers to _____.

7. sociology — the study of society
sociologist — a person who studies society
pianist — a person who plays the piano
economist — a person who studies the economy
economic — about the science of economics

   a. *socio* probably refers to _____.

   b. *–ist* is probably the ending for _____ (part of speech)

   c. *–ic* is probably the ending for _____ (part of speech)

8. transcontinental — across a continent
transport — to move from one place to another
transmit — to send
transform — to change
transformation — a change

   a. *trans-* probably means _____.

   b. *form* probably refers to _____.

   c. *–ation* is probably the ending for _____ (part of speech)

A C T I V I T Y . 14   Read the following sentences. Use your knowledge of stems and affixes to guess the approximate meanings of the italicized words.

1. He lost his job because he was *chronically* late.

   Chronically means _____.

2. The unemployment rate is a strong *predictor* for the state of the economy.

   A *predictor* probably is _____.

3. There are laws against the *mistreatment* of animals.

   Mistreatment probably means _____.

4. It would be exciting to take a trip on the *Trans-Siberian* Railway.

   Trans-Siberian means _____.

5. The president said that anyone who didn't agree with him was a *disloyalist*.

   A *disloyalist* probably is _____.

Recognizing Common Phrases

Collocations, or arrangements of words, can have a literal meaning you can figure out, or an idiomatic one you can't. Some dictionaries list them in bold. Many do not list them at all. What do you do when you come across a phrase you don't know? Smart readers are prepared: They learn common phrases as they learn ordinary vocabulary.

Understanding the Strategy

Whether you can find a phrase in the dictionary or not, it takes valuable time trying to figure it out. Keep a list of phrases from your reading, and memorize them. This saves you trouble the next time you see them. Read the examples and the explanation about them. Then read the sentences and write the meaning of the underlined phrases.

Learn expressions as you learn ordinary vocabulary: by memory.

Examples

My job has many **fringe benefits**.

I was surprised when I heard from Mike. He wrote me **out of the blue**.

Fringe benefits can be figured out. Look up the words in the dictionary; or, if you know *benefits*, guess the meaning. *Out of the blue* can't be figured out. This phrase does not have a literal meaning but is an idiom for "without warning."

1. Ask Maria. She has all the information <u>at her fingertips</u>.

   _____

2. He told me that he was <u>ready, willing, and able</u> to play tennis despite the fact that he was still <u>black and blue</u> from the last game.

   _____

   _____

3. It's too bad that Eric is quitting. Good accountants are <u>few and far between</u>.

   _____

4. Marta <u>knows</u> the subway system <u>inside out</u>.

   _____

5. The police can't find the thief. He <u>covered his tracks</u> well.

   _____

ACTIVITY. 15 How many collocations do you recognize? Choose the best word to complete each common phrase.

1. It's faster than the speed of _____.
   a. sun   **b.** horses   **c.** light

2. The man kept walking back and _____.
   a. forth   **b.** up   **c.** in

3. He went _____.
   a. messy   **b.** sick   **c.** insane

4. Wait here. I'll be down right _____.
   a. away   **b.** what   **c.** down

5. She built this school from the ground _____.
   a. on   **b.** to   **c.** up

6. He didn't have enough money to settle his _____.
   a. accounts   **b.** debts   **c.** bills

7. Don't talk to her. She's in a bad _____.
   a. time   **b.** day   **c.** mood

8. It is illegal to commit _____.
   a. suicide   **b.** killing   **c.** unsafe driving

9. This house has changed _____ many times.
   a. hands   **b.** families   **c.** owners

10. I'm very fond _____ animals.
    a. with   **b.** to   **c.** of

11. They are going to lift the _____ on smoking in restaurants.
    a. law   **b.** ban   **c.** veto

12. Suddenly the car disappeared from _____.
    a. view   **b.** scene   **c.** vision

13. In the 1930s, times were _____. There were few jobs.
    a. strong   **b.** long   **c.** hard

More Practice Guessing the Approximate Meaning of a Word

Chapter 1 introduced strategies to guess the meaning of new terms. However, the challenge is not only to guess, but to guess correctly. You can guess by:

1. using your background knowledge.
2. looking for context clues.
3. analyzing words.
4. recognizing internal definitions.
5. recognizing names and abbreviations.

A C T I V I T Y. **16**   Look at the underlined words. Read the entire paragraph and then complete the sentences that follow.

1. The Ventana, which is Spanish for "window", is a <u>submersible robot</u> that helps scientists explore places under the sea that humans cannot easily reach. The scientists stay on a ship on the <u>surface</u> and use remote controls to guide the Ventana, which is 2,000 feet below them. Today they are looking for coral. One scientist uses the remote control to extend the Ventana's arm so that it can break off a <u>chunk</u> of rock with coral attached to it.

   a. *Submersible* probably means something that _____.

   b. A *robot* probably is a _____.

   c. *Surface* probably refers to _____.

   d. *Chunk* probably means _____.

2. Every year, 120 million <u>minuscule</u> <u>inhabitants</u> of Christmas Island <u>swarm</u> across their tiny island just south of Indonesia. Starting in November, the harmless red crabs <u>emerge</u> from their hidden homes to take over the cliffs, beaches, and <u>headlands</u>. There the <u>crustaceans</u> meet, mate, and finally <u>cast</u> their eggs back into the ocean. Then each crab somehow manages to find its way back home. By March it's over and the 2,000 human islanders can <u>reclaim</u> their roads, golf courses, and even their houses—until next year.

a. *Minuscule* describes the _____.

b. An *inhabitant* is probably _____.

c. *Swarm* probably means to _____.

d. *Emerge* probably means to _____.

e. *Headlands* probably are a kind of _____.

f. *Crustaceans* refers to _____.

g. *Cast* probably means to _____.

h. *Reclaim* probably means to _____.

Reading:
Diamonds!

6

Getting Started

Look at the photo of the diamonds. Discuss the questions in pairs or small groups. Share your ideas with the class.

1. Name the jewelry that you wear. Which gemstones would you buy if you had the money: diamonds, sapphires, emeralds, pearls, turquoise, or rubies? Why?

2. In your country, does anyone wear diamond jewelry? Where do they wear it?

Strategies Reminder

Comprehension Strategies

Prepare
- Predicting from Illustrations and Photos
- Predicting from Thesis Statements

Read
- Using Topic Sentences to Identify Main Ideas
- Reading with a Purpose (with Questions in Mind)
- Using Illustrations and Photos to Aid Comprehension
- Using Signal Words to Predict Ideas
- Using Referring Words and Referents to Follow Ideas
- Using Punctuation to Aid Comprehension

Critical Reading
- Evaluating Arguments

Remember
- Paraphrasing

Vocabulary Strategies
- Using a Dictionary
- Recognizing Names, Abbreviations, and Acronyms
- Recognizing Internal Definitions
- Analyzing a Word for Meaning
- Recognizing Common Phrases
- Guessing the Approximate Meaning of a Word

1 . READING

Prepare

Work with a partner. Look at the title, subtitles, and illustration of the reading. Which of these questions do you think the article will answer? Explain your choices to the class.

1. How should you choose a diamond?
2. How are diamonds formed?
3. Where can you buy diamonds?
4. How much do diamonds cost?
5. Where are diamonds found?
6. Why are diamonds so expensive?
7. What are diamonds used for?
8. How are diamonds mined?
9. When do people wear diamonds?
10. Why do people wear diamonds?

Read

Read the text to get a general idea of the meaning. Try to identify the topic sentence in each paragraph. Look at the diagram to help you understand the reading. Choose one of the questions from the *Prepare* section, and read to find the answer.

The Science of Diamonds

The Geology of Diamonds

1 Diamonds are the crystalline form of carbon that has been changed by extreme heat and pressure. There is only one natural environment in which diamonds form: in molten rock 75 to 120 miles below the surface of the earth.
5 Diamonds in the form of crystals then come to the surface in volcanic eruptions. This process doesn't always produce diamonds, however. The carbon crystals may become free carbon atoms, carbon dioxide, or graphite (the "lead" in pencils) instead. If the carbon crystal is cooled quickly near
10 the surface of the earth, it becomes the stone we call a diamond.

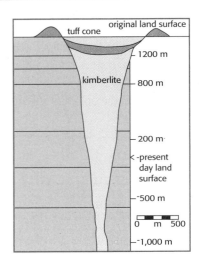

Kimberlite comes up through the earth in carrot-shaped cones.

Diamonds form under large, stable, cooler plates of earth called "cratons." Cratons are usually found in rock called kimberlite, named after the town of Kimberly, South
15 Africa. Kimberlite comes up through the earth in carrot-shaped cones known as "pipes." In South Africa there are more than 3,000 kimberlite pipes in the area of the Orange River. Diamonds from these sites are called "dry earth" diamonds. In fact, it is only since the South African diamond rush in the 1870s that diamonds have been mined from the earth. For thousands of years, the world's finest diamonds came from riverbed mines in India.
20 Diamonds can travel by river to the sea. At present, one of the richest of the world's diamond sources is on a beach. Although originally from South Africa, these diamonds appeared on a 100-mile stretch of beach south of Namibia. The river had transported them to the Atlantic Ocean. The larger diamonds sank to the ocean floor, while others were left on the beach. It is thought that Antarctica, with its large cratons, may be a rich potential source of diamonds.
25 However, international agreements prohibit mining there.

The Physics of Diamonds

A diamond is the hardest substance known on earth. There are two kinds of diamonds: industrial diamonds, and gem-quality diamonds. Industrial diamonds have a variety of manufacturing uses. For example, because of their hardness, they are often used in cutting tools. The best diamonds, however, are used to make jewelry.
30 Gemstone diamonds have a wide range of transparency and color. Color in diamonds is caused by the presence of minor elements. Not all colors are of equal value. Colorless stones, known as white diamonds, are extremely valuable, while yellow or brown stones are considered imperfect. Green and blue diamonds are very rare, red diamonds are the rarest of all, and all three are more expensive than the white.

35   Gemstone diamonds are valued for their sparkle and brilliance, characteristics caused by the way light moves in a diamond. Light travels at 186,000 miles per second in a vacuum. In contrast, when light travels through matter—air, water, glass, or diamond, for example—it travels more slowly. Most clear and colorless objects slow the speed of light by only a small amount. For example, light in water and ice travels about 140,000 miles per second—30 percent

40 slower than in a vacuum. Window glass drops the speed of light to 120,000 miles per second. The kind of glass used in chandeliers and cut glass slows light to about 100,000 miles per second. Light travels through a diamond at less than 80,000 miles per second. That's more than 100,000 miles per second slower than in air. Diamonds slow the speed of light more than any other colorless substance.

45   Why do diamonds slow down light? Cut diamonds have many different sides, so light enters the stone from many directions. As a result, the light bounces back and forth several times inside before it finds a way out. This is the secret to the diamond's beauty. White light contains all the rainbow's colors: red, blue, green, yellow, and violet. When the light changes direction several times, the colors of the light separate, creating the perfect brilliance and sparkle of a diamond.

Read Again

Read the text at least two more times. As you are reading, do the following:

1. Think of two or three more questions and find the answers.

2. Predict ideas. Circle the signal words and use them to predict the next idea.

3. Note unfamiliar words and phrases. Decide if they are important. If so, try to figure out their meanings, and notice which vocabulary strategies you are using. If you cannot figure out the meanings, list the terms on a separate piece of paper. After you finish reading, decide if you need to look up the definitions.

4. Note punctuation.

5. Follow ideas. Underline the referring words and circle their referents.

Post-Reading Activities

A. Comprehension Check

Answer these questions about Reading 1.

1. What are diamonds made of?

2. What is necessary for the formation of diamonds?

3. What form are diamonds in when they come up through the earth?

4. How are diamonds mined today?

5. How did people get diamonds 100 years ago?

6. What are the characteristics of a good diamond?

7. What causes color in diamonds?

8. How fast does light travel in a diamond? Why?

9. What is a result of light entering a cut diamond from many directions?

10. In paragraph 2, why do quotation marks enclose *pipe* and *dry earth*?

B. Vocabulary Check

A. You may have used your background knowledge of science, world affairs, or diamonds to guess the meanings of new words in the reading. Choose three terms that you figured out. Write a brief explanation of how you did so. The first two are done for you.

1. volcanic eruption

I figured that volcanic had to be related to volcano, and I know what a volcano is; here it comes before eruption so it probably means a kind of eruption. Volcanoes explode, so I guessed that eruption was probably "explosion."

2. perfect

I remembered this word from Chapter 5, so I knew that it meant "the best possible."

3. surface

4. transported

5. diamond rush

6. international agreements

7. transparency

_____

_____

_____

8. sparkle

_____

_____

_____

9. brilliance

_____

_____

_____

10. imperfect

_____

_____

_____

B. There are several scientific words in this reading. All of them are explained within the reading itself. Find and mark the explanation or definition of the following words.

cratons   dry earth diamonds   kimberlite   pipe

C. Following Ideas

Find the referents, or antecedents, of the following words and phrases. Look back at the reading and complete the chart.

Word/Phrase	Line	Refers to	No referent
1. it	10		
2. it	18		
3. these diamonds	21		
4. it	23		
5. all three	33		
6. it	37		

Word/Phrase	Line	Refers to	No referent
7. it	47		
8. this	47		

Remember

Restate in writing some of the article's ideas to clarify them in your mind. Paraphrase the following passages. Then, without looking at your paper or book, explain the ideas to a partner or group.

 a. how diamonds are formed
 b. why diamonds sparkle

Discuss

 1. Identify and discuss three or four other uses diamonds have besides decoration.
 2. Why do people value diamonds? Do you value them? Why or why not?

Thinking About Strategies

How well did you understand this reading? Did you use a dictionary to look up any words? Work with a partner. Compare your answers to the following questions.

 1. What kind of dictionary did you use?
 2. Which words did you look up?
 3. Was your dictionary helpful? Why or why not?

2 · READING

Prepare

Work with a partner. Look at the title and chart of the reading. Read the first sentence of each paragraph. Then think of three questions the reading will answer. Compare your questions with your classmates' questions.

Read

Read the text to get a general idea of the meaning. Try to identify the topic sentence in each paragraph. Look at the chart to help you understand the reading. Choose one of your questions from the *Prepare* section and read to find the answer.

The History of Diamonds

The name *diamond* is derived from the Greek word *adamas,* which means "unbreakable." People have valued diamonds for thousands of years, perhaps as a result of the fact that until the 20th century only a few diamond deposits were known. For a thousand years, starting in roughly the 4th century BCE, India was the only source of diamonds. At that time, diamonds were used
5 in two ways: for decoration, and as a talisman for good luck because people used to think that diamonds had extraordinary powers. In fact, there are even records of people eating diamonds as medicine. During the early Middle Ages, Pope Clement tried this treatment; it was unsuccessful, and he died.

During the Middle Ages, more
10 attention was paid to the value of diamonds than to their mystical powers. In the 13th century, Louis IX of France instituted a law saying that only the king could own diamonds. Nevertheless,
15 slowly the distribution of diamonds became less unfair and more democratic. First, other members of the royal family were allowed to own them. Then, by the 17th century, wealthy merchants were
20 wearing them.

In 1726, diamonds were discovered in Brazil, and in 1866 they were found in South Africa. By the mid-19th century, the discovery of diamonds near the
25 Orange River in South Africa sparked the world's biggest diamond rush. There have been large discoveries in the 20th century as well. The last one was in Australia in 1979, when geologists found
30 the Argyle Pipe near Lake Argyle: the richest diamond deposit in the world.

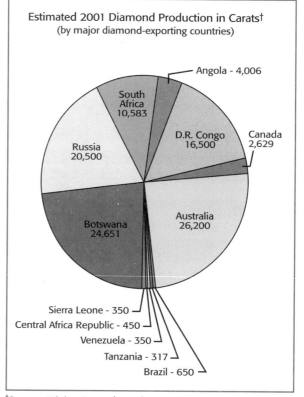

Estimated 2001 Diamond Production in Carats[†]
(by major diamond-exporting countries)

Angola - 4,006
South Africa 10,583
D.R. Congo 16,500
Canada 2,629
Russia 20,500
Botswana 24,651
Australia 26,200
Sierra Leone - 350
Central Africa Republic - 450
Venezuela - 350
Tanzania - 317
Brazil - 650

[†]Source: *Mining Journal,* London, August 17, 2001

Since then, Argyle has become the world's largest producer of diamonds and is responsible for producing over a third of the world's diamonds every year.

The monumental increase in diamond production in the last century is shown on this graph.
35 India's maximum production, perhaps 50,000 to 100,000 carats* annually in the 16th century, is very small by modern standards. Brazil's and Venezuela's are barely visible compared with South Africa's. For the most part, except for major wars and economic recessions, diamond production has been steadily increasing since then, with non-African sources growing in relative proportion. Major production is now dominated by Australia, Botswana, Russia, and the Congo
40 Republic (Zaire). However, although other countries produce more diamonds than South Africa, when you look at statistics for both quality and quantity, South Africa is still the world's leading diamond producer.

---

*The carat is the traditional measuring unit of a diamond's weight. One carat equals 200 milligrams.

Read Again

Read the text at least two more times. As you are reading, do the following:

1. Think of two or three more questions and find the answers.
2. Predict ideas. Circle the signal words and use them to predict the next idea.
3. Note unfamiliar words and phrases. Decide if they are important. If so, try to figure out their meanings, and notice which vocabulary strategies you are using. If you cannot figure out the meanings, list the terms on a separate piece of paper. After you finish reading, decide if you need to look up the definitions.
4. Note punctuation.
5. Follow ideas. Underline the referring words and circle their referents.

Post-Reading Activities

A. Comprehension Check

1. Make a chronology of events for the history of diamonds. Put the information on this timeline.

   4th century BCE   13th century   17th century   19th century   20th century

2. How have people used diamonds in history?
3. Until the last century, only a few diamond deposits were known. What is a possible result of this fact?
4. What comes out of the Argyle Pipe? Where is this pipe?
5. Has diamond production always steadily increased?

B. Vocabulary Check

Find the proper names and abbreviations in the reading. What do they refer to? Compare your list with your classmates' lists.

Remember

Choose one paragraph of the reading and write a paraphrase of it. Don't forget: Simplify the meaning, but don't change it. Include the most important information.

Discuss

Discuss the following questions in groups of four or five.

1. Does your country invest in diamond mines? Where are they?
2. Where are Brazil, Venezuela, and Russia? In what kind of environment would you expect to find diamond deposits in these countries? Are there any environments like this in your own country? If so, where?

Thinking About Strategies

Were you able to use the graph to help you understand the reading?

A. Study the graph. It has information that illustrates two of the following points about global diamond production. Which point is not illustrated by the graph? Why?

   1. Major production is now <u>dominated by</u> Australia, Botswana, Russia, and the Congo Republic (Zaire).

   2. Production in Brazil and Venezuela is <u>barely visible</u>.

   3. South Africa is still the world's <u>leading</u> diamond producer.

B. Use the information in the graph to guess the meanings of the underlined words or phrases when possible.

3 ⁝ READING

Prepare

Work with a partner. Look at the title and subtitle of the reading. Can you guess the meaning of *cursed*? Share your ideas with your class.

Read

Read the text to get a general idea of the meaning. Try to identify the topic sentence in each paragraph. While you are reading, find the answers to these questions.

   What evidence is there that the owners were lucky?

   What evidence is there that the owners were cursed?

The Story of the Hope Diamond

Were the Owners Lucky or Cursed?

1   The legend of the Hope Diamond began with a theft. Several centuries ago, a man named Tavernier made a trip to India. While there, he stole a large blue diamond from the forehead of a statue of the Hindu goddess Sita. According to the legend, for his crime, Tavernier was killed by wild dogs on a trip to Russia many years later. This was the first death caused by the curse. Before he died, and 26 years after he acquired the large blue
5   diamond, Tavernier sold it to French King Louis XIV, the Sun King.

   In 1673, King Louis XIV decided to recut the diamond. Sixty-seven and an eighth carats, the newly cut gem was of the most superior quality. Louis XIV officially named it the "Blue Diamond of the Crown." He was quite fond of the gem and often wore it on a long ribbon around his neck. The diamond was then passed down from king to king until the reign of King Louis XVI and Queen Marie Antoinette. The crown jewels, including the
10   blue diamond, were stolen during the French Revolution. According to the legend, Marie Antoinette and Louis XVI were beheaded because of the curse of the blue diamond. Though it is true that they were killed, their deaths

had much more to do with the peasants' anger at them than with any curse. In addition, they were certainly not the only royals who lost their heads during the Reign of Terror.

The blue diamond was next seen in London about 20 years later. The owner was a jeweler named Daniel
15 Eliason. At that time, the diamond was estimated at only 44 carats. It is likely that someone had recut it in order to hide its origin. King George IV of England bought the blue diamond from Daniel Eliason. After he died, the diamond was sold to pay off debts.

The "cursed" stone then disappeared from view. By 1839, it resurfaced once more. It was now owned by Henry Philip Hope. Some people say that the Hope family suffered from the diamond's curse because they went
20 bankrupt after they bought it. However, these people were misinformed. The bankruptcy occurred three generations later and it was most likely gambling, rather than the curse, that caused it.

The next owner was Simon Frankel, an American jeweler, who bought the Hope diamond in 1901 and brought it to the United States. The diamond changed hands often during the next several years, ending with Evalyn McLean, who thought it brought luck. She wore the diamond all the time. In fact, according to one story,
25 she did not even want to take it off when she went into the hospital. Though Evalyn McLean wore the Hope Diamond as a good luck charm, it doesn't seem to have helped her. McLean's son, Vinson, died in a car crash, her daughter committed suicide, and her husband went insane.

Evalyn McLean had wanted her jewelry to go to her grandchildren, but it was sold in order to settle debts. The buyer was a famous jeweler named Harry Winston, who donated the Hope Diamond to the Smithsonian Institution
30 in 1958. On November 10 of that year, the most famous diamond in the world traveled by ordinary mail in a plain brown box to Washington, D.C. There it was met by a large group of people at the Smithsonian who celebrated its much anticipated arrival. It remains on display at the Smithsonian Institution today.

Read Again

Read the text at least two more times. As you are reading, do the following:

1. Think of two or three more questions and find the answers.

2. Predict ideas. Circle the signal words and use them to predict the next idea.

3. Note unfamiliar words and phrases. Decide if they are important. If so, try to figure out their meanings, and notice which vocabulary strategies you are using. If you cannot figure out the meanings, list the terms on a separate piece of paper. After you finish reading, decide if you need to look up the definitions.

4. Note punctuation.

5. Follow ideas. Underline the referring words and circle their referents.

Post-Reading Activities

A. Comprehension Check

Answer these questions about the reading.

1. What is the legend of the Hope Diamond?

2. In what century did Tavernier steal the diamond from the Hindu statue?

3. To which countries did the Hope Diamond travel? What country is it in now?

4. Write the names of the owners of the Hope Diamond in order.

5. Put an "X" next to the names of owners who suffered from the "curse."

B. Vocabulary Check

Work alone or with a partner, and do the following.

A. Look at this list of proper nouns. Which ones are identified in the reading? Which ones do you recognize from background knowledge? Briefly explain to a partner who or what each one is.

1. Sita
2. French Revolution
3. Sun King
4. Reign of Terror
5. Smithsonian

B. You may not know the exact meaning of these words. However, there are enough clues in the reading for you to guess approximately. Decide if each word or phrase represents something generally good or bad. Then check the appropriate column.

Word/Phrase	Probably Good	Probably Bad
1. superior		
2. curse		
3. good luck charm		
4. suicide		
5. bankruptcy		
6. insane		

C. Following Ideas

A. The writer refers to the Hope Diamond in several different ways. Go back to the reading, and underline them. Compare your answers with a partner's.

B. Did you follow the referring words and their referents, or did they confuse you? Look back at the reading and complete the chart. Write an "X" if the word has no referent.

Word/Phrase	Line	Refers to	No referent
1. it	11		
2. it	15		
3. he	16		
4. these people	20		

Word/Phrase	Line	Refers to	No referent
5. it	26		
6. it	28		
7. its	31		

D. Critical Reading Check

Evaluate the legend. Is there any truth in it? Does the writer believe in a curse? Find evidence in the reading that supports your opinion. Be sure to separate fact from opinion.

Remember

Retell the legend of the Hope Diamond. Highlight key points, then orally restate them in short paraphrases. When you can remember them all, close your book and write down the legend.

Discuss

1. Do you believe in curses? Why or why not?
2. What are other objects or places that people believe are cursed?

Thinking About Strategies

Answer the following question, and be ready to explain the reasons for your choice. Share your opinion with the class.

> If you had to illustrate the information in this text, which of the following graphic organizers would you use?
>
> * a circle graph
> * a painting
> * a timeline
> * a diagram

4 . READING

Prepare

Work with a partner. Look at the title of the reading. Skim the first paragraph and try to identify a thesis statement. Answer the questions, and share your ideas with the class.

1. Complete this sentence:

   This reading is about _____.

2. Do we usually think of selling a tradition? What does the title tell you about the reading?

Read

Read the text to get a general idea of the meaning. Try to identify the topic sentence in each paragraph. While you are reading, find the answers to these questions.

What is the tradition?

In what ways is the tradition sold?

The Selling of a Tradition

1   For more than a century the DeBeers Corporation of South Africa has controlled the world's supply of uncut diamonds. In fact, today when people hear the name DeBeers, they think of diamonds. The DeBeers company was founded in 1888 by Englishman Cecil Rhodes. He owned a diamond mine in Kimberly, South Africa. Thousands of people had rushed to mine diamonds after the discovery of the great diamond deposit
5   in the 1870s. By 1885, there were so many diamonds for sale that the price had fallen from $500 a carat to just 10¢ a carat. Times were hard. Rhodes knew that the only way to make money with diamonds was to make them rare. The only way to do this was to control the supply of diamonds. The company started the Central Selling Organization (CSO), which still exists today. CSO was a diamond cartel that made sure that there were never too many diamonds available. Rhodes's plan worked very well. By 1900, the CSO
10   controlled about 90 percent of the world's supply of diamonds, and DeBeers controlled the CSO.

By the early 20th century, however, DeBeers had figured out that controlling the supply was not enough. To increase profits, you also had to increase the demand. According to diamond expert Matthew Hart, the next step showed DeBeers' true genius. They took something useless—diamonds—and connected it to something of great value—human love.

15   In order to do this, they hired an advertising agency that began marketing a diamond as a symbol of love: the bigger, the better. They were even able to get famous artists such as Pablo Picasso, Salvador Dalí, and others to create art for DeBeers' ads. They also gave diamonds to famous movie stars to use as symbols of their indestructible love. Then they put stories in magazines and newspapers that stressed the size of these diamonds. They even used Queen Elizabeth, who visited diamond mines in South Africa and accepted a
20   diamond from DeBeers.

The most effective part of the advertising campaign was the slogan that they still use today: "A diamond is forever." This statement was perfect even though it was a lie. Diamonds actually can be destroyed. And even though 50 percent of the marriages in the United States end in divorce, people want to believe that theirs will last forever. As a result of this brilliant strategy, within three years, the sale of diamonds increased by 55
25   percent. Over the next 50 years, DeBeers repeated this marketing miracle in countries like Japan that previously had had no diamond tradition.

Experts say that diamonds are not rare today. In fact, they estimate that more than 100 million carats a year of diamonds come out of the ground. That might be as many as 800 million separate stones. So why are diamonds still so expensive? Because almost every diamond mine sells part of its output to DeBeers, and
30   DeBeers sells only a small amount and keeps the rest. DeBeers officials claim that the company controls its diamond supplies the same way that a manufacturer controls its inventory. Still, the central question remains: Is it fair to create demand and then refuse to meet it?

Read Again

Read the text at least two more times. As you are reading, do the following:

1. Think of two or three more questions and find the answers.
2. Predict ideas. Circle the signal words and use them to predict the next idea.
3. Note unfamiliar words and phrases. Decide if they are important. If so, try to figure out their meanings, and notice which vocabulary strategies you are using. If you cannot figure out the meanings, list the terms on a separate piece of paper. After you finish reading, decide if you need to look up the definitions.
4. Note punctuation.
5. Follow ideas. Underline the referring words and circle their referents.

Post-Reading Activities

A. Comprehension Check

Answer these questions about the reading.

1. Why did Cecil Rhodes found the DeBeers Company?
2. What was the company's first business strategy?
3. What did the company try to do next?
4. How successful were they?
5. Why are diamonds so expensive today?
6. What genre is this article? How do you know?

B. Vocabulary Check

A. Match the words in the reading with their definitions.

Words	Definitions
1. supply	a. a phrase that expresses a company's main message
2. demand	b. paying to talk in newspapers, television, or radio, etc., about a product's good points
3. marketing	c. the amount of a product that is available
4. advertising	d. an organized effort to reach a goal
5. slogan	e. how much a product is wanted
6. campaign	f. the money left after business expenses
7. profits	g. selling

B. What does "Times were hard" mean?

C. Identifying Main Ideas

For each of the paragraphs, circle the letter of the answer that states the main idea.

Paragraph 1

a. how important the DeBeers company is

b. how many diamonds South Africa has

c. how the DeBeers company became powerful

Paragraph 2

a. how the advertising agency marketed diamonds

b. the importance of advertising

c. the role of artists in advertising

Paragraph 3

a. why 50 percent of U.S. marriages end in divorce

b. the most successful part of the advertising campaign

c. other countries DeBeers targeted

Paragraph 4

a. the rarity of diamonds

b. the quantity of diamonds mined each year

c. how DeBeers keeps diamond prices high

D. Critical Reading Check

1. How does the writer feel about the DeBeers Company? Find evidence in the editorial to support your opinion.

2. Do you agree with the writer? Why or why not? Did the writer influence your opinion? How?

Remember

Reread the text, adding your own comments. Underline important or surprising information. Paraphrase points that are difficult.

Discuss

Discuss the following questions in groups of three or four:

1. Should a company completely control a product? Why or why not?

2. Knowing that DeBeers thought up the "tradition" of diamond engagement rings, would you give or accept one when you become engaged? Why or why not?

Thinking About Strategies

Did you predict the topic of the reading correctly? How would you define the word *selling* in the title now?

Reviewing Your Reading

A. Look at the following list of readings in this chapter. Check the column that shows how easy or difficult the material was for you.

Name of Reading	Type of Reading	Easy	Average	Difficult
1. The Science of Diamonds	textbook			
2. The History of Diamonds	textbook			
3. The Story of the Hope Diamond	magazine article			
4. The Selling of a Tradition	editorial			

B. Read the following list of strategies that you have practiced in this chapter. Review the readings. Which strategies did you use, and how often did you use them? Check your answers in the chart.

Strategy	Always	Often	Sometimes	Never
Prepare				
Predicting from illustrations and photos				
Predicting from thesis statements				
Read/Read Again				
Using topic sentences to identify main ideas				
Reading with a purpose				
Using signal words to predict ideas				
Using referring words and referents to follow ideas				
Using illustrations and photos to aid comprehension				
Using punctuation to aid comprehension				

Strategy	Always	Often	Sometimes	Never
Critical Reading				
Evaluating arguments				
Remember				
Paraphrasing				
Vocabulary Strategies				
Using a dictionary				
Recognizing names, abbreviations, and acronyms				
Recognizing internal definitions				
Analyzing a word for meaning				
Recognizing common phrases				
Guessing the approximate meaning of a word				

C. Compare your chart with a partner's.

D. Did you use any other strategies while reading? If so, share them with the class. Explain where you learned them.

Reading:
Marks of Beauty

Getting Started

Discuss these questions in pairs or small groups. Share your ideas with your class.

1. Read the chapter title and look at the man in the photo. Then look at the titles of the readings in this chapter. What do you think this chapter is about?

2. Do you think the man in the photo is attractive? Why or why not?

3. Do you know someone with a tattoo? What do you think of that person's decision to get it?

4. Why do people get tattoos?

Strategies Reminder

Comprehension Strategies

Prepare
- Predicting from Illustrations and Photos
- Predicting from Thesis Statements

Read
- Using Topic Sentences to Identify Main Ideas
- Reading with a Purpose (with Questions in Mind)
- Using Illustrations and Photos to Aid Comprehension
- Using Signal Words to Predict Ideas
- Using Referring Words and Referents to Follow Ideas
- Using Punctuation to Aid Comprehension

Critical Reading
- Evaluating Arguments

Remember
- Paraphrasing

Vocabulary Strategies
- Using a Dictionary
- Recognizing Names, Abbreviations, and Acronyms
- Recognizing Internal Definitions
- Analyzing a Word for Meaning
- Recognizing Common Phrases
- Guessing the Approximate Meaning of a Word

1 . READING

Prepare

Work with a partner. Look at the title, subtitles, and photo of the reading. Try to determine the thesis statement of the article, and complete the following predictions. Explain your choices to classmates.

1. This article came from a/an _____.
   a. newspaper
   b. encyclopedia
   c. magazine

2. The next subheading might be _____.
   a. the dangers of tattooing
   b. tattooing in the West
   c. popular tattoo designs

3. Agree on a question the reading will answer. Write the question down to remember it correctly.

Read

Read the text to get a general idea of the meaning. Try to identify the topic sentence in each paragraph. Look at the photo to help you understand the reading. Don't try to figure out unfamiliar terms. While you are reading, find the answer to the question you wrote in the *Prepare* section.

Tattoos Around the World

American teenagers see them as a symbol of rebellion,
but they actually are an ancient art.

Popularity Around the World

The Polynesian word *tattoo* became part of the English vocabulary after an English explorer, James Cook, visited the Pacific island of Tahiti. "Both sexes," he wrote, "paint their bodys. Tattow, as it is called in their language, is done by inlaying the colour of black under their skins . . ." Although the term *tattoo* came from the South Pacific, tattoos and other kinds of body paint have been part of cultures around the world. Native Americans tattooed themselves with bird blood. Mayans in Mexico tattooed themselves with pictures of their gods. Scientists have even discovered tattoos on Egyptian mummies. In 1991, hikers in the Alps found the tattooed mummy of a man who died 5,000 years ago.

Meanings of Tattoos

What do tattoos mean to the people who get them? The meaning can depend upon the culture. Tattoos may serve to connect people with ancestors or gods. In parts of Indonesia, tattoos are sometimes used as protection against evil. Tattoos can also be used to identify people as members of a social group. For instance, Japanese tattooing started among men in lower socioeconomic groups who could not afford to buy the expensive clothing that upperclass people wore. In parts of Polynesia, on the other hand, geometric tattoos showed high social class: The most powerful people had the most complicated tattoos. In many cultures, body art such as tattoos defines the transition from childhood to adulthood. An Indian bride's hands and feet are decorated with henna, for example, to bring her good luck. In many cultures, tattooing is a tradition.

The Return of a Tradition

Perhaps nowhere was tattooing a more important tradition than in the Marquesas, a group of volcanic islands in the South Pacific. In the Marquesas, tattoos were used to signify a number of things. One was beauty. The more complex designs were considered more beautiful. They were also a symbol of courage because the tattooing process was painful. Finally, tattoos showed wealth because the tattoo artist was well paid. Marquesan men often had their entire bodies tattooed, while women usually only had tattoos on their hands, lips, shoulders, ankles, and behind their ears. As important as this tradition was, however, it died out because of pressure from Europeans. In 1842, the islands were taken by the French, who made tattooing illegal.

Most of the Marquesan designs would have been forgotten by now except for the work of a German anthropologist, Ivan Kruesentern. Kruesentern's work has helped make tattoos popular in the United States and has influenced body art in Western cultures today. Kruesentern spent 20 years taking photographs of tattoos. His photographs have gained importance since the 1970s, when tattooing came in vogue again. Tattoo artists now may use modern battery-operated tools, but they often use the traditional designs they find in Kruesentern's work.

Read Again

Read the text at least two more times. As you are reading, do the following:

1. Think of two or three more questions and read to find the answers.
2. Predict ideas. Use signal words from Chapters 1 and 5 and other clues to help you.
3. Note unfamiliar terms. Decide if they are important. If so, try to figure out their meanings, and notice which vocabulary strategies you are using. List difficult terms and common phrases on a separate piece of paper. After you finish, decide if you need to look up definitions.
4. Note punctuation.
5. Follow ideas. Underline the referring words and circle their referents.

Post-Reading Activities

A. Comprehension Check
Answer these questions about the reading.

1. Identify these people and places:

   James Cook _____

   Tahiti _____

   Marquesas _____

   Ivan Kruesentern _____

   mummies _____

2. How long have people been getting tattoos?
3. What, if any, is the connection between tattooing and cultures?
4. Do people get tattoos for the same reason? How are their reasons similar and different?

B. Vocabulary Check

A. The following words are in Reading 1. Analyze each one. Then write the word or word part that helped you figure out the meaning.

1. *Volcanic*   is probably related to _____ .

2. *Geometric*   is probably related to _____ .

3. *Socioeconomic* is probably related to _____ .

4. *Transition*   is probably related to _____ .

5. *Europeans*   is probably related to _____ .

6. *Tradition*   is probably related to _____.

7. *Signify*   is probably related to _____.

8. *Themselves*   is probably related to _____.

B. The word *tattoo* is used as five parts of speech in the reading. Identify the part of speech of the word in bold for each phrase.

1. Native Americans **tattooed** their bodies. _____

2. We saw the **tattooed** mummy of a man. _____

3. **Tattoos** have different meanings. _____

4. They made **tattooing** illegal. _____

5. Men often had their bodies **tattooed.** _____

Remember

What do tattoos mean? Explain in your own words. Paraphrase key points in the reading and write them down. Exchange your paraphrase with a partner's and find out if you said the same thing.

Discuss

1. Describe some interesting tattoos you have seen.
2. Will people always get tattoos, or are they just a fad? Defend your opinion.

Thinking About Strategies

Work with a partner and answer these questions.

1. How well did you understand the reading? What helped or hindered you?
2. Could you find the thesis statement and the topic sentences? Why or why not?

2 · READING

Prepare

Work with a partner. Look at the title and subtitle of the reading. Make predictions about the following questions, and explain your answers to the class.

1. What genre is the article?
2. What is the thesis statement, or the main idea, of the article? Where is it stated?

Read

Read the text to get a general idea of the meaning. Try to identify the topic sentence in each paragraph. While you are reading, find the answer to this question.

What does it mean to fight for a right?

Fighting for the Right to Tattoo

An Ohio Tattoo Artist Takes the City to Court

1   A professional tattoo artist who has tattoos on 45 percent of his body is challenging a law that bans tattooing in the city of Cleveland. The artist, Tony DeRigo, claims that tattooing should not be illegal because it is simply an expression of ideas. He says,
5   "I have every right to do it and that's the way I feel. I'm not looking for glory or fame. I just want to do my art form wherever I feel I can."

Harvey Schwartz, a lawyer for the American
10   Civil Liberties Union, agrees. "People who have tattoos use their bodies as billboards to express their views to the world: who they love, who they hate. . . their religious beliefs, their political beliefs. Such tattooed messages should have the same protections
15   as other art forms."

Cleveland has had a ban on tattoos since 1976. It states "no person shall tattoo another person or permit himself or herself to be tattooed." This is the first time anyone has seriously challenged the law.

20   DeRigo owns and operates a tattooing business in Elyria, a suburb of Cleveland where tattooing is legal. Interestingly, although tattooing is illegal in the city of Cleveland, it is legal in the state of Ohio. The law of the state of Ohio provides health and safety regulations for tattoo shops, but does not ban   25   tattooing. DeRigo says that he wants to open a tattoo parlor in Cleveland because more than 80 percent of his customers are from there.

DeRigo's lawyer, Daniel Margolis, said that he had been working with the city for the past several   30   months. In the beginning, city officials were cooperative and told him that the ban would be lifted. However, they then stopped returning his phone calls, so Margolis told his client to file the lawsuit. "The art of tattooing stretches back into the depths of   35   prehistory, and is widely recognized today as a legitimate art form," said the Cleveland attorney.

Lawyers in Massachusetts filed a similar suit last year. In that case, a federal judge said that the state's 38-year-old ban on tattoos was illegal. DeRigo   40   said that he had followed that case closely. "For many, many people, this is art and this art is part of you," he argues.

Brian Rothenburg, spokesperson for the Cleveland mayor's office, said that city officials   45   would have no comment until they have had a chance to review the lawsuit.

Read Again

Read the text at least two more times. As you are reading, do the following:

1. Think of two or three more questions and read to find the answers.
2. Predict ideas. Use signal words from Chapters 1 and 5 and other clues to help you.
3. Note unfamiliar terms. Decide if they are important. If so, try to figure out their meanings, and notice which vocabulary strategies you are using. List difficult terms and common phrases on a separate piece of paper. After you finish, decide if you need to look up definitions.
4. Note punctuation.
5. Follow ideas. Underline the referring words and circle their referents.

Post-Reading Activities

A. Comprehension Check
Answer these questions about the reading.

1. What does Tony DeRigo want to do?
2. Why can't he do it?
3. Why does he think he should be able to do it?
4. Who are Daniel Margolis and Harvey Schwartz?
5. What happened in Massachusetts last year?

B. Following Ideas
Find the referents, or antecedents, of these words and phrases. Look back at the reading and complete the chart.

Word/Phrase	Line	Refers to	No referent
1. it	5		
2. they	12		
3. it	23		
4. there	28		
5. they	33		
6. his client	34		
7. that case	39		

C. Paraphrasing

A. Write a paraphrase of each statement.

1. The law bans tattooing. _____

2. Tattooing should not be illegal. _____

3. DeRigo owns and operates a tattooing business. _____

_____

4. Margolis told his client to file a lawsuit. _____

_____

5. The art of tattooing stretches back into the depths of prehistory, and is widely recognized today as a legitimate art form. _____

_____

B. Write another paraphrase of (5). Make it shorter. _____

_____

Remember

Are tattoos art? Find quotations in the article that support this opinion. Underline and paraphrase them. Compare your answers with a partner's.

Discuss

Discuss these questions in small groups.

1. Should tattooing be illegal? For whom, or for what reason?
2. If you got a tattoo today, how would you feel about it ten years from now?

Thinking About Strategies

News articles are organized differently from other readings. What paragraph of a news article usually contains all the important facts of the article? Did you use your knowledge of this organization to help you understand the reading? If so, did it help you?

3 · READING

Prepare

Work with a partner. Look at the title and subtitle of the reading and the first paragraph. Make predictions about the following questions, and explain your answers to the class.

1. What genre is this reading from?
2. What is the writer's purpose?
3. Who is the expected audience?

Read

Read the text to get a general idea of the meaning. Try to identify the topic sentence in each paragraph. While you are reading, find the answer to this question.

Why does the writer think that tattoos should be illegal for teenagers?

My Way

by Julia Foster

Tattoos Must Remain Illegal for Teens

1 Teenagers are crossing the state border to get tattoos, and the pressure is mounting for the legislature to do something about it. Last week, liberal fanatic Representative Stephen Armitage put forward a bill
5 that will put our children at risk. This one would change the laws regarding tattoos and teenagers. At the moment, no one under the age of 18 can get a tattoo in this state. Armitage proposes that the legal age for getting a tattoo should be 16 with the
10 approval of the teenager's parents. Responsible parents must work together to fight this bill.

The most important reason teens should not get tattoos is that it is dangerous to their health. Although tattoo artists are supposed to sterilize their equipment
15 after each use, there is no one to make sure that they do it. In these days of incurable diseases such as AIDS, only qualified medical personnel such as doctors and nurses should be allowed to use needles.

In addition to health concerns, there are other
20 reasons why teens should not be allowed to get tattooed. Getting a tattoo is a decision that may last for a lifetime because removing it is a painful, expensive process. Teenagers are not ready to make such decisions. Society admits that teenagers are not always responsible. That is why they are not allowed
25 to smoke and drink. Why should they be allowed to make other life-changing decisions? How will they feel about their tattoo a few years (or even a few months) down the line? Will having a tattoo affect their ability to get a certain job? Surely it will affect
30 how people react to them in the future.

Proponents of Armitage's bill say that parents should be the ones to help teenagers decide if they should get a tattoo. All of us know how difficult it can be to say no to a 16-year-old. Parents have enough
35 battles to fight with their teenaged children. The legislature should not make their jobs harder just because they themselves are under pressure. In summary, the current law should not be changed; it protects teenagers from themselves. No one under
40 the age of 18 should be allowed to get a tattoo, with or without a parent's approval.

Read Again

Read the text at least two more times. As you are reading, do the following:

1. Think of two or three more questions and read to find the answers.
2. Predict ideas. Use signal words from Chapters 1 and 5 and other clues to help you.
3. Note unfamiliar terms. Decide if they are important. If so, try to figure out their meanings, and notice which vocabulary strategies you are using. List difficult terms and common phrases on a separate piece of paper. After you finish, decide if you need to look up definitions.
4. Note punctuation.
5. Follow ideas. Underline the referring words and circle their referents.

Post-Reading Activities

A. Comprehension Check

Answer these questions about the reading.

1. Why are teenagers crossing the state border to get tattoos?
2. Why should the state mind if teenagers cross the border to get tattoos?
3. What is the Armitage bill?
4. How does the writer feel about teenagers getting tattoos?
5. What is the main reason for her opinion?
6. What are the secondary reasons for her opinion?
7. Who is currently "under pressure"? Why? From whom?
8. Why does the writer say that passing the bill will make parents' jobs harder?

B. Vocabulary Check

The following words are in Reading 3. Write the suffix and/or prefix of each word in the second column. If you know the root, write it in the third column. In the fourth column, try to define the word without using a dictionary.

Word	Suffix/Prefix	Root	Meaning
1. sterilize			
2. incurable			
3. qualified			
4. medical			
5. proponents			

C. Identifying Main Ideas

Go back to the reading and underline the thesis statement. Then underline the topic sentences of paragraphs 2–4.

D. Critical Reading Check

Work with a partner. Re-examine the reading, and answer the following questions.

1. Is the writer's argument persuasive?
2. Does she base her argument on fact or opinion?
3. Evaluate her points for logic, relevance, bias, and dependability.

Remember

Write a letter to the editor of your newspaper about tattooing for teenagers. Argue for a teen's right to get a tattoo. Argue against the points the author makes in her letter. Make notes from the reading to help you argue your case.

Discuss

1. How old is the author of the letter? Support the reason for your answer.
2. Would you allow your teenager to get a tattoo? Why or why not?

Thinking About Strategies

Were your predictions about the reading correct? If so, how did they affect the way that you read? What did you do with common phrases and idioms?

4 · READING

Prepare

Work with a partner. Look at the title and photo of the reading. Make predictions about the following questions, and explain your answers to the class.

1. What is the purpose of this article?
2. Who is the intended audience?
3. What genre does the article belong to?

Read

Read the text to get a general idea of the meaning. Try to identify the main idea in each paragraph. Look at the photo to help you understand the reading. Don't try to figure out unfamiliar terms. While you are reading, find the answers to these questions.

What is henna?

How do people use it to make designs?

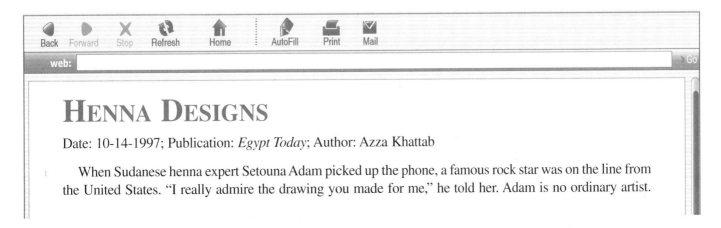

HENNA DESIGNS

Date: 10-14-1997; Publication: *Egypt Today*; Author: Azza Khattab

When Sudanese henna expert Setouna Adam picked up the phone, a famous rock star was on the line from the United States. "I really admire the drawing you made for me," he told her. Adam is no ordinary artist.

She creates her exotic geometric drawings on people rather than canvas. And instead of paint, she uses a special dye made from the leaves of the
5   Sudanese henna plant. Unlike permanent tattoos, the beautiful drawings she puts on hands, ankles, necks, backs, and even waists fade after a couple of weeks. Henna designs have become so popular with Egyptian women that brides will often get their bridesmaids together for a "henna night" before the wedding, when each woman gets a henna design.
10 Mention henna to fans of the traditional Sudanese art and the name Setouna Adam will probably come up. Since she came to Egypt eight years ago, Adam has become known as the queen of henna and henna nights. "I can proudly say that I've made henna a trend in Egypt," Adam says.

Adam first gained her fame at the American University in Cairo when she performed at International Day
15 with a Sudanese group demonstrating their country's marriage traditions. Adam was the henna woman in the show. "In Sudan, the bride doesn't have to have a dowry, but she's got to be painted with henna."

Since then, Adam has worked for brides, universities, hotels, and embassies. Local and international celebrities are among her clients, many of whom travel to Egypt to visit her. One famous rock musician and his wife went to Egypt only to have her decorate their hands and arms. Sherihan, a famous Egyptian actress
20 who used to travel to the Gulf to be painted with henna, is now a customer of Adam's. Others send for Adam from around the world.

Such demand comes from the good quality of her henna, the unique designs she provides, as well as her accurate and fast drawings.

A large drawing on the whole arm takes about ten minutes, and a small one, covering half the hand, takes
25 from three to five minutes.

Adam uses a Sudanese henna she brings from El-Dammer, an area in Sudan known for its henna trees. She mixes this with a perfume called mahalyya, made specifically for this purpose, which makes the henna stronger so that it will stay on the skin longer.

For a typical henna night, Adam will travel to the bride's home if at least ten girls are attending; otherwise,
30 the group comes to her. Each girl chooses her own design, and the bride pays accordingly. "If I have one hundred girls sitting in front of me, I'll provide every one of them with a unique drawing but, most often, girls like to have the same drawing as their friends," says Adam. Bridegrooms aren't excluded. Those who wish to have a henna drawing are welcome.

Read Again

Read the text at least two more times. As you are reading, do the following:

1. Think of two or three more questions and read to find the answers.

2. Predict ideas. Use signal words from Chapters 1 and 5 and other clues to help you.

3. Note unfamiliar terms. Decide if they are important. If so, try to figure out their meanings, and notice which vocabulary strategies you are using. List difficult terms and common phrases on a separate piece of paper. After you finish, decide if you need to look up definitions.

4. Note punctuation.

5. Follow ideas. Underline the referring words and circle their referents.

Post-Reading Activities

A. Comprehension Check

Answer these questions about the reading.

1. How did the writer of the article probably get her information?
2. Who is the article about?
3. How are henna designs different from tattoos?
4. What is henna and where does it come from?
5. Where are henna designs popular?
6. Who gets henna designs?

B. Vocabulary Check

Find the following words in the reading. For each word, write a synonym or make up your own definition. Compare your answers with your classmates'.

1. geometric _____

2. fade _____

3. traditional _____

4. trend _____

5. unique _____

6. exotic _____

7. fans _____

8. dowry _____

C. Following Ideas

Find the referents, or antecedents, of these words and phrases. Look back at the reading and complete the chart.

Word/Phrase	Line	Refers to
1. he	2	
2. the traditional Sudanese art	10	
3. she's	16	
4. their	19	
5. a small one	24	

Word/Phrase	Line	Refers to
6. the group	30	
7. those	32	

Remember

In your own words, write how henna designs are made.

Discuss

1. Have you ever seen a henna tattoo? If so, where?
2. Have you ever gotten a henna tattoo? Would you get one? Why or why not?

Thinking About Strategies

Were you able to correctly identify the several speakers in this reading? How?

Reviewing Your Reading

A. Look at the following list of readings in this chapter. Check the column that shows how easy or difficult the material was for you.

Name of Reading	Type of Reading	Easy	Average	Difficult
1. Tattoos Around the World	magazine article			
2. Fighting for the Right to Tattoo	newspaper article			
3. My Way	editorial			
4. Henna Designs	Website article			

B. Read the following list of strategies that you have practiced in this chapter. Review the readings. Which strategies did you use, and how often did you use them? Check your answers in the chart.

Strategy	Always	Often	Sometimes	Never
Prepare				
Predicting from illustrations and photos				
Predicting from thesis statements				

Strategy	Always	Often	Sometimes	Never
Read/Read Again				
Using topic sentences to identify main ideas				
Reading with a purpose				
Using signal words to predict ideas				
Using referring words and referents to follow ideas				
Using illustrations and photos to aid comprehension				
Using punctuation to aid comprehension				
Critical Reading				
Evaluating arguments				
Remember				
Paraphrasing				
Vocabulary Strategies				
Using a dictionary				
Recognizing names, abbreviations, and acronyms				
Recognizing internal definitions				
Analyzing a word for meaning				
Recognizing common phrases				
Guessing the approximate meaning of a word				

C. Compare your chart with a partner's.

D. Did you use any other strategies while reading? If so, share them with the class. Explain where you learned them.

Reading:
Home Sweet Home

Getting Started

Work in pairs or small groups, and answer the following items. Share your ideas with the class.

1. Discuss different types of homes. Brainstorm ways of describing homes. Include size, shape, rooms, building materials, and locations.

2. Look at the photo, and discuss these questions with classmates.
   a. Where would you find this kind of home?
   b. How is it different from the homes in your country?

Strategies Reminder

Comprehension Strategies

Prepare
- Predicting from Illustrations and Photos
- Predicting from Thesis Statements

Read
- Using Topic Sentences to Identify Main Ideas
- Reading with a Purpose (with Questions in Mind)
- Using Illustrations and Photos to Aid Comprehension
- Using Signal Words to Predict Ideas
- Using Referring Words and Referents to Follow Ideas
- Using Punctuation to Aid Comprehension

Critical Reading
- Evaluating Arguments

Remember
- Paraphrasing

Vocabulary Strategies
- Using a Dictionary
- Recognizing Names, Abbreviations, and Acronyms
- Recognizing Internal Definitions
- Analyzing a Word for Meaning
- Recognizing Common Phrases
- Guessing the Approximate Meaning of a Word

1 READING

Prepare

Work with a partner. Look at the features of the reading, such as the title, subtitles, and illustrations, and skim the first paragraph. Complete the following predictions. Explain your choices to the class.

1. This reading is from a/an _____.
   a. newspaper
   b. textbook
   c. encyclopedia

2. Most of the information in this reading will be _____.
   a. facts
   b. opinions

3. The main idea of this reading will be _____.
   a. to describe the effect of weather on housing
   b. to talk about clever architects
   c. to show how native peoples solved housing problems

Read

Read the text to get a general idea of the meaning. Try to identify the topic sentence in each paragraph. Look at the illustrations to help you understand the reading. While you are reading, find the answer to this question.

In what ways are homes different around the world?

Global Homes

What if you had to build a house out of what you could find nearby? What materials would you use? How would you design your home to fit your lifestyle—not to mention the local weather conditions? Here are some interesting examples of how clever architects around the world solved their housing problems.

by Rachel Dickinson

Houses on Skis

Northern Siberia has a harsh climate. Winter brings strong winds, severe cold, and snow. Summers aren't a whole lot better. Many ethnic groups live here, though, and several of them, including the Dolgans, traditionally herd reindeer. As the reindeer are moved from spot to spot in search of grazing land, Dolgan herders bring their homes with them. In summer they use tents, but about 100 years ago they began using huts on sleds pulled by teams of two to four reindeer in the winter.

Igor Krupnik, an anthropologist with the Arctic Studies Center of the Smithsonian Institution, says the early 20ᵗʰ-century *balock* looks like a small cabin. It has a wooden, rectangular frame that's attached to a special sled. The frame is first covered with cloth, then reindeer skin. Then they put on a canvas outer cover to protect the skin from moisture. It has small windows and a wood-burning stove. Balocks are small: about 10 feet by 5 feet for a small family, and 30 feet by 6½ feet for a large one.

Families move into the balock from the portable summer tents in late October, when the snow cover is fully in place. They return to their tents in May. The balocks are usually left at storage sites while people move farther north with their tents and herds to summer pasture and hunting and fishing grounds.

According to Dr. Krupnik, some Dolgans who herd reindeer still live in movable balocks. But it's such strenuous work to pull them, and the weather is often so extreme—temperatures falling several degrees below zero—that after a reindeer team has pulled a balock 10 kilometers (6 miles), the animals have to rest for a full week.

Dome Homes

For hundreds of years, the Inuit of eastern Canada and Greenland built *igloos* for both permanent and temporary housing. Now most are igloos only built for temporary shelter on hunting trips; still, the Inuit have never forgotten their techniques.

To build an igloo, the Inuit first search snowfields for the perfect type of snow—flat layers of hard-packed snow. Then they draw a circle in the snow that is from 9 to 15 feet in diameter. With long knives, they cut angled snow blocks from within the circle and stack them so the walls lean inward. This makes the walls stronger.

After the igloo is built, the Inuit make it safe. A narrow doorway is left—large enough for a person, but too small for a polar bear. Soft snow is packed into the cracks to keep out the wind. Sometimes small, translucent windows are added, made of seal intestines or sheets of freshwater ice.

Igloos may look cold, but skilled Inuits can build them with an interior temperature of 60°F. They then further heat up from a combination of body heat and warmth from oil lamps and small stoves (a hole in the top of the igloo lets smoke escape). As unlikely as it sounds, the heat makes the walls stronger by turning the snow walls to ice within a few weeks. Although skilled builders can make one in about an hour, an igloo is so strong that someone could stand on top of it and it wouldn't break.

Houses of Wool

For the past thousand years, Mongolian herders in Asia have used movable homes called *yurts,* large circular tents 16 to 30 feet in diameter. As nomads, these herders move hundreds of miles each year looking for fresh pasture for their sheep, goats, cattle, camels, and yaks. Because they move so often, they must be able to take their homes with them. Mongolian herders live in high desert plains surrounded by treeless mountains where it can be warm during the day but very cold and windy at night; consequently, they need sturdy shelters. Yurts are made from wood and felt. A round, wooden roof ring braced with wooden rafters forms the top of the yurt frame. This sits on top of a larger wooden framework. The walls are about four feet tall. Wool felt panels cover the entire structure to block the wind. The wood for the shelters is cut from trees that grow in the river valleys.

Herdsmen furnish their yurts with beds, chests of household goods, and a small iron stove for cooking and heating. Rugs cover the floor for warmth. Beds placed along the sides leave the center of the floor clear for the stove.

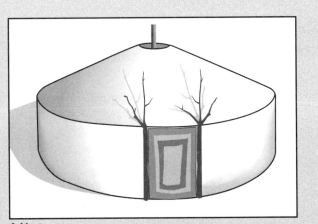

A Yurt

Herders may build yurts near one another to create temporary yurt "villages." When it's time to move, they disassemble their yurts. The wooden walls are rolled up in sections, and rafters are bundled. The yurts are transported by camel, or by horses on a *travois*—a platform supported by two poles, the ends of which drag on the ground.

After finding the next grazing spot, the herdsmen seek flat ground, sheltered if possible. In an hour they reconstruct their yurts, which can serve as home for a night or several months.

Read Again

Read the text at least two more times. As you are reading, do the following:

1. Think of more questions and read to find the answers.

2. Predict ideas. Circle signal words as you go, and use them to predict the next idea.

3. Note unfamiliar terms. Decide if they are important. If so, try to figure out their meanings, and notice which vocabulary strategies you are using. If you cannot figure out the meanings, list the terms on a separate piece of paper. After you finish reading, decide if you need to look up the definitions.

4. Examine the use of punctuation.

   a. What kind of information comes after the colon and the long dash? Is it important?

   b. Which words are italicized? Why?

   c. Which word is enclosed by quotation marks? Why?

5. Follow ideas. Underline the referring words and circle the referents.

Post-Reading Activities

A. Comprehension Check

Look at the diagrams and label the following parts of each structure.

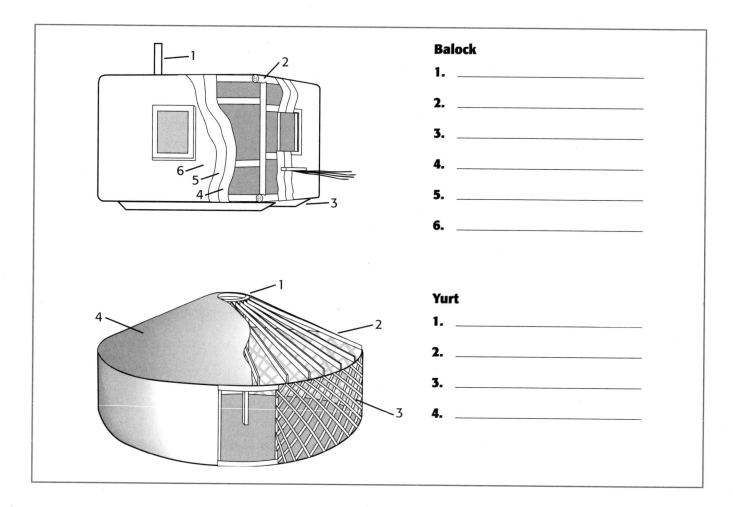

Balock

1. _____
2. _____
3. _____
4. _____
5. _____
6. _____

Yurt

1. _____
2. _____
3. _____
4. _____

B. Vocabulary Check

A. The following chart lists words from Reading 1. Match the words with their definitions.

Words	Definitions
1. harsh	a. can be moved
2. severe	b. a group of animals
3. herd	c. cruel
4. nomads	d. very bad
5. portable	e. to feed on grass
6. graze	f. people who move from place to place

B. The following words are also from Reading 1. Write their roots on the lines.

1. rectangular   _____

2. housing   _____

3. storage   _____

4. circular   _____

5. movable   _____

6. reconstruct   _____

C. Following Ideas

Underline each referring word in the paragraph below. Then find the correct referent and circle it. Put an "X" above a pronoun that has no referent.

Igloos may look cold, but skilled Inuits can build them with an interior temperature of 60° F. They then further heat up from a combination of body heat and warmth from oil lamps and small stoves (a hole in the top of the igloo lets smoke escape). As unlikely as it sounds, the heat from the stoves makes the walls stronger by turning the snow walls to ice within a few weeks. Although skilled builders can make one in about an hour, an igloo is so strong that someone could stand on top of it and it wouldn't break.

Remember

Look at the following chart. Go back to the reading and highlight the information missing from the chart. Then complete the chart. For the first line, be sure to write in the name of the people and the place.

	Balock	**Igloo**	**Yurt**
1. Used by/ Used in			
2. Made of			
3. Benefits			

Discuss

1. Are there any unusual types of housing in your country? What are they? What benefits do they have?

2. Would you like to live in any of the homes described in the reading? Why or why not?

Thinking About Strategies

Explain how these fields of knowledge helped you understand the text. Begin by identifying information in the reading that comes from each field.

anthropology   architecture   biology   geography

2 . READING

Prepare

Work with a partner. Look at the features of the reading, such as the title, subtitles, and photo, and skim the first and last paragraphs. Complete the following predictions, and explain your choices to the class.

1. This reading is from _____.
   a. a magazine
   b. a textbook
   c. an encyclopedia

2. Most of the information in this reading will be _____.
   a. facts
   b. opinions

3. The main ideas of this reading will be about _____.
   a. France, China, outback Australia, Turkey
   b. cavemen
   c. people making caves their homes

Read

Read the text to get a general idea of the meaning. Try to identify the topic sentence in each paragraph. Look at the photo to help you understand the reading. While you are reading, find the answers to these questions.

Where and why do people live in caves?
How are the caves made into homes?

Home Sweet Cave

Caves aren't just for cavemen. They make comfortable homes in many places around the world.

1   Most of us think that people stopped living in caves thousands of years ago. You might be surprised to discover the number of places around the world where people today are living in caves — France, China,

the Australian Outback, and Turkey. In these countries, cave dwellers have made use of geological architecture, sometimes called *geotecture,* suited to home-shaped excavation.

Caves with All the Modern Conveniences

5   In Spain's southeastern countryside, nature has provided a variety of strange rock formations made from red sandstone and volcanic limestone. For centuries, poor Spaniards have used the soft, raw material to create homes. They just dig a deep hole in the face of a cliff, cut windows and doors, and move in.

In the village of Guadix, a typical cave has whitewashed brick outside edged with a fringe of roof tiles. Outside of each home you can also see electric wires and television aerials along with strings of drying red
10   chilies, vines, flowers, and strips of green plastic door curtain.

One homeowner told us that her cave is more than 200 years old. She was using a large bucket and a brush to whitewash the floors and walls of her home. She explained that the surfaces of her underground rooms need constant painting—twice a year at least, to keep fungus from growing. She then showed us the beds covered with several wool blankets. Cave dwellers use them all year round because even in the heat of a dry Spanish
15   summer, caves have a comfortable temperature of 20°C.

Underground Churches

The volcanic rockscapes of Turkey's Cappadocia region attract tourists from all over the world. Cappadocia has a long history of cave dwelling. The soft, white volcanic limestone is the perfect building material because it is easy to work with but hardens when exposed to air. For thousands of years, the locals have made multi-story homes out of natural rock formations. Somewhere around 600–800 B.C., the Christian Hittites built about
20   400 cave churches, of which 100 are still open to the public.

Millions of Cave Dwellers

It is estimated that 70 million Chinese live in caves following a tradition extending back thousands of years. Most of them live in the northwest, where the fertile loess soil makes it easy to carve out rooms. While cave dwellers in Spain and Turkey are trying to escape the heat, cave homes in China are known for their warmth. Even in the middle of the harsh winter, visitors can curl up nice and warm on a *kang,* a fire-heated brick bed.
25   Three types of cave dwellings are found in northern Shaanxi province: stone caves, brick caves, and others dug directly into the cliffs. Known as earthen caves, this last type is ready for use right after the doors and windows are in place. These earthen caves are extremely firm because the loess cliffs are solid, the air in the northwest is dry, and the cave dwellers usually cook indoors, which helps to cure the walls and ceilings and keep the inside dry. In fact, it is said that after withstanding 1,300 years of severe weather, the cave dwelling
30   of famous General Xue Rengui on the banks of the Yellow River is still in good condition.

An Underground Town

The town of Coober Pedy in the Australian Outback is recognized as the largest producer of opals in the world. The name of the town is an anglicized version of the aboriginal
35   words *kupa piti,* said to mean "white man in a hole." However, the mining pits aren't the only underground openings. Fifty percent of the population of this town of 3,500 people live in caves.

Living underground became popular when soldiers
40   returning from World War I came to Coober Pedy looking for opals. They were used to living in trenches during the

Cave Dwellings

war. And they quickly discovered they could avoid hot desert days and cold nights by living underground. At first, they only built homes, but eventually other services such as hotels, restaurants, and churches went underground as well. As a result, people could live and work underground in comfort compared to the 50°C
45   heat on the surface.

Benefits of Cave Living

Outsiders often find it difficult to understand the cave dwellers' passion for their homes. They cannot comprehend why they would not trade their cave for a modern home anywhere. However, the benefits of cave living are easy to see. Because they have thick, solid walls and roofs, caves are never cold in winter or hot in summer. They are also relatively inexpensive because they are made of materials that are within easy reach. In
50   addition, they do not occupy valuable farmland. With all these advantages, caves have attracted the attention of architects throughout the world. Environmentalists are also impressed at their ecological soundness.

Read Again

Read the text at least two more times. As you are reading, do the following.

1. Think of more questions and read to find the answers.
2. Predict ideas. Note signal words and use them to predict the next idea.
3. Note unfamiliar terms. Decide if they are important. If so, try to figure out their meanings, and notice which vocabulary strategies you are using. If you cannot figure out the meanings, list the terms on a separate piece of paper. After you finish reading, decide if you need to look up the definitions.
4. Note punctuation.
5. Follow ideas. Underline the referring words and circle their referents.

Post-Reading Activities

A. Comprehension Check

Answer these questions about the reading.

1. What is the main reason that people live in caves?
2. How long have people been living in caves?
3. What kinds of rock are caves often made of?
4. What is unusual about the caves in Turkey?
5. Why are the earthen caves in China strong?
6. What is unusual about Coober Pedy?
7. What are some of the benefits of cave homes?

B. Vocabulary Check

The following words are in Reading 2. Write words that might help you guess their meanings.

1. geotecture _____

possible meaning _____

2. volcanic _____

possible meaning _____

3. rockscape _____

possible meaning _____

4. multi-story _____

possible meaning _____

5. earthen _____

possible meaning _____

6. outsider _____

possible meaning _____

7. inexpensive _____

possible meaning _____

8. ecological _____

possible meaning _____

9. aerials _____

possible meaning _____

Remember

Complete this chart on cave homes.

	Spain	Turkey	China	Australia
1. made of				
2. location				
3. interesting fact				

Discuss

1. Do any people in your country live in caves? Where?
2. Would you like to live in a cave? Why or why not?

Thinking About Strategies

Answer the following questions. Consider the strategies that helped you find the answers. Explain your choices to a partner.

1. What are the writer's main ideas?
2. Where are they stated?

3 READING

Prepare

Work with a partner. Look at the features of the reading, such as the title and subtitles. Complete the following predictions, and explain your choices to the class.

1. This reading is from _____.
   a. an advertisement
   b. a guidebook
   c. a tourist brochure

2. Most of the information in this reading will be _____.
   a. facts
   b. opinions
   c. bias

3. Write three predictions about the information you will find in the text. Keep them for later.

Read

Read the text to get a general idea of the meaning and try to identify topic sentences. While you are reading, think about these questions.

Would you like to stay in the Ice Hotel? Why or Why not?

The Ice Hotel

Imagine a hotel that is built from the ground up every year. A new design, new rooms, a brand-new lobby—in fact, everything in it is brand new. Well, there is such a hotel: the Ice Hotel, situated on the shores of the Torne River, in the old village of Jukkasjärvi in Swedish Lapland.

Ten thousand tons of crystal clear ice from the "ice manufacturing plant," the Torne River, and 30,000 tons of pure snow supplied by Mother Nature are needed to build the Ice Hotel every year. The hotel sleeps over 100 guests, and every bedroom is unique.

Covering more than 30,000 square feet, the Ice Hotel includes an Ice Chapel, the hotel itself, an ice art exhibition hall, a cinema, and last but not least, the world famous "Absolut Ice Bar."

Accommodations

Our guests always have lots of questions about what it is like to stay in a hotel of ice. Well, first of all, you can be sure that you will be warm and comfortable. The temperature in the Ice Hotel varies between −4° and −9° Centigrade, depending on the temperature outside and the number of overnight guests. However, you do not need to worry: Warm outer clothing is included in the price. In addition, each room has a specially made sleeping bag. In the morning a hot drink will be brought to you, after which you can enjoy an early morning sauna followed by breakfast.

There are several different types of accommodations.

Double Room

You sleep in a thermal sleeping bag on a special bed built of snow and ice, covered with reindeer skins. You are awakened in the morning with a cup of hot lingonberry juice at your bedside. Breakfast buffet and morning sauna included.

Suite

Unique rooms are decorated with ice art and sculptures. You sleep in a thermal sleeping bag on a special bed of snow and ice, covered with reindeer skins. You are awakened in the morning with a cup of hot lingonberry juice at your bedside. Breakfast buffet and morning sauna included.

Aurora House Cabins

The Aurora House cabins have two separate bedrooms for three persons with a single bed and a double bed. The rooms have a ceiling skylight for a view of the Midnight Sun or the Aurora Borealis. There is a sitting room with a refrigerator, a water heater, a TV, a telephone, and a bathroom with shower and toilet. Breakfast is included.

Chalet Cabins

The Chalet cabins have two separate bedrooms with four beds in total. There is a sitting room with kitchenette, a TV, a telephone, and a bathroom with shower and toilet. Breakfast is included.

Read Again

Read the text at least two more times. As you are reading, do the following:

1. Think of more questions and read to find the answers.
2. Predict ideas as you are reading. Use signal words and other clues to help you.
3. Note unfamiliar words. Decide if they are important. If so, try to figure out their meanings, and notice which vocabulary strategies you are using. If you cannot figure out the meanings, list the terms on a separate piece of paper. After you finish reading, decide if you need to look up the definitions.
4. Examine the use of punctuation.
5. Follow ideas. Underline the referring words and circle their referents.
6. Mark topic sentences that state main ideas.

Post-Reading Activities

A. Comprehension Check

Check the features for each type of accommodation.

Type of room	Bed of of snow and ice	Hot drink	Breakfast	Sauna	Sitting room	Skylight	Kitchenette	Toilet with shower
1. Double room								
2. Suite								
3. Aurora House cabins								
4. Chalet cabins								

B. Vocabulary Check

A. The following words are in Reading 3. Write an approximate meaning for each word.

1. unique _____

2. situated _____

3. brand new _____

4. lingonberry _____

5. reindeer _____

6. "the ground up"   _____

7. bedside   _____

B. Why is "ice manufacturing plant" in quotations?

C. Critical Reading Check

1. Find words and phrases in the text that show the writer's opinion. Is the writer's opinion surprising? Why or why not?

2. Arguments are intended to persuade. Has the writer persuaded you to stay at the Ice Hotel? Why or why not?

Remember

You are gathering facts for a vacation to Sweden. Your friend doesn't want to go the Ice Hotel, but you do. Highlight the features that might persuade your friend to stay at the hotel.

Discuss

Discuss this question in pairs or small groups. Then share your ideas with your classmates.

If you were going to build an unusual hotel from your environment, what kind would it be? Describe it.

Thinking About Strategies

Look back at the predictions you made in the *Prepare* section for this reading. Were you correct?

4 · READING

Prepare

Work with a partner and answer the questions. Share your ideas with the class.

1. Look over the text, and skim for main ideas. Make predictions about the following.

   a. what genre it is _____

   b. whether it will contain facts and/or opinions _____

   c. what you will learn about the Hearst Castle _____.

2. Think of one question to ask as you are reading the article for the first time. Write it down so you can remember it correctly.

Read

Read the text to get a general idea of the meaning and try to identify topic sentences. While you are reading, find the answer to the question you wrote in number 2 in the *Prepare* section.

Hearst Castle®

San Simeon, Cambria

1   Hearst Castle® is located a few miles from the town of Cambria on Highway 1, northwest of the city of San Luis Obispo in California. It is easily reached by car, and the route passes through the beautiful coastal areas of Central California.

   William Randolph Hearst called his beautiful dream home La Cuesta Encantada®, or the
5   "enchanted hill." Its construction was a huge undertaking. The main house contains more than 60,000 square feet of space. There are 115 rooms, including 38 bedrooms and 41 bathrooms. It also has 30 fireplaces, a theater, 2 swimming pools, and 120 acres of gardens. It is estimated that the main house cost about $10 million, including the artwork—a very small amount by today's standards.

10   Hearst began construction on the main house in 1922. When he left it for the last time in 1947, it was still incomplete, and so it remains today. Even though it was unfinished, he loved it and enjoyed spending time there with friends and family. Hearst Castle® is like a wonderful museum with tapestries, art, furniture, ceilings, walls, statues, and other architectural items brought to the site from many parts of the world. The mansion sits high on a hill surrounded by luxuriant
15   gardens, terraces, and hillsides. It combines several different architectural styles and was designed by Julia Morgan, who supervised the total construction for at least 25 years.

   Hearst Castle® is a must-see attraction. It is a combination of art museum and incredible landscaping. There is even a zoo. Hearst loved exotic animals. In fact, one can still see some of the descendants of the original zebras roaming the hills in the area.

20   In 1958, the Hearst Corporation presented La Cuesta Encantada® to the state of California with the agreement that it be preserved as is, as a memorial to Hearst and his mother, Phoebe Apperson Hearst. It is operated by the California State Park System, and four different tours are available. They are all fascinating and very interesting! If you plan on staying a few days in the area, lodging and restaurants are available at San Simeon and Cambria, just a few miles away.

San Simeon

25   San Simeon is located along Highway 1, about 40 miles north of San Luis Obispo. It offers treasures you won't want to miss. In addition to William Randolph Heart's lavish mansion, there are beautiful beaches and campsites in San Simeon State Park.

Cambria

   Cambria is located on the coast halfway between Los Angeles and San Francisco, just six miles from the famous Hearst Castle®. Cambria offers visitors wonderful restaurants, art galleries,
30   antique and specialty shops, and numerous nearby wineries. This picturesque village has a variety of hotels, motels, B & Bs, inns, and vacation home rentals.

San Simeon Chamber of Commerce
9255 Hearst Dr., San Simeon, CA 93452-9723
Telephone: (805) 555-3500

Cambria Chamber of Commerce
767 Main St., Cambria, CA 93428
Telephone: (805) 555-3624
(Hearst Castle® tickets can be purchased here.)

Hearst Castle® Tickets (phone orders)
MISTIX: 1(800) 555-7275

Read Again

Read the text at least two more times. As you are reading, do the following:

1. Think of more questions and read to find the answers.
2. Predict ideas. Use signal words and other clues to help you.
3. Note unfamiliar terms. Decide if they are important. If so, try to figure out their meanings, and notice which vocabulary strategies you are using. If you cannot figure out the meanings, list the terms on a separate piece of paper. After you finish reading, decide if you need to look up the definitions.
4. Examine the use of punctuation.
5. Follow ideas. Underline the referring words and circle their referents.
6. Find and mark the main ideas.

Post-Reading Activities

A. Comprehension Check

The following numbers appear in Reading 4. Explain the importance of each one. (Note: Some numbers may be written as words in the text.)

1. 1922   _____

2. 25   _____

3. 1958   _____

4. 30   _____

5. 1947   _____

6. 115 _____

7. 41 _____

8. 60,000 _____

9. 120 _____

10. 10,000,000 _____

11. 38 _____

12. 6 _____

Words	Line #	Approximate Meaning or Idea	Strategy #
1. coastal	3		
2. enchanted	5		
3. undertaking	5		
4. tapestries	13		
5. luxuriant	14		
6. exotic	18		
7. roaming	19		
8. preserved	21		
9. lodging	24		
10. lavish	26		

B. Vocabulary Check

Work with a partner and complete the chart. Choose the strategy or strategies that you used to guess the meanings from the following list of strategies. Write X if you knew the word before you read the text.

1. background knowledge

2. context clues

3. word analysis

4. internal definition

5. other

Remember

Underline the most astonishing facts about the Hearst Castle®. Paraphrase the facts. Share your answers with the class, and find out how many of you gave the same answers.

Discuss

1. What is your opinion of William Randolph Hearst and his castle?
2. Would you like to live in the Hearst Castle®? Why or why not?

Thinking About Strategies

Who is the expected audience for this text? Is it necessary that they understand the text completely? If not, what information is probably important for them?

Reviewing Your Reading

A. Look at the following list of readings in this chapter. Check the column that shows how easy or difficult the material was for you.

Name of Reading	Type of Reading	Easy	Average	Difficult
1. Global Homes	newspaper feature			
2. Home Sweet Cave	magazine article			
3. The Ice Hotel	tourist brochure			
4. Hearst Castle	guide book			

B. Read the following list of strategies that you have practiced in this chapter. Review the readings. Which strategies did you use, and how often did you use them? Check your answers in the chart.

Strategy	Always	Often	Sometimes	Never
Prepare				
Predicting from illustrations and photos				
Predicting from thesis statements				
Read/Read Again				
Using topic sentences to identify main ideas				

Strategy	Always	Often	Sometimes	Never
Reading with a purpose				
Using signal words to predict ideas				
Using referring words and referents to follow ideas				
Using illustrations and photos to aid comprehension				
Using punctuation to aid comprehension				
Critical Reading				
Evaluating arguments				
Remember				
Paraphrasing				
Vocabulary Strategies				
Using a dictionary				
Recognizing names, abbreviations, and acronyms				
Recognizing internal definitions				
Analyzing a word for meaning				
Recognizing common phrases				
Guessing the approximate meaning of a word				

C. Compare your chart with a partner's.

D. Did you use any other strategies while reading? If so, share them with the class. Explain where you learned them.

Reading Skills and Strategies

Overview of the Strategies

PART 1 . COMPREHENSION STRATEGIES

Prepare

Predicting Organization

Writers organize ideas in different ways depending on their purpose. There are different organizations for comparing, contrasting, telling a story, describing, defining, explaining, and giving examples, among other purposes. Understanding organization helps you identify a reading's ideas.

Before you read, scan the text for terms indicating organization.

Understanding the Strategy

Methods are often mixed in a reading, although main ideas are usually organized in one basic pattern. Certain terms are used with each method. Learning them will help you predict the information coming—for example, a description, definition, or explanation.

Match the lists of terms with the types of organization.

_____ **1.** *before, after, until, again, then, first, next, last, when, next*

_____ **2.** *kinds, types, divided into, a number of, parts, categories, sections, there is/are*

_____ **3.** *as a result, then, therefore, so, cause, consequently, effect*

_____ **4.** *for example, for instance, such as, as, to illustrate, show*

_____ **5.** *likewise, in the same way, different from, compared to, on the other hand*

a. definition/classification/division

b. example

c. chronological order

d. comparison/contrast

e. cause/effect

A C T I V I T Y . 1   Scan each paragraph for organizational terms. Then predict the organization of the reading. It may use more than one type.

1. Books serve a variety of functions. Some types may be regarded primarily as a storehouse of information. To some extent, school textbooks fit this category. Certainly this is true of encyclopedias and other kinds of reference books. Then, there are books written for the specific purpose of presenting a point of view so as to influence the reader to think in a certain way. Other kinds of books, such as novels and volumes of poetry, have the primary purpose of pleasure and entertainment.

2. Many people who would like to have gardens complain that they don't have enough space or time. Putting plants in pots is an easy solution for people with busy lives or small homes. Potted plants are almost weed-free; consequently they do not require a lot of care. Today it is even possible to plant vegetable seeds that do well in containers. Therefore, don't feel that you are restricted to flowering plants. If you have a sunny backdoor area, plants in containers right outside the door can be easy to water or harvest.

3. One example of dangerous cancer-causing materials is asbestos. What is asbestos? Asbestos is a fibrous mineral found in rocks and soil throughout the world. It is used in construction because it is strong, durable, and fire retardant. It is also a good insulator. Asbestos can be used alone or in combination with other materials. It is found in numerous products within the building industry—for instance, floor tiles, ceiling tiles, and as a fire retardant for heating and electrical systems.

Predicting from First and Last Paragraphs

In most readings the key point, or main idea, is stated twice: once in the beginning and once at the end. This technique is used to help readers understand the idea and remember it.

Understanding the Strategy

The first paragraph of a reading is usually an introduction. It tells you what the writer is going to talk about. The last paragraph is usually a conclusion. A conclusion summarizes the main ideas in the reading. Some genres require more information in the beginning than in the end or vice versa.

To get the gist of a reading, read the first and last paragraphs first.

A. Look at the following types of readings. Decide if predicting from first and last paragraphs of each type of reading would be an effective strategy.

Types of Readings	Is predicting from first and last paragraphs effective?		
1. a newspaper editorial	yes	no	perhaps
2. directions on how to paint a room	yes	no	perhaps
3. the history of space travel	yes	no	perhaps
4. a short story	yes	no	perhaps
5. a movie review	yes	no	perhaps
6. a description of an ancient temple	yes	no	perhaps

A C T I V I T Y . 2   Read the first and last paragraphs of each item. Complete the predictions about the reading.

1. *(First)*

    Newspapers in the United States have long been seen as a strong influence on public opinion. Because they are privately owned, they do not serve as the voice of the government. One writer has even called newspapers the "bible of democracy." Their power to persuade causes them to be criticized by those who disagree with their views and actions.

    (Last)

    Much of the criticism of newspapers is valid. However, their negative effects must be balanced against the crucial role they play in a democracy. Without privately owned and independent newspapers, citizens would have to depend solely on government news sources. It would severely decrease the amount of public debate on any issue. Therefore, despite their faults, newspapers serve an invaluable function in today's world.

    a. topic of the reading _____

    b. predicted content _____

    c. writer's opinion _____

2. *(First)*

In most developing regions, governments are hard-pressed to provide the services needed to keep civic and cultural life functioning. Schools often lack supplies, health care may not be available in the community, and community members often feel isolated and alone. One courageous attempt to change this pattern is underway in Costa Rica.

(Last)

No one knows if LINCOS will work. The government is still testing its ability to offer less expensive public services and new economic opportunities for residents. If it succeeds, communities that are far from large cities may no longer feel such isolation.

a. topic of the reading _____

b. predicted content _____

c. writer's opinion _____

3. *(First)*

Most of India's rural areas are still untouched by modern technology. There are few permanent, year-round jobs. Information about employment opportunities, crop prices, or candidates for traditional arranged marriages is hard to find. Now, however, with the help of the Internet and a new company called TARAhaat.com, all that may be changing.

(Last)

TARAhaat.com hopes to make money and to create jobs and raise incomes. This will unlock the buying power of rural communities. The company believes that opening villages to the world outside will widen perspectives, enabling India's people to become better-educated citizens and more active in shaping India's future.

a. topic of the reading _____

b. predicted content _____

c. writer's opinion _____

Read

Using Supporting Details to Identify Main Ideas

In Chapter 5 you practiced using topic sentences to identify the main ideas of a paragraph. In *Predicting Organization,* you learned that main ideas are organized by certain methods. Main ideas have supporting details that support or prove a thesis statement or topic sentence.

Understanding the Strategy

Facts, statistics, examples, quotations, or even anecdotes (little stories) often serve as supporting details. Generally, they are given after a statement to prove or illustrate it. At times, they are given before it, leading the reader to a conclusion, that is, the point stated in a thesis or topic sentence.

Read the paragraph and complete the idea map. Write the main idea and the supporting details of the paragraph.

> To understand a reading's main ideas, study its general organization. To know whether to believe them, study the supporting details.

A female sea turtle may migrate thousands of miles to find a suitable nesting beach. After depositing her eggs, she uses her flippers to cover them with sand. Why? The threats to turtle eggs and young hatchlings are so great that a clutch of more than 100 eggs may never make it to adulthood. These threats include wildlife predators, such as foxes and sea birds, that eat eggs or hatchlings. Humans are also a threat—some humans steal turtle eggs for food, and the lights of human dwellings often disorient the hatchlings, causing them to race toward human habitations instead of into the sea.

Main Ideas and Supporting Details

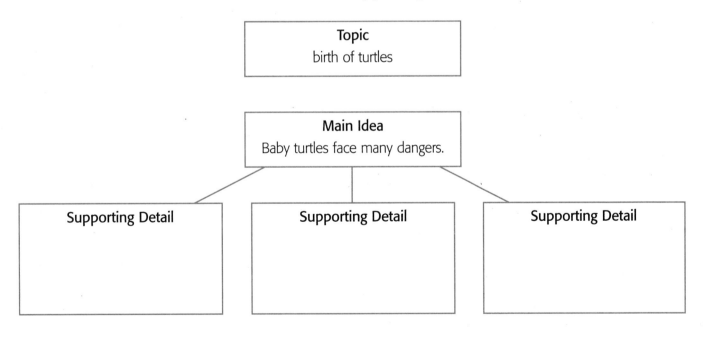

Topic
birth of turtles

Main Idea
Baby turtles face many dangers.

Supporting Detail

Supporting Detail

Supporting Detail

ACTIVITY. **3**   Read the following paragraphs and draw a diagram for each one.

1. The greatest evidence of the value of ancient Greek civilization is that the Romans, who defeated the Greeks in war, also greatly admired them. The first Roman literature, for example, was Homer's Odyssey, which was translated into Latin. Greek art, architecture, philosophy, and religion also inspired Roman artists and thinkers who used them as starting points for developing their own style of building, thinking, and believing. All educated Romans learned to read and speak Greek. In addition, the Greek philosophy of stoicism became the most popular Roman philosophy of life.

2. African Americans fought for equal rights for decades. In the early 1960s, the civil rights movement began to gain strength. Individuals and civil rights organizations criticized segregation in the south and discrimination everywhere. They protested with marches, boycotts, and refusals to tolerate segregation. Many organizations conducted their protests with nonviolent resistance. Civil rights protesters often faced harsh confrontations with their opponents. These confrontations, which appeared on network television, exposed the struggle for civil rights to a large national audience.

3. Plastics have a wide variety of useful characteristics. They are much lighter than metals because they are not as dense. Most plastics vary in density from 0.9 to 2.2 g/cm^3, compared with steel's density of 7.85 g/cm^3 (5.29 oz/cu in^3). Plastic can also be mixed with glass and other fibers to form incredibly strong materials. For example, nylon combined with glass can have a tensile strength (resistance of a material to being pulled apart) of up to 165 Mega Pascal (24,000 psi).

    Plastics also have some disadvantages. When they are burned, some plastics produce poisonous gases. Although certain plastics are made to withstand temperatures as high as 288°C, in general, plastics are not used in high heat conditions. In addition, plastics do not easily break down into simpler components. As a result, disposal of plastics creates a solid waste problem.

More Practice Using Signal Words to Predict Ideas

Study the following signal words and the sample sentences. Then answer the questions by filling in the blanks with the correct signal word(s). Note the punctuation: Some words can begin an independent clause; some cannot.

Categories and sample signal words

Addition:	*furthermore, moreover*
Condition:	*as long as*
Contrast:	*despite*
Counterargument:	*even so*
Effect or result:	*accordingly*
Similarity:	*similarly*
Time:	*eventually*

Sample Sentences

She loved her class; **furthermore**, she learned a lot.

She loved her class **despite** its inconvenient schedule.

She loved her class. **Moreover**, she never missed a day.

She loved her class; **similarly**, she enjoyed her new job,

She loved her class **as long as** it was easy. When it got difficult, she quit.

She loved her class; **accordingly**, she did very well.

She loved her class. **Even so**, she was homesick.

She loved her class. **Eventually**, she became the best student in it.

Which signal word(s) introduce(s):

a. an addition?   _____   _____

b. a contrasting idea?   _____

c. a condition?   _____

d. a result?   _____

e. a similarity?   _____

f. a counterargument?   _____

g. time?   _____

A C T I V I T Y . 4   Complete the following sentence(s). Circle the letter of the correct answer.

1. Henry Morse decided to quit writing despite _____.
   a. his great success
   b. his books' poor sales
   c. his work

2. I believe that everyone should do some volunteer work. Furthermore, _____.
   a. they shouldn't be paid
   b. no one should
   c. the government should make it mandatory

3. The computer industry has made great progress in recent years; similarly, _____.
   a. software has increased
   b. there have been many advances in communications
   c. there have been great losses in profits

4. The company invested millions on new computer equipment; even so, _____.
   a. they spent a lot of money
   b. it was no more efficient than before
   c. there were too many computers

5. Daniel won the national championship. Moreover, _____.
   a. he was unable to win in the following year
   b. he became one of the most famous athletes in the world
   c. he fired his coach

6. Your performance has been unacceptable. Accordingly, _____.
   a. you will be able to take your vacation
   b. you are being given one month's notice
   c. you are going to get a raise

7. The students will be allowed to leave campus as long as _____.
   a. they want
   b. they stay on the campus
   c. they sign out first

8. Tomi studied hard. Eventually, _____.
   a. the class was difficult
   b. she passed the class
   c. she wore her favorite pair of blue jeans

Reading Difficult Material

You may often have to read material that is quite difficult. Good readers approach difficult material with a positive attitude, and search for what they can understand. You may get valuable information even if you only comprehend 50 percent of what you are reading.

Understanding the Strategy

When you have to read difficult material, do the following:

- Read the title, the first paragraph, and the last paragraph.
- Read the subtitles.
- Think about what you know about the subject matter.
- Read for main ideas.
- Read actively. Underline important ideas. Put question marks in sections that confuse you.
- Don't be afraid to skip over unknown words.
- Keep reading. If you are confused, reread the last few sentences.
- If a sentence is particularly confusing, identify the subject and the main verb, and then try to figure out the modifying clauses.

Read what you can understand before trying to figure out what you can't understand.

- Use diagrams and illustrations. They can help you.
- Try to restate difficult ideas in your own words.
- Stay positive!

A C T I V I T Y **. 5**   Read this passage on global warming. Answer the following questions.

1. What is the greenhouse effect?

2. What is happening to the greenhouse gases?

3. Why is this happening?

4. What is predicted for the future?

Global Warming

Energy from the sun drives Earth's weather and climate and heats Earth's surface; in turn, Earth radiates energy back into space. Atmospheric greenhouse gases (water vapor, carbon dioxide, and other gases) trap some of the outgoing energy, retaining heat somewhat like the glass panels of a greenhouse. Without this natural "greenhouse effect," temperatures on Earth would be much lower than they are now, and life as we know it today would not be possible. Instead, thanks to greenhouse gases, Earth's average temperature is a more hospitable 60°F. However, problems may arise when the atmospheric concentration of greenhouse gases increases, thus causing the condition known as global warming.

Since the beginning of the Industrial Revolution, atmospheric concentrations of carbon dioxide have increased nearly 30 percent, methane concentrations have more than doubled, and nitrous oxide concentrations have risen by about 15 percent. These increases have enhanced the heat-trapping capability of Earth's atmosphere. Sulfate aerosols, a common air pollutant, cool the atmosphere by reflecting light back into space; however, sulfates are short lived in the atmosphere and vary regionally.

Why are greenhouse gas concentrations increasing? Scientists generally believe that the combustion of fossil fuels and other human activities are the primary reason for the increased concentration of carbon dioxide. Plant respiration and the decomposition of organic matter release more than 10 times the CO_2 released by human activities, but these releases have generally been in balance during the centuries leading up to the Industrial Revolution, with carbon dioxide absorbed by terrestrial vegetation and the oceans.

What has changed in the last few hundred years is the additional release of carbon dioxide by human activities. Fossil fuels burned to run cars and trucks, heat homes and businesses, and power factories are responsible for about 98 percent of U.S. carbon dioxide emissions, 24 percent of methane emissions, and 18 percent of nitrous oxide emissions. Increased agriculture, deforestation, landfills, industrial production, and mining also contribute a significant share of emissions. In 1997, the United States emitted about one-fifth of total global greenhouse gases.

Estimating future emissions is difficult, because it depends on demographic, economic, technological, and institutional developments, as well as government policies. Several emissions scenarios have been developed based on differing projections of these underlying factors. For example, by 2100, in the absence of emissions control policies, carbon dioxide concentrations are projected to be 30 to 150 percent higher than today's levels. This scenario would greatly increase the rate of global warming. However, if governments are successful at controlling the production of greenhouse gases, then the global warming will not have as profound an effect.

Critical Reading: Making Inferences

We make inferences all the time. If your mother walks in the door holding a wet umbrella, you can infer that it is raining. If your best friend looks unhappy when your teacher hands him a test paper, you might infer that he failed. In life and in reading, you deduce a thought from clues. Inference helps you understand what is indirectly stated.

Infer actions, attitudes, beliefs. Search for clues in the text that reveal what is not stated directly.

Understanding the Strategy

Inferences, or conclusions, must be based on clues in a text.

Read this paragraph. What can you infer about this situation? What clues helped you make this inference?

> Marta and Daniel walked into the room holding hands. They both had huge smiles on their faces. Marta kept glancing down at the small diamond that glittered on the fourth finger of her left hand. Marta's mother took one look at them and walked out of the room, angrily shutting the door behind her.

A C T I V I T Y . 6   Read each paragraph. Make an inference, and write down the clue(s).

1. One of the oldest known breeds, their slender, muscular bodies are often seen in paintings and sculptures in ancient Egypt. They have long, arched necks, large ears, almond-shaped eyes, and tapered tails. They are particularly loyal and make good companions.

   Inferences   **Clues**

   _____   _____

   _____   _____

2. A man and his son are driving in a car. The car crashes into a tree, killing the father and seriously injuring his son. At the hospital, the boy needs to have surgery. Upon looking at the boy, the doctor says (telling the truth), "I cannot operate on him. He is my son."

   Inferences   **Clues**

   _____   _____

   _____   _____

3. Mikhail Renko is a former star of the Moscow Circus. A tightrope walker, he won several international competitions. In his homeland, top circus performers are as admired as Olympic athletes, and their training is taken seriously. Renko started training at age six. After defecting to the United States in 1992, he became a trainer himself. Then, four years ago, he opened a circus training center in midtown Manhattan. Normally Wall Street parents might not be happy at the thought of their children becoming circus performers. But in Manhattan now, they send their kids for lessons.

Inferences	Clues

4. Steve LaRosa still remembers the day he knew they had to leave Manhattan. It was May 16, 1998, his daughter's fifth birthday. That was the day he realized that they wouldn't be able to let her leave their apartment building alone for about another ten years. "The city's got a lot to offer," he thought, "but not to a kid." So Steve and his wife Melanie sold their two-bedroom condo and moved into a four-bedroom home in the suburbs.

Inferences	Clues

Remember

Summarizing

Summarizing is another strategy we use in our daily lives. When a friend asks about your weekend, you tell the things most important and interesting. When someone asks you about a movie, you do the same. You give them the general idea without most of the detail. Summarizing a reading text is similar: It gets the point across clearly and quickly.

Understanding the Strategy

When you write a summary, do not:

- include everything. Focus on key points.
- copy word for word. Use your own words.
- write too much or too little. Summaries are usually 50 to 75 percent shorter than the original article.
- include your own ideas and opinions.
- list facts or details; put them in paragraph form.

Summarize main points to understand them better, especially in difficult reading.

A C T I V I T Y . **7**   Reread this article on a missing parrot, and do the following:

> A. Underline the important ideas as you read.
>
> B. Paraphrase these points on paper when you are finished reading.
>
> C. Organize your paraphrases into a summary paragraph no longer than 100 words.
>
> D. Compare your summary with a classmate's. Did you both include the same information? Explain your reasons for including or excluding material.

July 26, 2002 11:02 AM ET

SYDNEY (Reuters)—Australian police have issued an APB (All Parrots Bulletin) for Hector the galah, a talkative pink-and-gray bird they fear was stolen from a Sydney pet shop.

Hector had sat cheerfully at the front door of Doug Eyre's suburban pet shop for 31 years, delighting passers-by with cheerful chatter that included "Give me a kiss," "Hector's got a cough," and "See you later, mate." But the galah, a bird similar to a cockatoo, went missing last Saturday. Police issued a statement earlier this week that said Hector was last seen being carried off in his cage by a gray-haired woman in her 50s and placed into a car. "Police are investigating reports that the galah may have been 'freed' by a welfare group concerned at Hector's caging," the statement said. "Hector is still missing," a police spokesman said on Thursday.

Eyre fears his feathered friend has become an ex-parrot. "Our family is not taking this too well, but a lot of people have been coming in, asking where he's gone, and crying when they find out he was stolen," Eyre said.

Hector's cause has been championed by *The Daily Telegraph*. The Sydney tabloid ran a front-page photo of the bird on Wednesday next to the headline "Give the Parrot Back."

"What kind of people steal a talking galah that has been part of a community for 31 years?" the newspaper demanded. On Thursday, *The Daily Telegraph* ran another front-page story containing pleas for his return from high-profile community members, including Prime Minister John Howard.

"I urge the culprit to return Hector for the continuing enjoyment of local passers-by," Howard told the newspaper. The New South Wales state premier, Bob Carr, added: "My simple plea is this: Bring Hector back safe and well."

Galahs are found across the Australian mainland and can live for up to 80 years. In rural Australia, flocks of hundreds of galahs are regarded as pests who eat stock feed.

A C T I V I T Y . **8**   Complete the following steps for the article on pages 11-12.

> A. Read (or reread) the article about a "dangerous" fish on pages 11–12 of the Introduction chapter. Underline the important ideas as you go.
>
> B. When you are finished, paraphrase the underlined points, write them on paper, and organize them into a summary paragraph no longer than 125 words.

C. Compare your summary with a classmate's. Did you both include the same information? Explain your reasons for including or excluding material.

P A R T 2 . **VOCABULARY STRATEGIES**

Recognizing Jargon

Jargon refers to specialized vocabulary. There are two types of jargon. The first consists of terms used in a particular field. Many of these words have Greek or Latin roots. The second type consists of common words with specialized meaning.

Understanding the Strategy

Study the following examples of both types of jargon. Then try to figure out the meaning of the jargon in the sample sentences.

Be on the lookout for jargon as you read.

Technical Jargon

This type of jargon is usually simpler to deal with for two reasons. First, it is easy to recognize. Second, the terms are often explained within the text.

Example

The cochlea is divided into the **scala vestibuli** and the **scala tympani**, in other words the . . .

"Common" Jargon

This jargon is harder to recognize than the technical, and often the terms aren't explained. In the following sentence, many native English speakers wouldn't understand the specialized meaning of *cover*, which here is jargon for *recorded by*.

Example

Elvis Presley's songs have been **covered** by thousands of singers and musicians.

Sample sentences

Which of the following sentences uses the word *hits* in its most common meaning? What does *hits* mean in the other two sentences?

Dave had more **hits** than anyone on his baseball team.

The drummer **hits** the timpani with a mallet.

The Beatles recorded numerous **hits** in the late sixties.

ACTIVITY. 9   Read the following sentences. Try to guess the meaning of the underlined terms. Some are jargon, some are not. Write your guesses on the lines.

1. Ten years ago, no one could have imagined the clock speed of computers today.

_____

2. High-performance sports cars are not cheap.

_____

3. The dog's long coat was soft and silky.

_____

4. My company has a generous family leave policy.

_____

5. When you invest your money, you should look for the best rate of return.

_____

6. Greenhouse gases such as carbon dioxide are the cause of global warming.

_____

7. The various components of crude oil vaporize at different temperatures and then can be condensed back into pure streams. Some streams can be sold as they are.

_____

8. A beam of light contains many parallel rays. If a beam of light strikes a parallel smooth surface, all of the rays will be reflected parallel to each other.

_____

More Practice Recognizing Common Phrases

In Chapter 5, you learned that collocations were common phrases. You also learned that many collocations are idioms.

A C T I V I T Y . 10   Read each sentence. Circle the letter of the answer to complete the italicized phrase.

1. I'm not sure that Tom can do the job, but I'm going *to take a* _____ on him.
   a. gamble   **b.** choice   **c.** decision

2. This is such a difficult problem that even the experts can't *figure* it _____.
   a. on   **b.** in   **c.** out

3. Sandra is very unhappy. I think she's *getting* _____ *to* quitting her job.
   a. on   **b.** close   **c.** up

4. If you need help in the future, I hope that you'll *keep me in* _____.
   a. touch   **b.** mind   **c.** sight

5. The symbol % *stands* _____ percent.
   a. for   **b.** with   **c.** on

6. We never expected him to leave. We were *caught by* _____.
   a. disbelief   **b.** astonishment   **c.** surprise

7. Let's *take* _____. You can go first, then Sally, and then me.
   a. time   **b.** goes   **c.** turns

8. Ask Dana about the accident. She was *on the* _____ when it happened.
   a. place   **b.** spot   **c.** position

9. They haven't found a cure for cancer, but some of the newest drugs have given some *promising* _____.
   a. results   **b.** outcomes   **c.** solutions

10. These tickets are only for members of our organization. They are not available to *the general* _____.
    a. people   **b.** public   **c.** residents

11. Changing jobs will be difficult, but *in the long* _____, I think I'll be better off.
    a. time   **b.** run   **c.** view

12. Sara called me for help because she had no one else *to turn* _____.

  a. with   **b.** for   **c.** to

13. I know you have a lot of work to do, but I wish you'd take a day off *all the* _____.

  a. reasons   **b.** way   **c.** same

14. I support John for re-election, and I'd like to say a few words *on his* _____.

  a. behalf   **b.** own   **c.** favor

More Practice Analyzing a Word for Meaning

As you learned in Chapters 1 and 5, word analysis can be a powerful tool. The more word parts you know, the better your chances of being able to figure out general meaning.

A C T I V I T Y . **11**   Study the words, their parts, and the meanings. Then write the meaning of the italicized root, prefix, and/or suffix.

1. in-spect   to look at carefully
   retro-spect-ive   look backward
   re-turn   to go back

  a. *spect*   probably means _____.

  b. *re-*   probably means _____.

2. vis-ion   sight
   vis-ible   able to be seen
   port-able   able to be moved
   trans-port-ation   movement from place to place

  a. *vis*   probably means _____.

  b. *port*   probably means _____.

3. intro-duce   to present two people to each other for the first time
   in-duct   to make someone part of a group
   con-duct   to lead an orchestra
   reduce   to make less

   duc   probably means _____.

4. matri-arch   the female head of a family
   matern-al   motherly
   patern-ity   fatherhood

   a. *arch*   probably means _____.

   b. *ma-*   probably means _____.

   c. *pa-*   probably means _____.

5. hetero-sexual   person who is attracted to people of the opposite sex
   hetero-geneous   made up of parts of different kinds

   hetero-   probably means _____.

6. syno-nym   word with same meaning as another word
   anto-nym   word with opposite meaning as another word
   nomen-clature   system of naming

   nym/nomen   probably means _____.

7. bene-factor   a person who helps another financially
   bene-ficial   helpful

   bene   probably means _____.

8. Buddh-ism   an Eastern religion venerating Buddha
   commun-ism   a political system in which members of community share ownership
   commun-ity   people who live together
   comm-ittee   a group of people elected or appointed to serve a function

   a. *comm*   probably means _____.

   b. *ism*   probably means _____.

9. mort-ician   a person who prepares dead bodies for burial
   mort-al   destined to die
   im-mort-ality   living forever

   mort   probably means _____.

10. metro-polis   city
     megalo-polis   very large city

    a. *polis*   probably means _____.

    b. *mega-*   probably means _____.

11. man-iac   an insane person
     pyro-mania   an irresistible urge to start fires
     pyro-technics   the art of making fireworks

    a. *mania*   probably means _____.

    b. *pyro-*   probably means _____.

A C T I V I T Y . **12**   Read the following sentences and analyze the italicized words. Then write their meanings.

1. There were more than 20,000 *spectators* at the game.

   Spectators probably are _____.

2. We had so much luggage that we had to pay a *porter* to help us at the airport.

   A *porter* probably is _____.

3. It would take a *megaton* bomb to blow up an entire city.

   Megaton probably means _____.

4. In the 1960s, many hippies went to live on *communes* in the country.

   A *commune* probably is _____.

5. She inherited $50,000 because she was a *beneficiary* in her uncle's will.

   A *beneficiary* probably is _____.

6. In Italy, the oldest male member of the family is usually the *patriarch*.

   A *patriarch* probably is _____.

7. Sandy isn't working now. She has three months of *maternity* leave.

   Maternity probably means _____.

More Practice Guessing the Approximate Meaning of a Word

In every reading, you have encountered unfamiliar words. Have you gotten better at guessing the meaning in context? Which of these strategies are the most helpful to you?

1. using your background knowledge
2. looking for context clues
3. analyzing words
4. recognizing internal definitions
5. recognizing names and abbreviations
6. recognizing that the word may be jargon

A C T I V I T Y . **13**   Read the following paragraphs. Use vocabulary strategies to guess the meanings of the underlined words.

1. Unfortunately, a majority of Americans are <u>apathetic</u> about politics. They don't know much or care about the details of the political process. They are much more concerned about the details of their personal lives than they are of <u>exploits</u> of far-off politicians. Only when the affairs of government <u>intrude</u> on their lives do people <u>sit up and take notice</u>. A prime indicator of this apathy is <u>voter turnout</u>. The United States has about the lowest voter turnout of any democracy.

   a. *Apathetic* probably means _____.

   b. *Exploits* probably are _____.

   c. *Intrude* probably means to _____.

   d. *Sit up and take notice* probably means to _____.

   e. *Voter turnout* is probably _____.

2. The goal of caloric <u>restriction</u> research is not to <u>promote</u> a diet that few people could tolerate, but to understand why restricting calories works, and then find drugs that give the benefits without the constant hunger.

   a. *Restriction* probably means _____.

   b. *Promote* probably means _____.

3. The Romans so admired Greek art that they made many reproductions of it. In fact, today it's almost impossible to tell what's <u>genuinely</u> ancient Greek art and what are Roman <u>forgeries</u>. Then, in the Renaissance, Europeans copied the Romans the way the Romans had <u>aped</u> the Greeks.

    a. *Forgery* is probably _____.

    b. *Genuinely* probably means _____.

    c. *Aped* is a likely synonym for _____.

4. The <u>inhabitants</u> of ancient Mesopotamia, where Iraq now stands, <u>are</u> usually <u>credited with</u> the invention of writing. Clay tablets from slightly before 3,000 B.C. show a <u>predecessor</u> of the script called cuneiform, which records the affairs of the early <u>Babylonians</u>.

    a. *Inhabitants* probably are _____.

    b. *To be credited with* probably means _____.

    c. A *predecessor* probably is _____.

    d. The *Babylonians* probably were _____.

5. Infants often listen longer to <u>novel</u> sounds rather than to ordinary ones. Scientists measured the time infants listened to known and unknown sounds. First they exposed seven-to-eight-month-old infants to a <u>nonsense</u> language for two minutes. This was actually a group of nonsense syllables with no <u>pauses</u> indicating word endings.

    a. *Novel* probably means _____.

    b. *Nonsense* probably means _____.

    c. *Pauses* probably are _____.

Reading: Photography

10

Getting Started

Complete the following items in pairs or small groups. Share your ideas with the class.

1. Look at the photo and discuss these points.
   a. when it was taken
   b. why it was taken
   c. the skill of the photographer

2. What can you guess about the photograph?

Strategies Reminder

Comprehension Strategies

Prepare
- Predicting Organization
- Predicting from First and Last Paragraphs

Read
- Using Supporting Details to Identify Main Ideas
- Reading with a Purpose (with Questions in Mind)
- Using Signal Words to Predict Ideas
- Using Referring Words and Referents to Follow Ideas
- Using Punctuation to Aid Comprehension

- Reading Difficult Material

Critical Reading
- Making Inferences

Remember
- Summarizing

Vocabulary Strategies
- Recognizing Jargon
- Recognizing Common Phrases
- Analyzing a Word for Meaning
- Guessing the Approximate Meaning of a Word

1 . READING

Prepare

Work with a partner. Discuss the following questions, and explain your answers.

1. What mistakes do you make when you take photographs? What is the worst shot you have ever taken?
2. Look at the title of the reading, and then examine the features of the article. How is the article organized?
3. Who is the intended audience for this reading?

Read

Read the text to get a general idea of the meaning. Use supporting details to determine main ideas. While you are reading, think of ways to improve your photographs. Read to find that information.

How To Take Good Pictures

It's not easy to take great photographs, but you can learn to take good ones if you remember these simple principles.

Number of Photographs

Take lots of photographs, and ask your subjects to try different poses. Don't take only one picture of the "gang" at a party; take three or four. Besides having a variety of poses, you will also be less likely to get a shot where your best friend has his or her eyes closed.

Keep the Camera Steady

Make sure the camera is well supported. Keep your elbows tight against your body. Keep well balanced, with feet apart, and lean on something if possible.

Surroundings

Always be aware of what is in the photo. Before taking the picture, see if anything you don't want is in the frame. Things you don't want might be a telegraph pole, parked cars, people—anything that takes attention away from the subject. If you can't change the view, look for another angle to take the shot from.

Focus Attention on the Subject or Theme

What can you do to create focus on your subject? Following are a few techniques.

1) **Placement.** You may have heard of the "rule of thirds." This is simply dividing the frame into thirds and putting your subject at the intersection of one of these imaginary divisions. Thus your subject will be slightly off center. This makes for a more interesting photograph, one that will help pull focus onto your subject.

2) **Relative size.** This is simple. Make sure that the subject is large in the frame relative to other elements in the picture. Fill the frame with your subject!

3) **Framing.** This is a versatile technique. There are many ways to "frame" your subject. For instance, if you are photographing your cat Fritz sitting on his favorite chair, frame him either by the vertical arms of the chair, or the horizontal seat of the chair, or both. There are several ways to do it. When you photograph a distant scene, such as a large landscape scene, try framing the subject with a nearby object—a tree or fence line, for example.

4) **Lighting.** You can use lighting to help create emphasis on your subject. For example, you can compose your photograph so that your intended subject is lit while other elements of the picture are in the shadows.

Read Again

Read the text at least two more times. As you are reading, do the following:

1. Think of more questions and read to find the answers.
2. Predict ideas. Circle signal words as you go. Use them to predict the next idea.
3. Look for jargon. Are there any common words with specialized meanings?
4. Note punctuation.
5. Follow ideas. Underline the referring words and circle their referents.

Post-Reading Activities

A. Comprehension Check

Look at these photographs. Each one has a problem. On a separate sheet of paper, identify which principle(s) the photographer forgot. Briefly support your answer.

B. Vocabulary Check

For each of the following definitions, choose the correct term from the list. Write the term on the line.

angle	composed	focus	frame	horizontal
intersection	lighting	off center	placement	relative
shot	steady	subject	vertical	view

1. not moving   _____

2. where two lines meet   _____

3. in relationship to   _____

4. made up of   _____

5. at a right angle (90°) to the horizon   _____

6. a border around a picture   _____

7. parallel to the horizon   _____

8. slang for photograph   _____

9. a person or object of attention   _____

10. not exactly in the middle   _____

C. Organization Check

1. Which diagram represents the organization of main ideas in Reading 1? Explain.

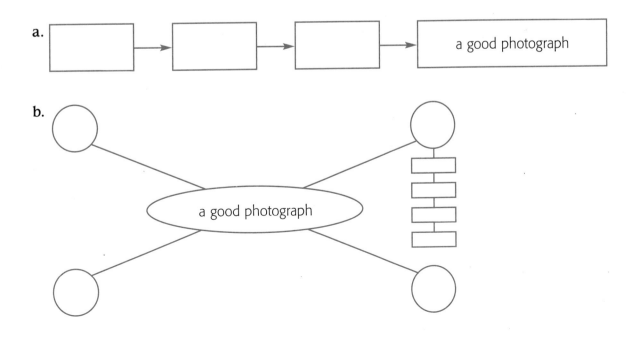

2. Draw the diagram on your own paper. Complete it with information from the reading.

D. Critical Reading Check

What can we infer about the author of Reading 1?

Remember

Write a one-sentence summary for each main point in the reading.

Discuss

1. Do you like to take photographs? Why or why not?
2. What is the best shot you have ever taken? What made it the best?
3. Will this reading help you to be a better photographer? How?

Thinking About Strategies

Work in small groups and answer the following questions.

1. What kinds of supporting details did the writer use?
2. Did you find them helpful in determining main ideas? Why or why not?

2 READING

Prepare

Work with a partner, and answer the following questions.

1. Look at the title and subtitles. How is the article organized?
2. Read the introduction and the conclusion. Compare the article with Reading 1. How is the audience different from the audience for Reading 1?
3. Think of a question that the reading will answer. Write it down so you will remember it correctly.

Read

Read the text to get a general idea of the meaning. Use supporting details to determine main ideas. While you are reading, find the answer to the question you wrote in number 3 of the *Prepare* section.

Take Great Photographs by Learning to Use Light

1   Most experienced photographers suggest taking pictures either early or late in the day. In other words, avoid taking photographs between 10:00 A.M. and 2:00 P.M. In order to understand the reasons for this, we need to look at three characteristics of light: color, quality, and direction.

Color

In the early hours, before the sun rises, the world is black and white. There are no shadows,
5   except those made by artificial light. Colors are vague in the early morning and intensify as the sun comes up. The low-lying sun must penetrate through a great deal of atmosphere that causes light to be "warmer" in color than it is at midday. The skies can contain hues of crimson, lavender, and orange. Shadows appear bluer for the first 30 minutes after sunrise.

Because of its very short duration, to take advantage of this light, you should have your
10   camera set up before sunrise. This little extra effort can produce dramatic landscapes and images. As the sun moves higher in the sky, we see a greater contrast between the colors, and shadows become blacker. The noon sun gives off white light, and colors appear purer, especially in the summer. Consequently, this has the effect of making light more harsh.

Dropping lower in the sky toward evening, the sun gives off light that begins to warm up
15   again. On clear days before the sun sets we again experience the warmer light of the "golden hour." This light appears to have magical qualities as it brings out textures that add special dimension to the subject.

Quality

The mood of a scene can also be changed by the quality of light. The strong light at midday can diminish a fabulous landscape because of the harsh shadows it creates. On the other hand, it
20   is beneficial in closeup work with interesting patterns and textures, as with photos of architectural details.

Clouds can soften and spread the light. The soft light of a misty morning brings subtle colors to life and makes strong colors more tranquil, reducing contrast and softening shadows. As a result, this type of light is preferred for portraits and many outdoor scenes, particularly for
25   flowers and garden images.

Direction

The direction where light comes from also affects the scene. Generally, sidelighting adds drama to your subject and brings out its pattern and texture. Shadows become more apparent, and the subject gains added dimension. Backlighting comes from behind the subject and toward the camera. It offers an opportunity to silhouette a scene, as with a dramatic sunset. Backlighting can
30   be very effective when doing portraits, but check to make sure the sun is not flaring into the lens . . . unless you want it to! In front lighting, the light strikes the subject directly, coming from

behind the photographer. Though commonly used, front lighting tends to flatten the scene, casting shadows behind the subject and reducing texture and form.

35 In conclusion, light is the key to the way we "see" a subject. For better or worse, it's changing every moment. You need to pay attention to its subtle changes to discover the enormous possibilities of photography. Learning how to use light to your best advantage will take time and experimentation. Be patient with the changing light and you'll be rewarded. Your photos will go from ordinary to extraordinary.

Read Again

Read the text at least two more times. As you are reading, do the following:

1. Think of more questions and read to find the answers.
2. Predict ideas. Use signal words and other clues to help you.
3. Note words that describe light. Think about what they mean in relation to photography.
4. Note punctuation. Why are certain words in quotation marks?
5. Follow ideas. Underline the referring words and circle their referents.

Post-Reading Activities

A. Comprehension Check

Complete the charts with information from the reading.

Time	Description of the light	Good for	Not good for
early morning			
noon			
later afternoon			

Type of lighting	Position of the light	Description	Used to
backlighting			
sidelighting			
frontlighting			

B. Vocabulary Check

Work with a partner. Think of two or three examples of each of the following terms. The examples can be real photographs or imagined ones. Exchange ideas with your partner. Write your ideas on the lines.

1. a portrait _____

2. an interesting pattern _____

3. an interesting texture _____

4. a landscape _____

5. a silhouette _____

6. a closeup _____

Remember

Paraphrase these five sentences from the reading. Compare yours with a partner's. Whose is more accurate? Easier to understand? Remember to use substitute terms.

1. Generally, sidelighting adds drama to your subject and brings out its pattern and texture.
2. The mood of a scene can also be changed by the quality of light.
3. Backlighting can be very effective when doing portraits, but check to make sure the sun is not flaring into the lens . . . unless you want it to!
4. Though commonly used, front lighting tends to flatten the scene, casting shadows behind the subject and reducing texture and form.
5. Most experienced photographers suggest taking pictures either early or late in the day.

Discuss

1. If you like to take photos, is this reading helpful? Did you learn information that you can use? Why or why not?
2. What other suggestions would you make to improve a photograph?

Thinking About Strategies

Work with a partner. In this article, the writer uses various adjectives to describe colors. Some of them are not usually used to describe colors. Look at the following words. What color(s) could each one describe? Explain your reasons.

1. vague _____

2. subtle _____

3. tranquil _____

4. warm _____

5. pure _____

6. strong _____

7. magical _____

8. harsh _____

3 • READING

Prepare

Work with a partner, and answer the following questions.

1. What do you know about the history of photography? Who is Edward Steichen?

2. Examine the article's title. Predict the text's basic pattern of organization.

3. Examine the features of the reading. What genre is this article?

4. Think of a general question the reading will answer. Write it down so you will remember it correctly.

Read

Read the text to get a general idea of the meaning. Use supporting details to determine main ideas. Don't try to figure out unfamiliar terms. While you are reading, find the answer to the question you wrote in number 4 of the *Prepare* section.

Edward Steichen
American; 1879–1973

Photographer and museum curator Edward Steichen was one of the most well known and influential figures of 20th century photography. During his long career he worked in a variety of styles in black and white and in color; his subjects ranged from portraits and landscapes, to fashion and advertising photography, to photography of dance and sculpture.

Steichen was born Eduard Jean Steichen in Luxembourg. His family came to the United States in 1881. Steichen was interested in art from an early age, and at 15 he began a four-year apprenticeship at Milwaukee's American Fine Art Company. He began to photograph in 1895, but continued to pursue a career as a painter for the next 20 years.

Steichen's photographs received their first public showing in Philadelphia in 1899. In 1901, 35 Steichen photographs were included in an exhibition of American photography in London and Paris. Steichen's first one-man show of photographs and paintings was held at La Maison des Artistes in Paris the following year.

Steichen began experimenting with color photography in 1904 and was an early user of the

Lumiere Autochrome process. He returned to Paris in 1906 and was responsible for selecting work to be exhibited at art galleries in New York. Among the artists whose work he selected were Picasso, Matisse, Brancusi, Cezanne, and Rodin.

In 1910, 31 Steichen photographs were exhibited at the International Exhibition of Pictorial Photography. The following year, Steichen made his first fashion photographs, but he began devoting much of his time to painting.

As commander of the photographic division of the Army Expeditionary Forces in World War 1, Steichen became acquainted with aerial photo-graphy, which required a new precision. After the war, he became chief photographer for the fashion magazines *Vogue* and *Vanity Fair*.

He was also employed as an advertising photographer by the J. Walter Thompson Agency. Among Steichen's famous subjects during these years were his brother-in-law the poet Carl Sandburg, movie stars Greta Garbo, Charles Chaplin, and Gloria Swanson, and journalist H. L. Mencken. At this point in his career, Steichen had a major disagreement with his long-time friend and mentor, photographer Alfred Steiglitz. While Steiglitz believed in "pure" photography, Steichen felt that fashion and other commercial photography could be raised to the level of art.

In 1938, Steichen retired from commercial photography. He became director of the U.S. Naval Photographic Institute in 1945, and was placed in command of all combat photography. From 1947 to 1962, Steichen was director of the Department of Photography at the Museum of Modern Art in New York. He did no photographic work of his own during these years, but was responsible for nearly 50 shows, including *The Family of Man*, for which he selected images from over 2 million photographs and which became the most popular exhibition in the history of photography.

In 1961, Steichen was honored by a one-man show of his photographs at the Museum of Modern Art; the Edward Steichen Photography Center was established at the museum in 1964. In 1967, Steichen wrote, "Today I am no longer concerned with photography as an art form. I believe it is potentially the best medium for explaining man to himself and to his fellow man." Steichen died in West Redding, Connecticut, shortly before his 94th birthday.

(from *The Encyclopedia of Photography,* 1984)

Read Again

Read the text at least two more times. As you are reading, do the following:

1. Think of two or three more questions and read to find the answers.
2. Examine the organization. Did you predict correctly? Look for key words and phrases that helped you follow the information. Underline major events in Steichen's life.
3. Look for jargon. Do you understand all the technical words? Do you need to?
4. Note punctuation.
5. Follow ideas. Underline the referring words and circle their referents.

Post-Reading Activities

A. Comprehension Check

Copy this timeline. Write the most important dates in Steichen's life on it.

```
┌──────────────────────────────────────────────────────────────┐
1879                                                          1973
```

B. Vocabulary Check

Work with a partner. Complete the chart.

	Part of Speech	Related Word	Part of Speech
1. influential			noun and verb
2. exhibition			
3. pictorial			noun
4. photographic			
5. aerial		air	
6. precision			
7. commercial	adjective		

Remember

Write a summary of the life of Edward Steichen. Your summary should contain no more than 175 words. Be sure to paraphrase key ideas.

Discuss

1. Is photography art? Why or why not?
2. Do you think that commercial photography is art? Why or why not?
3. Who are your favorite photographers? Describe some of the photographic art that you like.

Thinking About Strategies

What did you do with unfamiliar words in Reading 3? Complete the chart and then compare it with your partner's.

A. Check each column that applies. See step B for column B1.

Unfamiliar Words	A I knew this word.	B I was able to guess the approximate meaning.	B1 I used this vocabulary strategy.	C I couldn't guess the meaning, and it was an important word.	D I couldn't guess the meaning, but it wasn't an important word.
1. curator					
2. influential					
3. apprenticeship					
4. pursue					
5. one-man show					
6. precision					
7. retired					

B. For each word checked in column B, read the following list. In column B1, write the number of the strategy you used. If you are not sure, or if you used a strategy not listed, write "5."

   1. background knowledge
   2. context clues
   3. word analysis
   4. internal definition
   5. other

C. Did you find out the meaning of the words in column C. If so, how?

4 **READING**

Prepare

Work with a partner, and complete the following items.

1. Read the introduction and the conclusion. Predict the main idea of the reading.

2. Skim the article. Predict:

   a. the amount of supporting detail: Is there a little or a lot?

   b. the level of difficulty of the reading.

   c. how much of the reading you should try to understand (total comprehension or main ideas only).

   d. the best reading method for the material.

3. Think of a question the article may answer. Write it down so you will remember it correctly.

Read

Read the text to get a general idea of the meaning. Use supporting details to determine main ideas. While you are reading, find the answer to the question you wrote in number 3 of the *Prepare* section.

Photography
From Laboratory to Studio to Home

1   Cameras are everywhere today and photographs are almost mistake-proof; it's difficult to do it wrong. Even children as young as seven or eight can take good pictures. Therefore, it is hard to imagine that in the beginning taking photographs was a difficult process that could only be performed by scientists in a laboratory.

2   The idea of photography had been around for a long time before there were working cameras. In fact, Leonardo da Vinci drew a model for a *camera obscura* in 1519. However, the first photograph was not taken until 1827—more than 300 years later. This photograph was produced by a Frenchman named Niépce and required an exposure time of eight hours!

3   On January 4, 1829, Niépce became partners with Louis Daguerre to find a more efficient way to produce photographs. Niépce died only four years later, but Daguerre continued to experiment. He soon discovered a method that reduced the exposure time from eight hours to half an hour. Daguerre named this process the *daguerreotype*. Details of the process weren't published until 1839. At that point, Paul Delaroche, a leading scholar of the day, wrote about the invention saying that the daguerreotype "requires no knowledge of drawing . . ." and that "anyone may succeed . . . and perform as well as the author of the invention." This daguerreotype process moved photography from a laboratory experiment to the professional photography studio. (Thank goodness Sir John Herschel soon named the field photography—a shorter and easier term!)

4   People were fascinated by the invention, and daguerreotypmania swept across Europe and the United States. Everyone wanted their daguerreotype taken, and studios started opening up all over. However, some people were not enthusiastic. Some religious people felt that the invention was an instrument of the devil. Artists were also afraid that they would no longer be needed. Some even predicted that photography would bring the end of painting.

5   The daguerreotype process worked well, but it wasn't perfect. It was expensive, and produced only one print for each picture. If two copies were needed, the photographer had to use two cameras side by side. There was, therefore, a need for a method of taking photographs that could be easily and inexpensively reprinted. Calotype, invented by William Henry Fox Talbot, provided the answer to that problem. In 1844, he published a photographically illustrated book entitled *The Pencil of Nature*. Calotypes were not as detailed as daguerreotypes, but they had a great advantage—an unlimited number of photographs could be produced from the same negative.

6   The popularity of photography continued to grow by leaps and bounds. By 1850, there were 77 photographic studios in New York City alone. However, there were still no amateur photographers. Photography was a messy, expensive, time-consuming business. Very few people could afford to do it as a hobby.

7   In 1851, Frederick Scott Archer introduced the collodian process. This process was a boon for photographers and their customers alike. It was good for photographers because it reduced exposure times to two or three seconds. It was good for their customers because it dramatically reduced the price. The average price for a daguerreotype at the time was about 1.05 pounds. Photographs done with the collodian process cost as little as five pence.

8   Unfortunately, the collodian process still required a great deal of equipment because the photographs had to be developed while they were wet. This made it difficult to take photographs outside of the studio. It was clear that a dry method was required. The next major step forward came in 1871, when Dr. Richard Maddox discovered a way of using gelatin in the photographic process. This led to the development of the dry-plate process. The introduction of the dry-plate process marked a turning point in the science of photography because it took less equipment and was much simpler. Dry plates could also be developed much more quickly than with any previous technique.

9   The last two steps on the road from the studio to the home occurred when George Eastman introduced flexible film in 1884, and the box camera in 1889. Finally, photography was within the reach of the common man; hobbyists could now take photographs for fun.

Read Again

Read the text at least two more times. As you are reading, do the following:

1. Review the points about reading difficult material on page 176.
2. Think of two or three more questions and read to find the answers.
3. Watch for changes in organization as you read. Underline the major point of each paragraph. This text contains paragraphs that are organized in different ways.
4. Look for technical jargon. Decide which words are specifically about photography and which are common words with technical meanings.
5. Follow ideas. Underline the referring words and circle their referents.

Post-Reading Activities

A. Comprehension Check

A. Work with a partner. Write the main idea for each paragraph. Remember: a paragraph's main idea isn't exactly the same as the topic or thesis statement.

Paragraph 2 _____

_____

Paragraph 3 _____

_____

Paragraph 4 _____

_____

Paragraph 5 _____

_____

Paragraph 6 _____

_____

Paragraph 7 _____

_____

Paragraph 8 _____

_____

Paragraph 9 _____

_____

B. How does the article support and expand on the main idea of the reading?

C. Think about the title. Why did the author choose it? Is it a good title? Why or why not?

B. Vocabulary Check

A. There are several forms related to the word *photograph* in the reading. Find:

    a. two or more nouns   _____

                                      _____

    b. an adjective   _____

    c. an adverb (Hint: It ends in *-ly*.)   _____

B. Look for the following words and try to guess their meanings.

Word	Line	Idea introduced
1. mistake-proof	2	
2. exposure	15	
3. professional	31	
4. leaps and bounds	60	
5. amateur	62	
6. time-consuming	64	
7. boon	67	

Discuss

1. How do you feel about the impact of photography on our lives? Do you agree with the writer? Why or why not?

2. If someone showed you photographic "proof" of an event, would you believe it? Why or why not?

Thinking About Strategies

Work in small groups and answer the following questions. Then share your answers with the class.

How did you deal with this difficult reading? Did you:

- read more slowly than normal?
- skip over unfamiliar words and jargon?
- underline important words and phrases?
- put question marks next to confusing sections?
- go back and reread when you were confused?
- follow ideas by referents and antecedents?
- analyze words?
- paraphrase?

Reviewing Your Reading

A. Look at the following list of readings in this chapter. Check the column that shows how easy or difficult the material was for you.

Name of Reading	Type of Reading	Easy	Average	Difficult
1. How to Take Good Pictures	magazine article			
2. Take Great Photographs by Learning to Use Light	textbook			
3. Edward Steichen	encyclopedia entry			
4. Photography	newspaper article			

B. Read the following list of strategies that you have practiced in this chapter. Review the readings. Which strategies did you use, and how often did you use them? Check your answers in the chart.

Strategy	Always	Often	Sometimes	Never
Prepare				
Predicting organization				
Predicting from first and last paragraphs				
Read/Read Again				
Using supporting details to identify main ideas				
Reading with a purpose				
Using signal words to predict ideas				
Using referring words and referents to follow ideas				
Using illustrations and photos to aid comprehension				
Using punctuation to aid comprehension				

Strategy	Always	Often	Sometimes	Never
Critical Reading				
Making inferences				
Remember				
Summarizing				
Vocabulary Strategies				
Recognizing jargon				
Recognizing common phrases				
Analyzing a word for meaning				
Guessing the approximate meaning of a word				

C. Compare your chart with a partner's.

D. Did you use any other strategies while reading? If so, share them with the class. Explain where you learned them.

Reading:
The Odds Are

Getting Started

Discuss the following questions in pairs or small groups. Then share your ideas with the class.

1. What kind of gambling do you see in the photo?
2. Is gambling a good way of earning money? Why or why not?
3. What kinds of ways do people "take a gamble"?
4. Are there lotteries in your country? What is your chance of winning if you buy one ticket?

Strategies Reminder

Comprehension Strategies

Prepare
- Predicting Organization
- Predicting from First and Last Paragraphs

Read
- Using Supporting Details to Identify Main Ideas
- Reading with a Purpose (with Questions in Mind)
- Using Signal Words to Predict Ideas
- Using Referring Words and Referents to Follow Ideas
- Using Punctuation to Aid Comprehension
- Reading Difficult Material

Critical Reading
- Making Inferences

Remember
- Summarizing

Vocabulary Strategies
- Recognizing Jargon
- Recognizing Common Phrases
- Analyzing a Word for Meaning
- Guessing the Approximate Meaning of a Word

1 · READING

Prepare

Work with a partner, and then with your class.

1. Make predictions about the following aspects of the reading with your partner.
   a. the topic
   b. the intended audience
   c. the genre
   d. the organization
   e. the main idea

2. Talk about your predictions with the class. What did you look at in the reading to make your predictions?

3. With your class, think of two questions that the reading will probably answer. Write them down, so you'll remember them correctly.

Read

Read the text to get a general idea of the meaning. Use supporting details to determine main ideas. While you are reading, find the answers to the questions that you wrote in number 3 of the *Prepare* section.

Heads I Win, Tails You Lose

If I roll a pair of dice, what will the result be? Probability is the branch of mathematics that helps us answer that question. Let's look at how mathematicians determine probabilities.

Probabilities are expressed in numbers between 0 and 1. An event with a probability of 0 will never happen. An event with a probability of 1 is sure to happen. For example, coins have two sides—heads and tails. If you throw a coin into the air, the probability that it will land on a *particular* side is only about .5, or 50 percent.

To figure out the probability that an event will happen, therefore, you have to count the ways that it *can* happen and the ways that it *cannot* happen. In the coin example above, there are only two possibilities. Either the coin will land on heads, or it will land on tails. If you bet that the coin will land on heads, you have one chance in two of winning.

Just remember, probability doesn't tell you *what* will happen the next time you throw the coin. And this is where many gamblers make their mistake. Probability simply says that over time the likelihood of getting heads on any coin toss is 50 percent. Even if you flipped a coin 6 times and it landed on heads each time, the probability of it landing on heads the seventh time is still 50 percent. What about the 50-50 rule? According to mathematicians, the answer is that probabilities are more accurate with bigger numbers. For example, if you toss a coin ten times, you might get five heads and five tails, but you might not. However, if you toss it 100 times, you are more likely to get close to 50 percent heads and 50 percent tails. And if you do it 1,000 times, you will come even closer.

Finding Probabilities

Suppose we have a jar with four red marbles and six blue marbles, and we want to find the probability of choosing a red marble without looking in the jar. To find a basic probability, we use a fraction:

$$\frac{\text{number of favorable outcomes}}{\text{total number of possible outcomes}}$$

What's a favorable outcome? In our example, where we want to find the probability of drawing a red marble at random, our favorable outcome is *choosing a red marble*. What's the total number of possible outcomes? In our problem, the total number of outcomes is *all 10 marbles in the jar,* because we are equally likely to draw any one of them.

$$\frac{\text{number of red marbles}}{\text{number of total marbles in jar}} \quad \frac{4}{10}$$

The answer is 4/10, or expressed as a decimal, .4, and as a percentage, 40 percent.

Suppose we number the marbles 1 to 10. What is the probability of picking out number 5? Since there is only one number 5 marble, and there are still 10 marbles in the jar, the answer is 1 marble (favorable outcome) divided by 10 marbles (total of possible outcomes) = 1/10 or 10 percent.

What will happen, then, when you roll that pair of dice? Are you going to roll a 7? How likely is it you'll roll an 11? Probability can give you the answer.

Read Again

Read the text at least two more times and do the following:

1. Think of two or three more questions and read to find the answers.
2. The text contains many examples. Note them and the points that they illustrate.
3. Note technical jargon and common words used in specialized ways.
4. Note punctuation.
5. Note referring words and their referents.

Post-Reading Activities

A. Comprehension Check

Answer these questions about the reading.

1. What is probability?
2. If you toss a coin ten times and it lands on heads eight times and tails two times, what is the chance that it will land on heads on the 11th toss? How do you know?
3. Does probability help gamblers? Why or why not?
4. What is the probability that the sun will come up in the east tomorrow? Can you express this as a number between 0 and 1?
5. What can we say about an event that has a probability of .0001?
6. What do you have to know in order to figure out your chances of winning the lottery?
7. What academic subject studies probability?

B. Vocabulary Check

The following words are in Reading 1. Guess their meanings. Write a synonym, a definition, or a related word for each term.

1. outcome _____

2. favorable _____

3. random _____

4. likelihood _____

5. event _____

6. fraction _____

7. marble _____

Remember

With a partner or in a group, do the following.

1. Orally paraphrase the main ideas and supporting details of Reading 1. If you need to do so, briefly summarize them.

2. In your own words, write the steps for finding out the probability of an event when all outcomes are equally likely. Try not to look at the text.

Discuss

1. Has this article changed your feelings about gambling and the lottery? Why or why not?

2. In what ways do you take a gamble?

3. Is the study of probability a science?

Thinking About Strategies

Many people find statistics and probability difficult to understand. Do you understand it better than you did before you read the article? If so, why? Give specific reasons.

2 · READING

Prepare

Work with a partner or with your class.

1. Make predictions about the following aspects of the reading.
   a. the topic
   b. the intended audience
   c. the genre
   d. the organization
   e. the main idea

2. Talk about your predictions with your partner or your class. What did you look at to make your predictions?

3. List some English terms that you might use to talk about game shows.

4. Think of a question that the reading will answer.

Read

Read the text to get a general idea of the meaning. Use supporting details to determine main ideas. While you are reading, find the answer to the question you thought of in number 4 of the *Prepare* section.

There used to be a popular American TV game show called *Let's Make a Deal!* At the end of the program, the host showed a contestant three doors. First, he explained that behind one of the doors was a great prize, and behind the other two doors were worthless prizes. For example, there might be a car behind door 1, a chicken behind door 2, and some old shoes behind door 3. The contestant then picked a door. Next, the host opened one of the other two doors. Of course, he always opened a door that didn't have a good prize. After the host showed the worthless prize behind the door, he gave the contestant the opportunity to change doors. What do you think? Should the contestant change doors? What was the probability of winning a good prize if the contestant stayed with his original choice? What if he decided to change?

Let's assume that there is a car, a chicken, and a box of old shoes behind the doors. There are three options:

a. The contestant has chosen the door with the car behind it. The host asks him if he wants to keep what's behind the door. If he says yes, he wins the car. If he says no, he loses the car.

b. The contestant has chosen the door with the chicken behind it. He is shown the door with the box of old shoes behind it. If he changes doors and chooses the third door, he wins the car.

c. The contestant has chosen the door with the box of old shoes behind it. He is shown the door with the chicken behind it. Again, if he changes doors and chooses the third door, he wins the car.

Each of the above three options has a $\frac{1}{3}$ probability of occurring, because the contestant is equally likely to choose any one of the three doors. In two of the above options, the contestant only wins the car if he changes doors. There is only one option where the contestant wins by not changing doors. When he switches, he wins the car twice out of three possible options. Thus the probability of winning the car is $\frac{2}{3}$ if he changes doors, which means that the contestant should always change doors.

This result of $\frac{2}{3}$ may seem illogical. Why? We may believe that the probability of winning the car should be $\frac{1}{2}$ once the host has shown that the car is not behind door 1 or door 2. Many people think that since there are two doors left, one of which must have the car, the probability of winning must be $\frac{1}{2}$. This would mean that changing doors would not make a difference. As we've shown above through the three different options, however, this is not the case.

Still not convinced? Look at it another way. What if there were 1,000 doors? You would have a $\frac{1}{1,000}$ chance of picking the correct door. If the host opens 998 doors, all of them with worthless prizes behind them, the door that you chose first will still have a $\frac{1}{1,000}$ chance of being the winner. You would have to be pretty lucky to have made the correct choice out of 1,000!

One way to convince yourself that $\frac{2}{3}$ is the correct probability is to do a simulation with a friend. Have your friend be the host and you be the contestant. Keep track of how often you win the car by switching doors and then not switching doors.

Read Again

Read the text again and do the following:

1. Review the points about reading difficult material on page 176.
2. Think of two or three more questions and read to find the answers.
3. Predict ideas. Use signal words and other clues to help you.
4. Note unfamiliar words, and decide which vocabulary strategies to use to deal with them.
5. Note punctuation.
6. Find the sentence that states the main idea of the reading. For every key point, mark one detail that supports it through example, explanation, illustration, or other means.

Post-Reading Activities

A. Comprehension Check

Put these steps of the game in order.

_____ The host opens the other two doors.

_____ The contestant has a chance to change his or her mind.

_____ The host shows the contestant three doors.

_____ The host opens one of the doors.

_____ The contestant chooses a door.

B. Vocabulary Check

A. The following words are in Reading 2. Guess their meanings. Write a synonym, a definition, or a related word for each term.

1. contestant _____

2. host _____

3. convinced _____

4. illogical _____

5. worthless _____

6. option _____

7. switching _____

8. simulation _____

9. original _____

10. assume _____

11. prize _____

12. pick _____

B. Are all of these words equally important? Write 1 next to the most important words and 5 next to the least important words. Write 3 if you aren't sure.

Remember

If you were going to explain *Let's Make a Deal!* what would you say? Highlight key points about the game and the problem choices it offers the contestants.

Discuss

1. Are there any game shows like this in your country? How are they played?
2. Which game show would you like to play? Explain your reasons.

Thinking About Strategies

With a partner or in a small group, discuss the following questions. If you do not agree with your classmates, explain your reasons.

1. Which paragraphs were easiest to understand? Why?
2. What does "either of these" in option (c) of the reading refer to? Which strategy did you use to figure this out?

# 3 READING

Prepare

Work with a partner.

1. Examine the features of the text. Skim it and make predictions about the following aspects of the reading.
   a. the topic
   b. the type of major supporting detail that will be used
   c. the intended audience
   d. the genre
2. Talk about your predictions. Explain how you made them.
3. Think of some English terms that might be used to talk about this topic.
4. Think of a question the reading will answer. Write it down to remember it correctly.

Read

Read the text to get a general idea of the meaning. Use supporting details to determine main ideas. While you are reading, find the answer to these questions.

Who played Bul?

How did they play the game?

Play Bul, a Mayan Game of Chance

1   Games of chance were quite popular in a number of ancient Central American cultures. In the 16th century, a Spanish priest named Fra Diego Duran wrote that the stakes they played for sometimes rose so high that the loser had to sell himself into slavery to pay his debt. One should keep in mind that Father Duran may have been prejudiced; he fiercely disapproved of the games because the players prayed to Aztec gods for luck during

5   games.

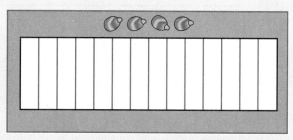

We know a lot about Mayan games of chance because game boards have been found scratched into the stone floors of Mayan ruins. The Mayan game of bul was played with a game board, "dice" made of

10   corn, and game pieces used to stand for players. The Mayans scratched the board onto a stone surface. Then they placed 15 grains of corn in a row on the board, the 14 spaces between grains being used for play. They marked 4 flat grains of corn on one side, and they used these like dice. When the corn was tossed, the count

15   was based on the number of grains that fell with the burned mark up (3 burned side and 1 unburned = 3, etc.). If all the kernels came up unburned, the count was 0.

Bul can be played with any even number of participants. The following example with only two players is the simplest arrangement. Each player has five game pieces. The two players each start with a single game piece at opposite ends of the board. Each player gets two throws of the corn in a row, then moves his piece the

20   number of spaces indicated after each throw. When the piece reaches the opposite end of the board, it is re-entered at the end where it started, as if the board were circular.

Bul is a game of strategy as well as a game of chance. What was the object of the game? To win a war. Players tried to land on spaces that their opponents already occupied. If they did, they captured their opponents' pieces. They then forced the captured pieces to go in the direction of home — that is, their own

25   end of the board. Once this was done, you could re-enter your piece into play, while the captive marker was "dead." Play continued in this way until all of one side's pieces were captured and dead.

Bul is no longer played on game boards etched in stone floors with grains of corn for dice. But versions of this ancient game can be played on the Internet at http://www.halfmoon.org/bul.html. Try testing your skill.

Read Again

Read the text again and do the following:

1. Think of two or three more questions and read to find the answers.
2. Predict ideas. Use signal words and other clues to help you.
3. Note unfamiliar words. Decide which vocabulary strategies to use to deal with them.
4. Note punctuation.
5. Examine the organization. Find sentences stating main ideas; note the supporting details.

Post-Reading Activities

A. Comprehension Check

Work with a partner. Draw a bul board on a piece of paper. Use four coins as dice, and paper clips to represent your pieces. Before you begin, decide which side will be the "burned" side of the dice.

B. Vocabulary Check

A. The following words are in Reading 3. Write a synonym, a definition, or a related word for each term.

1. games of chance   _____
2. slavery   _____
3. prejudiced   _____
4. participants   _____
5. arrangement   _____
6. opponent   _____
7. capture   _____
8. captive   _____
9. unburned   _____

B. Are all of these words equally important? Write 1 next to the most important words and 5 next to the least important words. Write 3 if you aren't sure.

C. Organization Check

Which of these charts best represents the organization of Reading 3?

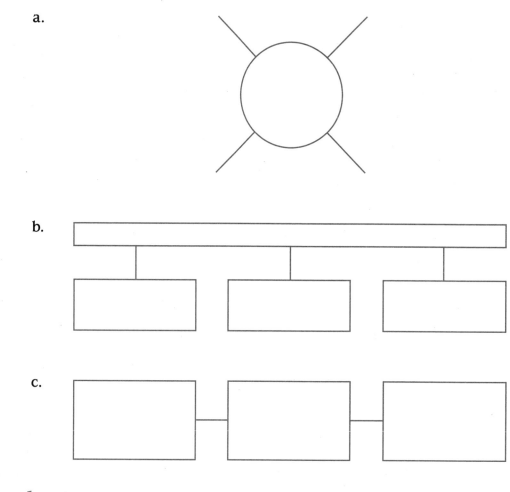

a.

b.

c.

Remember ─────────────────────────────────

Pretend that you are going to teach someone to play bul. Make notes for yourself.

Discuss ─────────────────────────────────

1. What are some other strategy games? How are they played?
2. Do you enjoy playing board games? Why or why not?

Thinking About Strategies

This reading has two separate sections. One is the introduction and summary, and the other is the body. Did you read both sections in the same way at the same speed? Why or why not?

4 · READING

Prepare

Work with a small group.

1. Make predictions about the following aspects of the reading.
   a. the topic
   b. the intended audience
   c. the genre
2. Talk about your predictions. What did you look at to make your predictions?
3. Think of a question that the reading will answer. Write it down so you will remember it correctly.

Read

Read the text and get a general idea of the meaning. Use supporting details to determine main ideas. While you are reading, find the answer to the question you wrote in number 3 of the *Prepare* section.

The Lady or the Tiger?

Once, in a kingdom long ago, a gardener's son loved the king's only daughter, the Princess Royal. That was bad enough. Unfortunately, the princess loved the boy in return. And that was worse. Of course, the two never had a chance to actually speak, but they exchanged many glances. Occasionally, they blew each other a kiss when they hoped nobody was looking. Even though they both knew that loving each other was not right, they loved each other all the same.

Oh, how they wanted to speak to each other, to whisper loving things to each other, or to kiss each other. Still, for many months they were happy with their secret love, watching each other from afar. At about the same time, however, the princess and the boy realized that this was not enough. In fact, it wasn't good enough at all. When he worked in the garden, the boy spent more and more time under the windows of the princess's bedroom. And the princess spent more and more of her time looking out her windows, hoping for a moment when the two could finally speak.

One lovely spring day, the moment finally arrived. The princess was in her room, staring out the window. The gardener's son was working near the palace walls, and the other gardeners were out of sight around the corner. The boy came near the princess's window just as she looked down. The princess leaned out the window, the boy stood up, and the two were just inches away. Caught by surprise, for a moment neither could say a word. Finally the boy spoke. He said the first thing he had ever said directly to the princess. "I love you," he said simply. "I love you," the princess replied. But that was their downfall. For as she spoke, the door to her bedroom opened and the king himself entered! He walked to the window and caught the gardener's son still standing outside the window, smiling at the Princess Royal.

The king had one method of dealing with all serious offenses, and it was used on all, rich or poor. There was a large arena right on the palace grounds. Prisoners were led into the center of the arena, where they were faced with two large doors. The prisoner was then to choose one of the doors, and open it.

45 Behind one door was always a lovely lady, and behind the other was always a fearsome tiger. The doors were well padded, so there was no way to hear the roars or rumblings of the ferocious animal. And nobody but the king himself ever knew which door held the lady 50 and which held the tiger.

If the prisoner opened the door with the lady, he must marry this lady, whoever she was, on the spot. If he opened the door with the tiger, he was eaten by the fierce beast. Thus, felt the king, luck alone would 55 determine the guilt or innocence of the prisoner.

Loving the king's daughter was, of course, a serious crime. The gardener's son was arrested on the spot, and led to prison to await his turn in the arena. As he was led away, he saw the princess form 60 a few words with her lips: "Trust me," she said.

Waiting in prison was horrible. As he waited, his hopes faded. At the same time, the king grew more pleased with himself and his system of justice. Both had the same thoughts: Whatever the outcome, the 65 boy would be separated from the princess forever. For if he chose the lady, he would be married on the spot to another woman, and if he chose the tiger, he would not live another ten minutes.

While the boy was waiting in the prison, the 70 princess was very busy. By the day the prisoner was to go into the arena, she had found out which door would contain the tiger and which the lady. All that next night, she couldn't sleep. What should she tell her love? She didn't know how to decide. If he chose the lady, how could she bear to watch him there, married 75 on the spot? And then, to see him forever around the palace but forever out of reach. Perhaps it would be easier to end things quickly. But oh! How could she possibly condemn him to the horrible death of the tiger's teeth and claws? The screams? The blood? 80

It was a terrible night for the princess, but by morning, she knew what she would do. She rose and dressed, and was sitting at her father's side in the arena, waiting for the prisoner to arrive. Then the boy came striding boldly out, and he walked directly over 85 toward the king, and bowed. As he stood up, he looked at the princess. One glance was enough. She sat calmly and with dignity, but she made a quick motion with her right hand. Without waiting or thinking, the gardener's son walked instantly to the 90 right-hand door and opened it.

And now, dear reader, I ask you the same question that the princess asked herself for all those long agonizing hours of the final night. What was her decision? Which came out? The lady or 95 the tiger?

Adapted from a Frank R. Stockton fable

Read Again

Read the text again and do the following:

1. Think of two or three more questions and read to find the answers.
2. Predict ideas. Use signal words and other clues to help you.
3. Remember to keep in mind that this is a story, so it will be organized chronologically.
4. Note unfamiliar words. Decide if they are important in figuring out the story. If so, try to guess them. For most people, a dictionary should not be necessary.
5. Note punctuation.
6. Examine the organization of the reading.

Post-Reading Activities

A. Comprehension Check
Put the events of the story in order.

_____ The boy opened the door.

_____ The king found them talking.

_____ The princess found out which door had the tiger.

_____ The princess and the boy fell in love.

_____ The princess and the boy spoke.

_____ The princess motioned to the boy.

_____ The gardener was arrested.

_____ The princess and the boy blew kisses to each other.

B. Vocabulary Check

A. The following words and phrases are in Reading 4. Many of them may be unfamiliar. Circle the ones that you didn't know before you started reading.

afar	condemn	fierce	kingdom	out of sight
agonizing	downfall	glances	leaned out	rumblings
arena	faded	guilt	offenses	staring
await	fearsome	in return	on the spot	striding
boldly	ferocious	innocence	out of reach	whisper

B. You were probably able to guess the approximate meaning of some of the new words and phrases listed in (A). Write them with your guesses.

_____   _____

_____   _____

_____   _____

_____   _____

_____   _____

_____   _____

C. Look at the words that you could not guess. Were you able to understand the story without knowing their meanings? Why or why not?

Remember

Write a summary of the story. Your summary should be no more than 300 words.

Discuss

What do you think happened? Did the young man get married or get eaten? Explain your reasons for your opinion.

Thinking About Strategies

Compare the way you read this text with the way that you read Readings 1–3 in this chapter. Did you read the story more quickly or more slowly than the others? Why or why not? Did you use any different strategies? Why or why not?

Reviewing Your Reading

A. Look at the following list of readings in this chapter. Check the column that shows how easy or difficult the material was for you.

Name of Reading	Type of Reading	Easy	Average	Difficult
1. Heads I Win, Tails You Lose	magazine article			
2. Let's Make a Deal!	magazine article			
3. Play Bul, a Mayan Game of Chance	Website article			
4. The Lady or the Tiger?	magazine article			

B. Read the following list of strategies that you have practiced in this chapter. Review the readings. Which strategies did you use, and how often did you use them? Check your answers in the chart.

Strategy	Always	Often	Sometimes	Never
Prepare				
Predicting organization				
Predicting from first and last paragraphs				
Read/Read Again				
Using supporting details to identify main ideas				
Reading with a purpose				
Using signal words to predict ideas				
Using referring words and referents to follow ideas				
Using illustrations and photos to aid comprehension				
Using punctuation to aid comprehension				
Critical Reading				
Making inferences				
Remember				
Summarizing				
Vocabulary Strategies				
Recognizing jargon				
Recognizing common phrases				
Analyzing a word for meaning				
Guessing the approximate meaning of a word				

C. Compare your chart with a partner's.

D. Did you use any other strategies while reading? If so, share them with the class. Explain where you learned them.

Reading:
The World of Money

Getting Started

Discuss the following questions in pairs or small groups. Then share your ideas with the class.

1. Describe what you see in the photo.
2. How important is money to you?
3. Can people be successful if they aren't rich?
4. What do you do with extra money?
5. What kinds of money are there?

Strategies Reminder

Comprehension Strategies

Prepare
- Predicting Organization
- Predicting from First and Last Paragraphs

Read
- Using Supporting Details to Identify Main Ideas
- Reading with a Purpose (with Questions in Mind)
- Using Signal Words to Predict Ideas
- Using Referring Words and Referents to Follow Ideas
- Using Punctuation to Aid Comprehension

- Reading Difficult Material

Critical Reading
- Making Inferences

Remember
- Summarizing

Vocabulary Strategies
- Recognizing Jargon
- Recognizing Common Phrases
- Analyzing a Word for Meaning
- Guessing the Approximate Meaning of a Word

1 · READING

Prepare

Work with a partner. Study the features of the reading, then do the following items.

1. Make predictions about the following aspects of the reading.
   a. the topic
   b. the intended audience
   c. the genre of the article
   d. the organization of the article
   e. the main idea
2. Talk about your predictions with your partner or with your class. What did you look at to make them?
3. Tell your partner three things that you know about this topic.
4. Think of a question that the reading will answer.

Read

Read the text to get a general idea of the meaning. Use supporting details to determine main ideas. While you are reading, find the answer to the question you thought of in number 4 of the *Prepare* section.

The Evolution of Money

Bartering

1 Consider this problem: You catch fish for food, but you're tired of eating it every day. Instead, you want to eat some bread. Fortunately, a baker lives next door. Trading the baker some fish for bread is an example of barter, the direct exchange of one kind of product for another.

However, barter is difficult when you try to obtain goods from a producer who doesn't want
5 what you have. For example, how do you get shoes if the shoemaker doesn't like fish? The series of trades required to obtain shoes could be complicated and time-consuming.

Early societies faced these problems. The solution was money. Money is an item, or commodity, that people agree to accept in trade. People have used a wide variety of items for money such as seashells, beads, tea, fishhooks, fur, cattle, and even tobacco.

Coins

10 Most early cultures traded precious metals. In 2500 B.C., the Egyptians produced metal rings for use as money. By 700 B.C., a group of seafaring people called the Lydians became the first in the Western world to make coins. The Lydians used coins to expand their vast trading empire. The Greeks and Romans continued the tradition and passed it on to later Western civilizations. Coins were useful since they were durable, easy to carry, and contained valuable metals.

15 During the 18th century, coins became popular throughout Europe. One of the most widely used coins was the Spanish 8-reale. It was often split into pieces or bits to make change. Half a coin was four bits; a quarter was two bits, a term still used today. Coins containing precious metals are an example of commodity money. The item was traded because it held value. In this case, the value of the coin depended upon the amount of gold and silver it contained.

Paper currency

20 The Chinese were the first to use paper money, beginning in the Tang Dynasty (A.D. 618–907). During the Ming Dynasty in A.D. 1,300, the Chinese placed the emperor's seal and signatures of the treasurers on a paper made from mulberry bark.

Representative money is tokens or pieces of paper that are not valuable themselves but can be exchanged for a valuable commodity such as gold or silver. In 1715, Maryland, North
25 Carolina, and Virginia issued a "tobacco note" that could be exchanged for a certain amount of tobacco. This type of money was easier to carry than coins or tobacco leaves.

Fiat money is similar to representative money except for one difference. Fiat money can't be exchanged for a commodity such as gold or silver. Currency issued by most governments today are examples of fiat money. In 1967, the U.S. Treasury stopped exchanging silver certificates for
30 silver dollars or gold. By 1970, silver was removed from coins altogether. The old coins were gradually replaced with new copper-cored coins covered in an alloy of 75 percent copper and 25 percent nickel.

People are willing to accept fiat money in exchange for the goods and services they sell only because they are confident that they will be able to use it to buy goods and services. The Federal Reserve is responsible for maintaining the integrity of U.S. currency by setting monetary policy—controlling the amount of money in circulation—to keep prices stable. If prices remain stable, people have confidence that the dollar they use to buy goods and services today will buy a similar amount in the future.

Summary

In summary, then, we have seen that coins and paper currencies are examples of three types of money: commodity, representative, and fiat. We have also seen that money in general serves three purposes:

1. **Medium of Exchange**
   People accept money in trade for goods and services.

2. **Standard of Value**
   The value of a good or service can be measured with money. For example, a car with a price of $2,000 is worth twice as much as a car with a price of $1,000.

3. **Store of Value**
   Money can be saved and used in the future.

As societies changed, payment for goods and services changed. From early bartering to modern paper currencies, money has evolved through the centuries.

Reprinted with permission from the Federal Reserve Bank of Dallas Business Review, *December 1975.*

Read Again

Read the text again and do the following:

1. Think of two or three more questions and read to find the answers.
2. Predict ideas. Use signal words and other clues to help you.
3. Look for money jargon. Most of these words will be explained within the reading.
4. Note punctuation, especially long dashes.
5. Note referring words and their referents.
6. Note the supporting details.
7. Note abbreviations and names.

Post-Reading Activities

A. Comprehension Check

A. Complete the chart with information from the reading.

Types of money	Made of	Advantages	Disadvantages
1.		durable, easy to carry	
2. representative money			
3.			People must have confidence in it.

B. Compare money and barter. What are the advantages of each?

B. Vocabulary Check

A. The following words and phrases are in Reading 1. Many of them may be unfamiliar. Does the author use any methods to help you remember them? Circle the ones that you didn't know before you started reading.

barter	durable	monetary	precious	stable
commodity	fiat money	money	representative	time-consuming
commodity money	integrity	obtain	seafaring	tokens
currency	medium of exchange	policy	split	

B. You were probably able to guess the meanings of some of the new words and phrases listed in (A). Write them with your guesses.

_____   _____

_____   _____

_____   _____

_____   _____

_____   _____

_____   _____

_____   _____

_____   _____

_____   _____

C. Look at the words that you could not guess. Were you able to understand the text without knowing their meanings? Why or why not?

C. Organization Check

Write the main idea for each supporting idea or example.

1. You can exchange fish for bread.

_____

2. Lydians made coins.

_____

3. Many people used the Spanish 8-reale.

_____

4. North Carolina and Virginia issued the "tobacco note."

_____

5. By 1970, silver was removed from coins altogether.

_____

6. The Federal Reserve is responsible for maintaining the integrity of U.S. currency.

_____

Remember

Make a timeline showing the evolution of money. Be sure to include the most important dates.

Discuss

1. What kind of money do you use in your country?
2. Who controls monetary policy in your country? Do they do it well?

Thinking About Strategies

Analyze Reading 1. Work with a partner, and discuss the following questions.

1. Did you correctly predict the main idea? Where is the main idea stated? What strategy can help you find this statement quickly?

2. Did you correctly predict organization? What basic method does the author use to organize ideas? Why?

2 · READING

Prepare

Work with a partner or with your class.

1. Make predictions about the following aspects of the reading.
   a. the topic
   b. the intended audience
   c. the genre of the article
   d. the main ideas

2. Talk about your predictions. What did you look at to make them?

3. Tell two things you know about this topic. Name some English terms that people might use when talking about the topic.

4. Think of a question that the reading will probably answer. Write it down to remember it correctly.

Read

Read the text to get a general idea of the meaning. Use supporting details to determine main ideas. While you are reading, find the answer to the question you wrote in number 4 of the *Prepare* section.

A Beginner's Guide to the Stock Market

A Simple Example

1 Suppose that you want to start a business, and you decide to open a restaurant. You buy a building, buy all the kitchen equipment, tables, and chairs that you need, buy your supplies and hire your cooks, servers, etc. Then you advertise and open your doors.

2 Let's say that:
- You spend $500,000 buying the building and the equipment.
- In the first year, you spend $250,000 on supplies, food, and the payroll for your employees.
- At the end of your first year, you add up all of the money you have received from customers

15 and find that your total income is $300,000. Since you have made $300,000 and paid out the $250,000 for expenses, your net profit is: $300,000 (income) − $250,000 (expense) = $50,000 (profit)

20 **3** At the end of the second year, you bring in $325,000, and your expenses remain the same, for a net profit of $75,000. However, at this point, you decide that you want to sell the business. What is it worth?

25 **4** One way to look at it is to say that the business is "worth" $500,000. If you close the restaurant, you can sell the building, the equipment, and everything else and get $500,000. This is a simplification, of course—
30 the building probably went up in value, and the equipment went down because it is now used. Let's just say that things balance out to $500,000. How do you determine worth? One way is by the asset value, or book value, of the
35 business—the value of all of the business's assets if you sold them today.

5 There is another way to determine worth, however. If you keep the business going, it will probably make at least $75,000 this year—you
40 know this from your history with the business. Therefore, you can think of the restaurant as an investment that will pay out something like $75,000 in interest every year. Looking at it that way, someone might be willing to pay $750,000
45 for the restaurant, since a $75,000 return per year on a $750,000 investment represents a 10 percent rate of return. Someone might even be willing to pay $1,500,000, which represents a 5 percent rate of return—or even more if he or she
50 thought that the restaurant's income would grow and increase earnings over time at a rate faster than the rate of inflation. An additional way to determine worth is, then, by potential earnings.

6 To decide your price for the restaurant, you,
55 as the owner, would consider asset value and potential value. Unfortunately, when prices go high, fewer people are able or willing to pay cash for a purchase. While they may not be able or willing to buy the entire purchase, they may buy
60 a share.

7 Let's say you price the restaurant at $1,500,000. What if 10 people come to you and say, "I would like to buy your restaurant, but I

don't have $1,500,000"? How do you sell?
65 Divide your restaurant into 10 equal pieces, and sell each piece for $150,000. In other words, sell shares in the restaurant. Each person who bought a share would receive one-tenth of the profits at the end of the year, and one out of 10 votes in
70 any business decisions. Or, you might divide ownership into 1,500 shares, and sell each share for $1,000 to make the price something that more people could afford. Last, you might divide ownership into 3,000 shares, keep 1,500 for
75 yourself, and sell the remaining shares for $500 each. That way, you keep a majority of the shares (and therefore the votes) and remain in control of the restaurant while sharing the profit with other people. In the meantime, you get to
80 put $750,000 in the bank when you sell the 1,500 shares to other people.

8 Stock, at its most basic, is really that simple. It represents ownership of a company's assets and profits. A dividend on a share of stock
85 represents that share's portion of the company's profits, generally dispersed yearly. If the restaurant has 10 owners, each owning one share of stock, and the restaurant makes $75,000 in profit during the year, then each owner gets a
90 dividend of $7,500. A large company like IBM has millions of shares of stock outstanding— around 1.1 billion in October, 1999. In this case, the total profits of the company are divided by 1.1 billion and sent to the shareholders as
95 dividends.

9 One measure of the value of a company, at least as far as investors are concerned, is the number of outstanding shares multiplied by the share price. This value is called the
100 "capitalization of the company."

The Stock Exchange

10 In the United States, if I am a private citizen who owns a restaurant, and I am selling my restaurant stock to other private citizens in the community, I could do it by placing an ad in the
105 newspaper. This makes selling the stock easy for me. However, it creates a problem for investors who want to sell their stock in the restaurant. The seller has to find a buyer, which can be hard. A "stock market" solves this problem.

110 **11**   Stocks in publicly traded companies are bought and sold at a stock market, also known as the stock exchange. The New York Stock Exchange (NYSE) is an example of such a market. In your neighborhood, you may have a
115 supermarket that sells food. The reason you go to the supermarket is for convenience: to buy all the food you need in one place—meat from the butcher, milk and yogurt from the dairy farmer, bread from the baker, vegetables and fruit from the produce market. A stock market is a 120 supermarket for stocks. It can be thought of as a big room where everyone who wants to buy and sell shares of stocks can go to do their buying and selling.

12   The stock exchange makes buying and 125 selling stocks easy. You don't have to travel to the stock market at all. You can call a stockbroker who does business with a stock market, and he or she will contact the stock market on your behalf to buy or sell your stock. 130 If stock markets did not exist, buying or selling stock would be much more difficult. You would have to place an ad in the newspaper, wait for a call, and decide on a price whenever you wanted to sell stock. Because there are stock exchanges, 135 you can buy and sell shares instantly.

Read Again

Read the text again and do the following:

1. Review the points about reading difficult material on page 176.
2. Think of two or three more questions and read to find the answers.
3. Predict ideas. Use signal words and other clues to help you.
4. Note the technical words about finances. They may be helpful in later readings.
5. Note punctuation.
6. Note referring words and their referents.
7. Note the supporting details.
8. Note abbreviations and acronyms.

Post-Reading Activities

A. Comprehension Check

Answer these questions about the reading.

1. What are two different ways to figure out the worth of a business?
2. How do people figure out the cost of a share of stock?
3. What do stockholders get for their money?
4. How does a stock market help stockholders?
5. What does a stockbroker do?

B. Vocabulary Check

This reading contains several terms in economics. Work with a partner. Look at the reading again, and find a definition or example for each of the following terms.

asset value   dividends   interest   rate of return

book value   expenses   investment   shareholders

capitalization   inflation   net profit   shares

C. Organization Check

Most of Reading 2 is an example. The example explains stock and stock market concepts. On the following lines, write the concept that each paragraph explains.

Paragraph 4 _____

Paragraph 5 _____

Paragraph 8 _____

Paragraph 9 _____

Paragraphs 10–12 _____

Remember

Imagine that you have a business that you want to sell. Review the reading, and summarize the key points for the following:

    a. determining the worth of your business.

    b. selling shares in your business.

Discuss

    1. What do you know about the stock market in your country?

    2. Do you know about the stock of any one company? How much does one share cost? Is the price going up or down?

Thinking About Strategies

    A. How well did you follow referring words? Find the referent for each of the following words.

Word/Phrase	Paragraph	Refers to
1. it	3	
2. this is	4	
3. it (is now)	4	
4. that way	5	
5. it	8	
6. this	10	
7. it (creates)	10	
8. you	11	

    B. Did you pay attention to the transition words and phrases? Which of these transition phrases are used to show time sequence?

        1. at this point

        2. at the end of the second year

        3. in this case

        4. in the meantime

        5. in other words

    C. What ideas do the other transitional phrases introduce?

3 · READING

Prepare

Work with a partner. This reading is divided into two parts. Study the features of both parts, then do the following items.

1. Make predictions about the following aspects of the reading.
   a. the topic
   b. the intended audience
   c. the genre of the article
   d. the organization of the article
   e. the main ideas of Part A and of Part B

2. Talk about your predictions with a partner or with your class. What did you look at to make your predictions?

3. Tell your partner something that you know about this topic.

4. Think of two questions that the reading will answer, one question for each part.

Read Part A

Read the text to get a general idea of the meaning. Use supporting details to determine main ideas. While you are reading, find the answer to the question you thought of in number 4 of the *Prepare* section.

Nella: The New Money?

THE OLDEST SYSTEM of exchanging goods and services has met the latest technology. Tokyo Website developer Hiromi Amano and his partner, New York architect Usman Haque, have started a Website that
5 will allow Internet users to barter online. Amano and Haque aren't just building a Website. They believe that they are laying the foundation of a new parallel economy.

Amano says that their aim is to provide a system
10 that the online community can use any way it wants. That system is based on the Nella, as they have christened their cybermoney. Although it is not actually equivalent to any currency, they suggest that one nella would be the equivalent of one US dollar.
15 (Why did they choose the name *nella*? It is a short form of marinella, the name of a fictional island in a novel Amano recently read.)

So, how would this parallel economy work? People who have information or services to "sell" would register themselves as cyberbusinesses. They 20 would then open an account at the Global Village Bank, also created by Amano and Haque. Everyone who opens an account will automatically receive 50 nellas. They can spend their nellas by purchasing information or services from other cyberbusinesses. 25 Nellas are then transferred from one Global Village Bank account to another.

Amano and Haque hope that nellas will eliminate the problem that other bartering systems have had—finding a mutually acceptable unit of value. "If it 30 became popular enough, nella would be just another currency on the world currency exchange," said Kevin McCabe, an associate professor of economics at the University of Arizona.

Will nellas fulfill their inventors' expectations? No 35 one can say. However, it's going to be tough to start a whole new economy from scratch even with the aid of the latest technology.

Read Part B

Read the text to get a general idea of the meaning. Use supporting details to determine main ideas. While you are reading, find the answer to the question you thought of in number 4 of the *Prepare* section.

Back Forward Stop Refresh Home AutoFill Print Mail

web: Go

Time Dollars FAQ

**Here are the answers to some of the most frequently
asked questions about Time Dollars.**

What are Time Dollars and how do they work?

Time Dollars are a new kind of money that helps people convert their personal time into purchasing power by helping others. An hour helping another earns one Time Dollar. From childcare to karate lessons to cooking, the ways of earning Time Dollars are endless. Everyone's contribution is valued the same: an hour for an hour. Time Dollars turn helping others from a one-way street to a two-way street. I help you, and
5   you help another—and someone else helps me. The recipients of help become, in turn, the providers of help.

How can Time Dollars be used?

The Time Dollars you earn can be used to receive services or help from someone else. When you spend your Time Dollars, someone else earns them. They can also be saved up for a rainy day. They can be given to a family member, friend, or neighbor who needs help. Or they can be donated to others in need.

Are Time Dollars a form of barter?

Barter almost always involves bargaining between two individuals to establish the worth of a good or a
10 service. There is no bargaining with Time Dollars. An hour is an hour is an hour. All contributions are valued equally. So Time Dollars are something different from barter.

Who can earn them?

Anyone can. You can join a Time Dollar program or start your own.

What kinds of help are offered?

Practically anything! Here is a sample: child care, karate lessons, children's activities, computer set-up, carpentry, plumbing, electrical work, cooking, delivered meals, meal planning, first aid classes, nursing,
15 tutoring, gardening, hairstyling, office help, house cleaning, translating . . . the list goes on and on.

Aren't Time Dollars just a way of paying people to volunteer?

In a way, but they are much more than that. They enhance volunteer programs by making it possible for those who traditionally have been recipients to now become givers and helpers, too. And they are a way of activating a new resource: the time of people who are retired or underemployed or undervalued so that we can begin to meet the needs of our communities.

Read Again

Read both texts at least two more times. As you are reading, do the following:

1. Think of two more questions for each part, and read to find the answers.
2. Predict ideas. Use signal words and other clues to help you.
3. Note unfamiliar words. When you find one, decide which vocabulary strategies to use to deal with it.
4. Note punctuation.
5. Note referring words and their referents.
6. Note the supporting details.

Post-Reading Activities

A. Comprehension Check

Answer the following questions about both parts of the reading.

Part A

1. Think back to the kinds of money listed in Reading 1. What kind of money is a nella?
2. What is the purpose of a nella?
3. How can you earn a nella?
4. Where can you keep your nellas?
5. How much is a nella worth?

Part B

1. What kind of money is a Time Dollar?
2. What is the purpose of Time Dollars?
3. How can you earn a Time Dollar?
4. How can you spend a Time Dollar?
5. How much is a Time Dollar worth?

B. Vocabulary Check

A. The following words and phrases are in both parts of Reading 3. Many of them may be unfamiliar. Circle the ones that you didn't know before you started reading.

Part A

christened	equivalents	fulfill	parallel
cyberbusiness	from scratch	mutually accepted	tough

Part B

convert	donate	endless	recipients

B. You were probably able to guess the approximate meaning of some of the new words and phrases listed in (A). Write them with your guesses.

_____   _____

_____   _____

_____   _____

_____   _____

_____   _____

_____   _____

_____   _____

C. Look at the words that you could not guess. Were you able to understand the text without knowing their meanings? Why or why not?

D. In the text about Time Dollars, the writer uses two metaphors. Can you explain what they mean?

". . . turns helping others from a one-way street to a two-way street"

". . . saved up for a rainy day"

C. Critical Reading Check

Read both parts of Reading 3 again. Summarize the key points and major supporting details for each of the following:

1. the similarity of Time Dollars and nellas
2. the differences of Time Dollars and nellas

Remember

Create a chart comparing Time Dollars and nellas.

Discuss

1. Do you think that either of these systems will become successful? Why or why not?
2. Have you ever used barter to purchase something?

Thinking About Strategies

Did you find one part of the reading easier than another? If so, what made it easier? Be specific in your answer. Consider level of difficulty, organization, jargon, and other points.

4 · READING

Prepare

Work with your class.

1. Read the first paragraph and the last paragraph. Make predictions about the following aspects of the reading.

   a. the topic

   b. the intended audience

   c. from the genre of the article

   d. the main idea

   e. the level of difficulty of the reading

2. Talk about your predictions. What did you look at to make your predictions?

3. If you think that the text is going to be difficult, what strategies will you use?

4. Think of a question that the reading will answer. Write it down to remember it correctly.

Read

Read the text to get a general idea of the meaning. Use supporting details to determine main ideas. While you are reading, find the answer to the question you wrote in number 4 of the *Prepare* section.

MICRO CREDIT, MACRO RESULTS

In El Salvador, Francisca Rojas—an orphan at age 9, a runaway at age 17, and a mother at age 18—seemed destined to stay poor and dependent on others. Instead, she became a businesswoman and a responsible member of her community—thanks to her first loan of $50 by a Salvadoran bank that believed in her when no traditional bank would.

Her first loan, or "micro credit," as it is referred to in the world of finance, literally revolutionized her life, helping her to lift herself out of poverty and into the world of self-reliance. Today, she earns about $53 a week, spends almost twice as much on food as she used to, lives in a much nicer home, buys medicine, and even saves.

Halfway around the globe, in Bangladesh, Noorjahan has a similar story. Abandoned by her parents at three months of age, again abandoned by her husband at age 12 while pregnant, she had nobody to turn to for help. Working as a domestic helper, she earned $37.50 a year and could not even think of owning or saving anything.

Today, however, her annual income is $250 (which is above the Bangladeshi national average), and she owns two goats, one cow, ten hens, and two-thirds of an acre of land. Thanks to a tiny loan of $50 from Grameen Bank, she was able to pull herself out of poverty. The best part, however, is that she has pulled the next generation along with her. In a country where the rate of children attending school is small—only 46 percent of children reach grade five—her son is now in the eighth grade.

Entrepreneurial "Evangelism"

20 From Bolivia to Indonesia, and from El Salvador to India, millions of poor people are taking control of their lives. The world is beginning to take notice. For example, the U.S. Agency for International Development (USAID) increased its funding of micro-credit programs from $80 million in fiscal year 1993 to $140 million in 1995. And last year, the World Bank set aside $200 million to give to lending organizations for ultrasmall-scale loans. It is estimated that micro-credit programs now reach about 10 million people worldwide, consequently altering every 25 aspect of their lives.

Why Micro Credit is Successful

Micro credit works for several reasons. "For one," says Sam Daley Harris, director of Results Educational Fund, "contrary to common belief, poor people are good credit risks." Banks such as Grameen Bank in Bangladesh and Banco Sol in Bolivia show that poor people's repayment rate is equal to or better than conventional borrowers. Typically, all these programs boast a 95 to 30 98 percent repayment rate—comparable with any large bank.

"Poor people have tremendous management capability," says Muhammad Yunus, the founder of Grameen Bank and one of the pioneers of the micro-credit movement. "They know exactly what they want to do and how they want to do it. They only lack the resources." Grameen Bank now disburses $500 million a year to 2 million borrowers, reaching 35,000 Bangladeshi villages.

Trickle-down vs. Bubble-up Economics

35 International agencies such as the United Nations International Children's Emergency Fund (UNICEF) and others have realized that most aid programs have failed to reach the poorest 20 percent of the world's people. Most of the aid provided by wealthy countries over the last 50 years has been used for large-scale development projects such as dams, highways, and power plants.

40 The greatest beneficiaries of these efforts are builders and people who hold political power. Even without corruption, most benefits go to managers and professionals. In contrast, micro credit reaches indigent people immediately, bypassing the usual barriers.

"Rather than injecting capital into the economy at the altitude of corporate investors, as tax cuts or special incentives, in micro credit, the capital is injected at ground level, as loans to the 45 poor," writes David Bornstein in his upcoming book, *Price of a Dream* (Simon & Schuster).

Call it a 'Bubble-Up' Economics

According to Bornstein, although the bubble-up economy initially seems to benefit only the poorest of the poor, it has the potential to eventually lift the spending power of millions of people, creating more demand for such consumer goods as soap and toothpaste. In the long run, then, everyone benefits.

50 Consider this. Since its birth in 1971, Bangladesh has received more than $25 billion in foreign aid—and yet the majority of its citizens have only grown poorer. But Grameen Bank has helped millions of villagers move from eating one meal a day to three, from owning one set of clothes to four, and has provided thousands of children with education and medicine. Throughout all of this, the bank has had a repayment rate of 97 percent, a rate comparable with Chase 55 Manhattan Bank.

Micro-credit programs have undergone an evolutionary growth at the grassroots level. Each lending organization in each country has developed a style and program tailored to its own environment. In fact, in many programs, micro credit is disbursed in the form of a "living loan" of farm animals, or takes the shape of training or in-kind resources to successfully carry out the

60 business. Each program is unique in its method of application, its clientele, the amount of the typical loan, and how the repayment is structured.

For example, ACCION International, a Cambridge, Massachusetts–based agency that provides micro credit to poor people in Latin America and the United States, has a system called the "solidarity group." The group chooses its leader, who is responsible for coordinating the loan

65 and bringing the payments to the ACCION office. If one member fails to repay, the whole group suffers.

"This is not just a peer-pressure technique, but it is also peer support, in which if a member is in some difficult situation, the other members help her out," says Gabriela Romanow, vice president of ACCION.

70 Because many of these organizations realize that long-term sustainability is the key to success, they take a very businesslike approach. For example, Grameen Bank charges market-competitive rates, never forgives a loan, and provides no free services to its borrowers.

Although it has been proven that micro credit is an excellent weapon against poverty, there are many hurdles to its expansion, ranging from legal barriers to insufficient funds and lack of

75 will. The largest barrier is, however, the fear that it can't be done.

"All too often, stereotypes about the poorest deter us from reaching out to them," says Daley-Harris, the Results Educational Fund director. "Poverty is often confused with a moral condition and its victims perceived as the perpetrators of their own conditions." But the goals are achievable, proponents say. Micro credit is a "socially conscious capital enterprise" where

80 everyone wins, according to Yunus, the Grameen Bank founder.

Perhaps one day, the banking official says, micro credit and other development programs will have won their goals and "our great-grandchildren will go to museums to see what poverty was."

Meenal Pandya, "Micro Credit, Macro Results." *The World & I*, Vol. 11, August 1, 1996, pp. 54.

Read Again

Read the text again. As you are reading, do the following:

1. Review the points about reading difficult material on page 176.
2. Think of two or three more questions and read to find the answers.
3. Predict ideas. Use signal words and other clues to help you.
4. Look for jargon.
5. Note punctuation, especially capital letters and long dashes.
6. Note referring words and their referents.
7. Note the supporting details. Pay attention to the examples and think about the purpose of each one.
8. Note abbreviations, names, and acronyms.

Post-Reading Activities

A. Comprehension Check

Answer these questions about the reading.

1. Explain the title.
2. What evidence does the author give that micro-credit programs are successful?
3. Why is micro credit better for poor people than normal aid programs?
4. What different kinds of loans might poor people get?
5. How does ACCION make sure that its loans are repaid?
6. Is Grameen Bank a charity? Why or why not?
7. What are some reasons why micro-credit programs might not expand?
8. What is the meaning of *trickle-down* and *bubble-up* economics?

B. Vocabulary Check

A. The following words and phrases are in Reading 4. Many of them may be unfamiliar. Circle the ones that you didn't know before you started reading.

abandoned	clientele	disburses	lack	rate
aid	comparable	funding	large-scale	repayment
altering	contrary	grassroots	literally	revolutionized
aspect	conventional	hurdles	orphan	runaway
barriers	corruption	in the long run	peer pressure	self-reliance
beneficiaries	destined	indigent	perpetrators	sustainability
bypassing	deter	initially	proponents	tailored

B. You were probably able to guess the approximate meaning of some of the new words and phrases listed in (A). Write them with your guesses.

_____   _____

_____   _____

_____   _____

_____   _____

_____   _____

_____   _____

_____   _____

_____   _____
_____   _____
_____   _____
_____   _____
_____   _____
_____   _____
_____   _____
_____   _____
_____   _____
_____   _____

C. Look at the words that you could not guess. Were you able to understand the text without knowing their meanings? Why or why not?

C. Critical Reading Check

Is the author in favor or against micro credit? Give evidence to support your opinion.

Remember

Write a paragraph describing micro credit and why it is good for poor people. Be sure to paraphrase and summarize key points.

Discuss

1. What do you have to do to get a loan from a bank in your country?
2. What is the interest rate?
3. Is micro credit available to people in your country? If not, do you think it should be?

Thinking About Strategies

Work with a partner, and answer the following questions.

1. How much of this reading were you able to understand?
2. Were there any sections that were easier than others? If so, why were they easier?
3. When you got confused, what did you do?

Reviewing Your Reading

A. Look at the following list of readings in this chapter. Check the column that shows how easy or difficult the material was for you.

Name of Reading	Type of Reading	Easy	Average	Difficult
1. The Evolution of Money	textbook			
2. A Beginner's Guide to the Stock Market	magazine article			
3A. Nella: The New Money?	newspaper article			
3B. Time Dollars FAQ	Website article			
4. Micro Credit, Macro Results	magazine article			

B. Read the following list of strategies that you have practiced in this chapter. Review the readings. Which strategies did you use, and how often did you use them? Check your answers in the chart.

Strategy	Always	Often	Sometimes	Never
Prepare				
Predicting organization				
Predicting from first and last paragraphs				
Read/Read Again				
Using supporting details to identify main ideas				
Reading with a purpose				
Using signal words to predict ideas				
Using referring words and referents to follow ideas				
Using illustrations and photos to aid comprehension				
Using punctuation to aid comprehension				

Strategy	Always	Often	Sometimes	Never
Critical Reading				
Making inferences				
Remember				
Summarizing				
Vocabulary Strategies				
Recognizing jargon				
Recognizing common phrases				
Analyzing words for meaning				
Guessing the approximate meaning of words				

C. Compare your chart with a partner's.

D. Did you use any other strategies while reading? If so, share them with the class. Explain where you learned them.

Appendix I

Scanning Practice

EXERCISE. 1   Scan the television schedule. Find the following information.

1. What time is *Sports Desk* on?
2. What channel is *Mercy General Hospital* on?
3. What is the topic of *Eyewitness to History*?
4. What program would be good for gardeners?
5. What's on Channel 2 at 8:30?

Television

Tonight's shows	7:00	8:00	8:30
2 WGBH	**Newshour with Jim Thompson** (CC)	**Eyewitness to History** The story of Hurricane Andrew. (CC)	**All About Animals** The animals of Australia are featured. (CC)
4 WBZ	**Hollywood Squares** (CC)	**Entertainment Tonight** An interview with director Samuel Cox. (CC)	**King of Hearts** Jack loses his job but pretends that he got a promotion. (CC)
5 WCVB	**Inside Edition** A look at the steel industry. (CC)	**Chronicle** A visit to a tobacco farm in North Carolina. (CC)	
9 WMUR	**Entertainment Today** An interview with director Samuel Cox. (CC)	**Sports Desk**	**Bobby's House** Bobby decides he needs to get a second job. (CC)
11 WVTA	**Nightly Business Report** (CC)	**Antique Hunt** (CC)	
12 FOXNET	**Plants for all Seasons** Gregg shows the best plants for an indoor garden. (CC)	**LAPD: Life on the Street** Sam investigates the murder of a famous actor. (CC)	
13 WNNE	**Crosswords** (CC)	**Money Wheel** (CC)	**Who's a Millionaire?** (CC)

Tonight's shows	7:00	8:00	8:30
14 WNDS	**News** (CC)	**Basketball** The Kansas City Kings play the Seattle Triumph. (CC)	
15 UPN38	**Mercy General Hospital** Dr. Thorndike tries to save the life of a convicted killer. (CC)	**Friends Forever** Joe and Mike buy an expensive television, but they don't want their girlfriends to know. (CC)	**What's Cooking?** Dinah makes dishes from Japan and Thailand. (CC)
16 WEKW	**Antique Hunt** (CC)	**Keeping Up with the Neighbors** Martha wants to buy a new car. (CC)	**Painting with Patty** Patty demonstrates how to paint flowers. (CC)

E X E R C I S E . **2**   Scan the bus schedule. Find the following information.

1. What time does the first bus leave Woods Hole?
2. How many buses leave from Bourne on Sundays?
3. What time does the last bus arrive at Logan Airport?
4. How much is the fare from Falmouth to Logan Airport?
5. How many stops are there in Wareham?
6. What does "X7" mean?

Express Bus Schedule Woods Hole–Boston, Logan Airport
COMBINED SCHEDULES EFFECTIVE JANUARY 1, 2004

	Leave Woods Hole	Leave Falmouth	Leave Otis Air Force Base	Leave Bourne	Leave Buzzards Bay	Leave Wareham Shore Road	Leave Wareham Mills Road	Arrive Boston	Arrive Logan Airport
X7	—	5:20	5:30	5:40	—	—	—	6:45	7:05
DAILY	—	6:10	6:20	—	—	—	6:30	7:30	7:50
X67 **H**	—	—	—	—	6:10	6:25	6:30	7:30	—
X7 **H**	6:45	7:00	7:10	7:20	—	—	—	8:25	—
DAILY	8:00	8:10	8:20	8:30	—	—	—	9:40	9:55
DAILY	10:30	10:40	10:50	11:00	—	—	—	12:05	12:25
DAILY	12:01	12:10	12:20	12:30	—	—	—	1:35	1:55
	2:30	2:40	2:50	3:00	—	—	3:10	4:05	4:25
X67 **H**	3:30	3:40	3:50	4:00	—	—	4:10	5:05	—
DAILY	5:00	5:10	5:20	—	5:45	6:00	—	7:30	7:50
7 **H**	6:00	—	—	—	—	—	—	7:25	—

CODES

Bold Face PM
6 Bus Operates on Saturday
X Except Saturdays, Sundays, & Holidays (upon request to driver)

7 Bus Operates on Sunday
H Bus Operates on Holidays

FARES

Woods Hole to Logan: one way–$22; round trip–$40
Falmouth to Logan: one way–$22; round trip–$40
Bourne to Logan: one way–$19; round–$34

For more information, please call 1-888-555-8800.

E X E R C I S E . 3   Scan the course schedule. Find the following information.

1. What course does Professor Peake teach?
2. What time does Chinese 301 meet?
3. Where does Biology 202 meet?
4. What days of the week does Computer Science 134 meet?
5. What class meets in Clark Hall 204?
6. Who teaches Astronomy lab on Monday afternoon?

Course Schedule

Astronomy

Subject/CRN		Day	Time		Building	Instructor
ASTR-101-01	LEC	TH	0955AM	1110AM	Physics Bldg 203	Pasachoff
ASTR-101-02	LAB	T	0100PM	0230PM		Souza
ASTR-101-03	LAB	T	0230PM	0400PM		Souza
ASTR-111-01	LEC	TH	1120AM	1235PM	Physics Bldg 203	Kwitter
ASTR-111-02	LAB	M	0100PM	0400PM		Souza
ASTR-217-T1	TUT	F	0235PM	0350PM	Clark Hall 204	Cox

Biology

Subject/CRN		Day	Time		Building	Instructor
BIOL-101-A1	LEC	MWF	0900AM	0950AM	Sparkman Hall 112	Lynch, D.
BIOL-101-A2	LEC	MWF	1100AM	1150AM	Sparkman Hall 112	Lynch, D.
BIOL-134-01	LEC	MWF	1000AM	1050AM	Sparkman Hall 112	Edwards, J.
BIOL-202-01	LEC	MWF	1100AM	1150AM	Chemistry Bldg 123	Altschuler

Chemistry

Subject/CRN		Day	Time		Building	Instructor
CHEM-151-02	LAB	M	0100PM	0500PM		Skinner
CHEM-151-03	LAB	T	0100PM	0500PM		Skinner
CHEM-151-04	LAB	W	0100PM	0500PM		Lovett
CHEM-153-02	LAB	M	0100PM	0500PM		Bingemann
CHEM-153-03	LAB	T	0100PM	0500PM		Bingemann
CHEM-155-01	LEC	MWF	0800AM	0850AM	Chemistry Bldg 202	Peack
CHEM-251-01	LEC	MWF	1000AM	1050AM	Chemistry Bldg 123	Richardson, D.
CHEM-251-02	LAB	M	0100PM	0500PM		Richardson, D.

Chinese

Subject/CRN		Day	Time		Building	Instructor
CHIN-101-01	LEC	MTWHF	1100AM	1150AM	Stetson 308	Chang, C.
CHIN-101-02	LEC	MTWHF	1200PM	1250PM	Stetson 308	Chang, C.
CHIN-201-01	LEC	MTWHF	0900AM	0950AM	Stetson 308	Silber

CHIN-275-01	LEC	H	0700PM	0940PM	Stetson 308	Lu
		W	0110PM	0350PM	Stetson 308	Silber
CHIN-301-01	LEC	MWF	1000AM	1050AM	Stetson 308	

Computer Science

Subject/CRN		Day	Time		Building	Instructor
CSCI-105-01	LEC	H	0955AM	1110AM	Chemistry Bldg 202	Murtagh
CSCI-105-02	LAB	H	0110PM	0225PM	Chemistry Bldg 217	Murtagh
CSCI-105-03	LAB	H	0235PM	0350PM	Chemistry Bldg 217	Murtagh
CSCI-134-01	LEC	MWF	0900AM	0950AM	Chemistry Bldg 206	Murtagh

E X E R C I S E . 4   Scan the menu. Find the following information.

1. What kind of pancakes are served?
2. How much is a side order of bacon?
3. What is the most expensive omelette that is served?
4. How much would two eggs with ham, a small apple juice, and a side order of sausage cost?
5. How many kinds of eggs are offered?
6. How many pancakes are in A short stack? A tall stack?

Breakfast Menu

Eggs
Served with fried potatoes and toast

Two Eggs Any Style	$2.75
Plus your choice of bacon, ham, or sausage	4.50
Two Eggs Scrambled with Ham	4.50
Two Eggs Any Style with Two Pancakes	3.25
The 2-2-2	
2 eggs, 2 strips of bacon, and 2 pancakes (with French toast instead of pancakes, add 50¢)	4.00

Omelettes
Served with fried potatoes and toast

Plain	$4.25
Ham	4.50
Mushroom and Cheese	4.75
Ham and Cheese	4.75
Popeye's Delight *(spinach, tomato, and jack cheese)*	5.75
Vegetarian *(tofu omelette with onion, bell pepper, mushroom, avocado)*	5.95

Bread Choices
Whole wheat, rye, and white bread

Hot from the grill

Buttermilk Pancakes
    Tall Stack (4) $3.25
    Short Stack (2)   2.50
    With bananas or berries, add 75¢
French Toast   3.50
Belgian Waffles with Bananas   3.25

Breakfast side orders

Cream Cheese   .75
Fried Potatoes $1.00
Toast   1.25
Sausage, Bacon, or Ham   1.50
Hot or Cold Cereal with Milk   1.85

Juices

	regular	large
Fresh Orange Juice	$1.50	$2.50
Fresh Grapefruit Juice	1.50	2.50
Apple Juice	1.25	1.95
Tomato Juice	1.25	1.95
Cranberry Juice	1.25	1.95

EXERCISE 5   Scan the chart. Find the following information.

1. How much does a room at the Pine Gardens Inn cost per night?
2. Does the Blain House have airport pick-up service?
3. Which hotels have kitchenettes?
4. Can you watch television at the Pine Gardens Inn?
5. Which hotels offer Internet access?
6. At which hotel can you go to a gym?

	Belvedere Hotel ($$$)	Blain House ($$)	Pine Gardens Inn ($$)
Hotel Facilities			
Restaurant	X		
Pool	X		X
Meeting Rooms		X	
Exercise Room	X		
Airport Pick-up Service	X	X	
Room Facilities			
Maid service	X	X	X
Kitchenette	X		X
Television	X	X	*
Hair dryer	X		X
Ironing board			X
Internet access	X	X	
In-room safe	X		**
Refrigerator	X	X	

Key
$ *$50–$75 a night*
$$ *$80–$100 a night*
$$$ *$110–$140 a night*
✻   *available in the lounge*
✻✻   *available at the front desk*

Appendix II

Reading for Speed

READING. 1 Read the following as quickly as you can, and time yourself. Look for the main points. Then answer the questions that follow. Do not look back at the reading.

462 words

In the spring of 1823, two men by the names of De Voe and Lozier told a group of butchers, farmers, and fishmongers an astounding tale: Manhattan Island was sinking. By the 1820s, burgeoning New York City had become America's most populous city, with 150,000 inhabitants, and the combined weight of all the additional people and the buildings, the two men claimed, had made
5 Manhattan too bottom-heavy, and the island was beginning to sink into the harbor.

De Voe and Lozier told the crowd not to worry. They had a plan. They were going to save Manhattan by sawing it in half, then towing the lower half out in the harbor, turning it around, and reattaching it. The new island would then be more balanced. Maybe it sounded a bit incredible, but to an audience of uneducated New Yorkers, nothing seemed beyond the abilities of dedicated, hard-
10 working men.

Such a mammoth project would require a tremendous number of workers and materials. The listeners were happy to provide both. With New York going through an economic depression, work was hard to find. The hope of steady employment at good wages was welcomed.

Hundreds of eager workmen and suppliers signed up. There were manual laborers to saw the
15 island in half, row it out into the harbor, turn it, bring it back in, and reattach it. There were carpenters to make twenty 100-foot-long saws with 3-foot teeth and two dozen 250-foot-long oars. There were ironworkers to make huge anchors to prevent the island from being swept out to sea; there were contractors to construct housing for all the workmen; and there were farmers and butchers to feed everyone.

20 On the first day of the project, men began to arrive early. Some were carrying tools—shovels, axes, picks. Some pushed wheelbarrows. Some came with their wives and children. Contractors and carpenters drove up in wagons full of lumber and hammers and saws. Butchers came with herds of cattle and hogs and carts loaded with chickens. Estimates were that between one and two thousand workers showed up. They stood around for some time, but nothing happened. Finally, after several
25 hours, people began looking for Lozier and De Voe. At the market, a message had been left. It said that the pair had had to leave town, owing to matters of their health.

Thousands of people had been fooled in one of the most famous and improbable hoaxes in American history. Or had they?

Although numerous accounts of this hoax have been written up throughout the years, they all
30 trace back to a single source: an account given over 30 years after the fact by John De Voe to his nephew Thomas, a member of the New York Historical Society. This is actually an example of a hoax about a hoax.

1. De Voe and Lozier told a group of New Yorkers that Manhattan Island was _____.
   a. falling apart
   b. sinking
   c. floating out to sea

2. De Voe and Lozier's "plan" was to _____.
   a. cut the island in half
   b. make many of the people move
   c. tear down the big buildings

3. The New Yorkers believed the men because they _____.
   a. weren't well educated
   b. needed work
   c. both (a) and (b)

4. On the day the work was supposed to start, _____.
   a. no one showed up
   b. between one and two thousand workers arrived
   c. De Voe and Lozier told people it was a hoax

5. The most surprising aspect of this story is that _____.
   a. people believed such an amazing tale
   b. De Voe and Lozier didn't go to jail
   c. it never happened

R E A D I N G   **2**   Read the following as quickly as you can, and time yourself. Look for the main points. Then answer the questions that follow. Do not look back at the reading.

514 words

In 1976, four students went on a camping trip in a wilderness area of northern Maine. One night they spotted a curious bright object in the night sky. Later they witnessed an oval object of brightly colored light above them. They then experienced a period of "missing time" in their conscious memory. It was not until years later in hypnosis sessions that they relived traumatic alien abductions
5 during that "missing" period. They reported being transported aboard a UFO, where strange humanoid creatures examined them.

Such sightings have a long history. At various times UFOs have been reported as chariots, ships, and religious visions. In the 1890s, there were widespread reports in the United States of cigar-shaped airships. Similar sightings came from England in 1909. During the 1930s, so-called *ghost*
10 *fliers* were spotted over Sweden, and during World War II reports of glowing objects called *foo*

fighters became common. The term *flying saucer* was coined in 1947 to describe strange objects spotted by a pilot over the American state of Washington. More recently, the UFO phenomenon has been dominated by stories of alien abduction.

15   While claims of alien abduction are relatively new, stories of contact with otherworldly beings are not. Visitations by angels have been reported throughout history. In many cultures there are beliefs about people being taken to other dimensions and/or rising to the heavens. Even before the abduction phenomenon, some individuals claimed to be in contact with extraterrestrials from advanced worlds. George Adamski, for instance, became famous in the 1950s for his stories of meeting beings from Venus and visiting the far side of the moon in their spaceship.

20   "Contactees" like Adamski claimed they traveled through space at their own volition. "Abductees," on the other hand, lack any choice in their encounters with aliens. Abductees might be taken in remote areas or simply "beamed up" from their own bedrooms. The alien abductors come in many different shapes and colors, but are typically short, gray, and hairless, with large black eyes. Frequently, memories of abduction are elicited through hypnosis.

25   The first abduction case to receive wide publicity in the United States involved a married couple, Betty and Barney Hill, in 1961. Since then, stories of alien abduction have multiplied. The phenomenon gained further prominence following the publication of Whitley Strieber's personal account in the bestseller *Communion* (1987). While the United States has by far the most abduction reports, followed by South America, the phenomenon in Britain dates from the mid-1970s. Some

30   researchers estimate that cases worldwide run into the millions.

    There is intense disagreement about whether abduction experiences relate to real physical events, psychological interaction, altered states of consciousness, or simply delusional fantasy. They may be compared, however, with other incidents where individuals suddenly find themselves in alien surroundings. For example, in earlier times, stories of people being captured by pirates or Indians

35   were very popular. In fact, there were many more stories than there were kidnappings. It is likely that the same is true of alien abductions. However, there is one important difference: Even one alien abduction would completely change our world.

1. The four students who went on a camping trip _____.
   a. saw people abducted by aliens
   b. realized that they were abducted years later
   c. saw a space ship and called the police

2. People have reported seeing strange sights in the sky _____.
   a. since the beginning of time
   b. for a long time
   c. for the last 50 years

3. Today, most reports are about _____.
   a. UFOs
   b. visiting with extraterrestrials
   c. alien abductions

4. The first well-known abduction case occurred _____.

    a. in the 19th century

    b. in the 1960s

    c. during World War II

5. The author compares stories of alien abductions with stories about _____.

    a. pirates capturing Indians

    b. aliens kidnapping pirates

    c. pirates and Indians as kidnappers

R E A D I N G . **3**

Read the following as quickly as you can, and time yourself. Look for the main points. Then answer the questions that follow. Do not look back at the reading.

508 words

1   Diamonds are judged on four characteristics: color, clarity, cut, and carat weight. These are also known as the four C's. A brief description of each characteristic will help you understand more about diamonds.

Color: Good Color Is No Color

    The best color for a diamond is no color. A totally colorless diamond acts as a prism, allowing

5 light to pass effortlessly through the diamond and transforming it into rainbows of color.

    The color grading scale goes from totally colorless to light yellow. The differences between one grade and another are quite small.

Clarity: A Rarity

    Diamonds can produce more brilliance than any other gemstone. A diamond that is virtually free of interior or exterior inclusions or flaws is of the highest quality because nothing interferes with the

10 passage of light through the diamond. To determine a diamond's clarity, an expert views it under a microscope to detect flaws.

    Clarity is broken down into different classifications. They range from Flawless (F1) and Very, Very, Small Inclusions (VVS) to Small Inclusions (SI) and Imperfect (I). The Flawless diamond is certainly the most expensive choice; however, the VVS class inclusion is not noticeable to the naked

15 eye.

Cut: The Brilliant Cut

    The type and shape of cut proportions, symmetry, and outer marks are taken into consideration when grading a diamond's cut. You should look for a stone that has the "Fine Brilliant Cut." There are also different classifications for cut. They are "Very Good," "Good," "Medium," and "Poor." "Very Good" means that the stone has exceptional brilliance, with few and only minor outer marks.

20 "Good" is the classification for stones that have good brilliance, with some outer marks. Stones ranked "Medium" are slightly less brilliant, with some larger outer marks. And finally, stones categorized as "Poor" have less brilliance, with large and numerous outer marks.

    In addition to the variation in ranking, diamonds are cut in several different shapes as well. Shapes include Round, Pear, Marquise, Emerald, Square, and Trillion.

Carat Weight: Bigger Is Bigger, But Not Necessarily Better

A diamond is measured in carats. One carat is divided into 100 points, so that a diamond of 75 points weighs .75 carats. Size is the most obvious factor in determining the value of a diamond. However, two diamonds of equal size can have very different values, depending on their quality. And diamonds of high quality can be found in all size ranges.

When purchasing a diamond at the quarter-carat intervals (1/4, 1/2, 3/4, 1.00, etc.), select a stone that weighs just below these intervals. For example, if you would like a 3/4 carat diamond, a .73-point carat diamond will save you hundreds of dollars.

In addition to educating yourself about the four C's, consider the following diamond buying tips.

Tip #1: Obtain a professional gemologist's *Diamond Grading Report.* This will give you confidence that you are getting what you are paying for.

Tip #2: Before you buy, inspect the stone unmounted—that is, not set in a ring. This will allow you to adequately and accurately inspect the diamond.

---

1. A good title for this article would be _____.
   a. Why Diamonds Are Expensive
   b. How to Buy a Diamond
   c. All About Diamonds

2. Match the diamond characteristics with the definitions:

1. clarity	a. size
2. cut	b. number of flaws it has
3. color	c. shape
4. carat	d. how good a prism it is

3. The best stones have _____.
   a. many outer marks
   b. a few outer marks
   c. no outer marks

4. The best diamonds are _____.
   a. big
   b. yellow
   c. flawless

5. You should inspect diamonds _____.
   a. after they are made into jewelry
   b. before they are mounted
   c. from a gemologist

READING · 4   Read the following as quickly as you can, and time yourself. Look for the main points. Then answer the questions that follow. Do not look back at the reading.

525 words

1   Numerous tribes of Indians lived on the Great Plains. Some were nomads and moved from place to place. Others farmed and built permanent villages.

Pawnees in what are now Kansas and Nebraska and the Arikaras in what is now South Dakota were farming tribes. And so were the Mandans. The Mandans were an Indian tribe that lived in the 5 northern Great Plains, an area that is now the state of North Dakota.

The Mandans were typical of the farming Indians of the Plains. They lived in settled villages. Each village was built on high ground overlooking the Missouri River, usually where a tributary stream joined the main river. The Mandans chose such places because the steep riverbanks gave them some protection against attack. On the open side of each village, the Mandans erected a high 10 fence of posts set vertically in the ground. Then they dug a broad ditch outside the fence. The Mandans fortified their villages to defend themselves against other warlike Indians.

Mandan families lived in large houses made of earth. These homes were arranged around a central plaza. In this plaza, they held religious ceremonies and competitive games. Mandan women tended gardens where they raised corn, beans, and tobacco. The men hunted buffalo and other 15 animals.

In the early days nearly all of the Plains Indians lived like the Mandans. Beginning in the 1700s, however, a different culture developed. It was based on two animals—the horse and the buffalo. Buffalo had always lived on the Great Plains, but the Spaniards imported horses to Mexico. Horses spread northward coming first to Texas. The Indians, who had had a hard time hunting animals on 20 foot, quickly learned to ride. Using a very simple bridle, Indian hunters began to ride horseback.

After horses were introduced to the Plains, most Plains Indians adopted the nomad culture. The tribes who did so became among the best known of all American Indians—the Cheyenne, the Crow, the Comanche, the Arapaho, and the Dakota (also called the Sioux).

The typical Plains Indians after the 1700s were nomads or wanderers. They moved about from 25 place to place and had no fixed location for their villages. In the spring and summer, large herds of buffalo ranged over the Great Plains. In those seasons, the Plains Indians followed the herds and lived off of them.

Plains Indians got almost everything they needed from the buffalo. They depended on the buffalo for meat. This meat had to last a long time since hunting during the cold winters on the Great Plains 30 was difficult. To preserve the buffalo meat, the Indian women cut it into strips and dried it. They pounded some of it into a food called pemmican. Indian hunters and warriors carried pemmican with them for food.

The Plains Indians used hides to make tepees, the cone-shaped tents in which most of the Indians lived. Women also made the hides into cooking devices on which they boiled food by dropping in 35 hot stones. Buffalo hides made good blankets. Buffalo fat was used to tan hides. Even buffalo tendons and sinews were used to provide thread for sewing.

1. The Mandan Indians were _____.
   a. farmers
   b. nomads
   c. warriors

2. The Mandan designed their villages so that they were _____.
   a. difficult to attack
   b. beautiful
   c. temporary

3. The Mandan way of life was changed by _____.
   a. the Spaniards
   b. the settlers
   c. the horse and the buffalo

4. In the 1700s many Plains Indians became _____.
   a. farmers
   b. nomads
   c. warriors

5. The buffalo gave the Plains Indians _____.
   a. food and clothing
   b. shelter and tools
   c. both (a) and (b)

R E A D I N G . **5**   Read the following as quickly as you can, and time yourself. Look for the main points. Then answer the questions that follow. Do not look back at the reading.

535 words

1   Any business that wants to sell shares of stock to a number of different people does so by turning itself into a corporation. The process of turning a business into a corporation is called incorporating.

    If you start a restaurant by using your own money to buy the building and the equipment, then what you have done is form a sole proprietorship. You own the entire restaurant yourself—you get
5 to make all of the decisions and you keep all of the profits. If three people put their money together and start a restaurant as a team, what they have done is form a partnership. The three people own the restaurant themselves. They will share the profits and the decision making.

    There is a whole body of law that controls corporations—these laws protect the shareholders and the public. The laws control a number of things about how a corporation operates and is organized.
10 For example, every corporation has a board of directors (if all of the shares of a corporation are owned by one person, then that one person can decide that there will only be one person on the board of directors, but there is still a board). The shareholders in the company meet every year to vote on

the people for the board. The board of directors makes the decisions for the company. It hires the officers (the president and other major officers of the company), makes the company's decisions, and
15 sets the company's policies.

From this description, you can see that a corporation has a group of owners—the shareholders. The owners elect a board of directors to make the company's major decisions. The owners of a corporation become owners by buying shares of stock in the corporation. The board of directors decides how many total shares there will be. For example, a company might have one million shares
20 of stock. In a privately held company, the shares of stock are owned by a small number of people who probably all know one another. They buy and sell their shares among themselves. A publicly held company is owned by thousands of people who trade their shares on a public stock exchange.

One of the major reasons why corporations exist is to create a structure for collecting lots of investment dollars in a business. Let's say that you would like to start your own airline. Most people
25 cannot do this because it would cost millions of dollars. A person who wants to start an airline will therefore form a corporation and sell stock in order to collect the money needed to get started.

A corporation is an easy way to gather large quantities of investment capital—money from investors. When a corporation first sells stock to the public, it does so in an Initial Public Offering (IPO). The company might sell one million shares of stock at $20 a share to raise $20 million very
30 quickly. The company then invests the $20 million in equipment and employees. The investors (the shareholders who bought the $20 million in stock) hope that with the equipment and employees, the company will make a profit and pay a dividend.

1. When people put their money together to form a company, this is called a _____.
   a. sole proprietorship
   b. corporation
   c. partnership

2. A corporation must _____.
   a. issue shares
   b. have a board of directors
   c. both (a) and (b)

3. The shareholders of a company _____.
   a. are the owners
   b. are the investment capital
   c. make the company's major decisions

4. One main reason why a company becomes a corporation is to _____.
   a. buy stock
   b. get investments
   c. form a board of directors

5. An Initial Public Offering (IPO) is when a company _____.
   a. buys or sells stock
   b. goes out of business
   c. issues stock for the first time